QUEEN O

EXPLORING THE

Haydn Paul has spent many years exploring the transpersonal way, and has been a practising Astrologer for over ten years.

QUEEN OF THE NIGHT

EXPLORING THE ASTROLOGICAL MOON

Haydn Paul

ELEMENT BOOKS

First published in Great Britain in 1990 by
Element Books Limited
Longmead, Shaftesbury, Dorset

Cover design by Max Fairbrother
Typeset by Selectmove, London
Printed and bound in Great Britain
by Billings Ltd, Hylton Road, Worcester

British Library Cataloguing in Publication Data
Paul, Haydn
Queen of the night: exploring the astrological moon.
1. Astrology
I. Title
133.5

ISBN 1-85230-142-2

'The Queen of the Night, riding in the majesty of her peerless light in heaven, throwing all into darkness, spreading her silver mantle over the whole world'.

Madame Blavatsky, *The Secret Doctrine*, Volume 1, *Cosmogenesis*

Dedicated to all who enter the initiation of the Temple of the Moon Goddess, and those who achieve the alchemical *mysterium coniunctio*. And to those special Moon reflections that inspire and help to lead me along the way, my wife Carol, and lovely daughters Sarah and Lauren. May you never run out of moon-beams. And not forgetting those whose influence directed me towards the depths, where the choice was learning how to swim or sink.

My love, appreciation and thanks to all embodiments of the Great Mother.

Contents

CHAPTER 1

Invocation: Dea Luna, Deus Lunus, The Reawakened Moon

DAY AFTER DAY, THEY LOOKED to the heavens above, watching the movement of the great orb of light rise at dawn and fall again at twilight. Night after night, they watched as another light cast an illumination into the darkness surrounding them, when mysterious shadows evoked fears of attack and animal noises eerily echoed in the distance, waiting for dreaming sleep to claim them during the night hours. Soon they realised that whilst one light in the sky was constant, blazing down and giving light to the day, the orb of night passed through mysterious and magical changes, apparently appearing and disappearing in a cyclic pattern. They observed these changes, and as time passed, watched the varying positions in the sky from which the lights would appear. They felt the changes occurring within their own bodies, emotions and minds and intuited that they were being influenced by the heavenly lights and the stars, those sparkling points of light in the black canopy of night. Slowly, the embryonic formulation of the later Hermetic axiom of 'As above, so below' began to be conceived, and the ancient wisdom of star-lore emerged through the consciousness of mankind.

In the mysterious and dangerous world that they inhabited, they felt that the lights in the sky were like eyes watching their every move. They were awed by their presence and reverential feelings arose, knowing that in some way, their lives depended on the rising of the sun each day, and the coming of the Moon-light at night.

The lights became sacred objects, and worship, ritual and propitiatory sacrifice were developed as means of ensuring heavenly goodwill. The Sun became identified as the King of Day, the God of Light; the Moon as the Queen of Night, the Goddess of Darkness.

Perhaps it was like this; certainly the sources of astrology lie deeply shrouded in the mists of antiquity, but even today we still look up at the same Sun, Moon and stars, and will until all human life passes away on Earth. They are constants in human experience across time and generations, transcending cultural and national barriers, looking down on the planet and humanity.

Ancient man studied the heavens, often measuring the linear progression of cyclic time by the transiting movements of the Sun and Moon, using marking stones aligned to indicate certain times of the year when crops could be successfully planted, or times when important religious rituals should be performed. The soli-lunar cycles became calendars and systems of organising time within cultures.

The rhythmic Moon pattern was especially useful as a model, forming the seven-day week and the twenty-eight-day lunar month. The average duration of human pregnancy is equivalent to ten lunar months (forty weeks). The twenty-eight-day Moon cycle is related to the female menstrual cycle. Various studies have shown that the onset of the monthly period is more likely to occur at either the New Moon or the Full Moon than at other times, and it is likely that in the past the correlation was even more marked than it is in our present era of chemical contraception and other interference with natural physiological patterns.

Our ancestors considered the 'dark of the Moon', when the Moon disappeared from sight, to be a phase when certain actions and thoughts should be avoided for fear of displeasing the Goddess. Physical contact with menstruating women was regarded as taboo, as it still is in some cultures. The shape-shifting quality of women during pregnancy was seen as echoing that of the Moon through its phases, and so in most cultures the Moon became identified with the Goddess and with the feminine principle. Women became priestesses of the Moon, which was perceived to be the source of life on earth, a heavenly gateway akin to the physical gateway of the female sexual organ.

To ancient man the Sun and Moon seemed to be the same size. We now know that in reality the Sun is far larger – four hundred times larger in fact, though also four hundred times further from the Earth. The Moon orbits at a distance of some 239,000 miles from Earth, some 92 million miles away from the Sun. It is approximately a quarter the size of the Earth, with a diameter of 2,160 miles and a much reduced mass and gravitational force, about one-sixth of Earth's gravitational field. The Moon's revolution around the Earth takes 27⅓ days (the sidereal period), and it rotates on its axis (a process called 'synchronous rotation'), which is why only one face of the Moon is presented to onlookers from the Earth.

Whilst the Moon is considered to be a satellite of the Earth, there are certain peculiarities about the relationship, especially concerning its relative size. Out of all the known satellites or moons associated with other planets in our solar system, there are none of such a proportionately large size. Also the Moon does not revolve around the Earth in the manner in which one would normally expect a satellite to revolve around its centre of gravitational attraction. It is the Sun which is the actual centre of gravitational pull for both the Earth and the Moon, and the Sun's influence on the Moon is considerably greater than that of the Earth. In that sense, the Earth and Moon act as a double planet system, with the Moon symbolically representing a position of dualism, one 'face' looking towards the Sun and the attraction of the light and spirit, and the other attracted to the pull of Earth and the absorption in physical bodies and material life. This symbolises the human dilemma. The Moon responds to its mediating role with a cycle of transformation reacting both to the Earth and the Sun, one consequence of this being the tidal ebb and flow of the Earth's oceans.

The fact that the Sun and Moon appear equal in size has been interpreted in astrology as an indication that both planetary principles are of equal importance in the human psyche, collectively and individually. A theme that will be considered throughout this book is the importance of achieving a balance between these principles, for both individual and society. Traditionally, the solar principle has been associated with the 'higher nature', and the lunar principle with the 'lower nature'; but these distinctions only apply within a dualistic and polarised consciousness, and need a more transcendant view to reconcile the opposites. The implication of the optical symbolism is that the light-radiating solar self needs to be perceived as being not superior but complementary to the light-reflective lunar and psychic self of humanity, and that a union between the two factors is vital in creating a whole human being.

The role of the Moon is that of a mediator between the Sun and the Earth. In the lunar cycle, nothing really changes except our geocentric perspective. The Moon's phases are only seen from Earth, which implies that their meaning is related purely to issues within human consciousness. It is only the relationship between the Moon and the Sun that actually changes. To the astrologer, this suggests that it is a change in the manner of how the solar light is being transmitted to us, by the Moon stepping down the sun's potency and intensity, and serving as a translator and transformer. This is achieved through an alternating current reflected in the dualistic nature of life on Earth – in sexual polarity, left-brain and right-brain activity, day and night, light and dark, life and death, and matter and spirit. Were this not so, we might be unable to cope with the brilliance of the solar light; we might be blinded instead of enlightened.

THE MOON LANDING AND THE REAWAKENED GODDESS

For thousands of years, the Moon had attracted the fascinated gaze of mankind and evoked many myths, legends and dreams. It was appropriate that the rupturing of the spatial planetary barriers should be achieved by the physical landing on the Moon. The solar impulse for outer expansion and exploration had resulted in the technological progress necessary to reach out into space, and on 9.18 BST, 20 July 1969, the Eagle lunar module from the aptly named Apollo 11 mission safely descended onto an area named the Sea of Tranquility. Neil Armstrong spoke those famous words during the first Moon walk: 'That's one small step for man, one giant leap for mankind.' Within an hour of the landing of the Eagle module, a Russian spacecraft Luna 15 crash-landed into the Sea of Crises. Those two areas of Tranquility and Crises symbolise the ambivalence of human response to the influence of the Moon and the mutability of emotional balance.

Whilst the physical planetary Moon may have appeared passive and lifeless in outer space, the corresponding inner Moon within the depths of consciousness was not so unresponsive to man's presence. A membrane, or veil, had been penetrated and man had broken free of his planetary restrictions; in standing free of the protective embrace of Earth and looking back on the home world slowly turning in space, a larger vision had been attained. The image of Earth that resulted from the Moon missions embodies a visual symbol of our planetary reality, reminding us of the One World and One Human Family, dissolving petty concepts of national barriers and racial antagonisms. That photograph of the beauty of Gaia symbolises an important turning-point for humanity, with the possibility of a renewed connection between Earth and the Moon being forged.

Lifting that spatial veil simultaneously opened an inner channel within the collective psyche which has grown ever wider in twenty years. This involves the rebirth of the inner Moon so that balance can be restored between lunar qualities and the qualities that are now threatening planetary health.

As the matriarchal cultures faded and were replaced by patriarchal hierarchies, the lunar principle retreated further into the unconscious mind. Over the centuries, the Great Mother has become secondary to the power of the Father God, resulting in a devaluing and denial of the virtues of the Feminine principle in life. Male fears of a resurgence of feminine power have resulted in purges of those holding pagan beliefs, with Christianity seeking to repress heretical and matriarchal attitudes by an abuse of social power and the use of physical aggression. The witch trials and inquisitions are an ineradicable stain on the Church's expression of Christ's teachings.

Under the domination of masculine exploitative, assertive and exploratory attitudes, mind and intellect have conditioned world-views so that rationality has gained the ascendancy over instinct, intuition and feelings. Inner connections to the depths of the personal nature and the vitality of the natural life have withered away over centuries of patriarchal power. Whilst this has helped to bring about certain major advances, such as the expansion of scientific knowledge and technology, we are now reaching the point where a new way needs to be discovered before the negative consequences of these advances destroy the planet.

Since the 1960s the influence of the Goddess, symbolised by the Moon, has been gathering strength once more. We live in a time when the values of emotions, instincts, feelings, irrationality, connectedness and nurturing need to be rediscovered and expressed within the collective. We need the vitalising energy of the Moon Goddess to renew those spiritual needs in man, so that heart values begin to play a more powerful role again. We need the importance and potential of the individual to be acknowledged as necessary to the well-being of society.

Signs of this shift towards the fulfilment of inner needs are apparent in the growth of the New Age movement, which is attempting to inculcate new attitudes, visions and approaches within all spheres of life in an effort to revitalise and transform unfulfilling ways of life. Since the inner Moon Goddess was reawakened, there has been a rapid growth in demands for personal and planetary nurturing. The emphasis has changed towards satisfying inner needs by creating a better quality of life, the search to explore inner consciousness and to walk the paths of self-understanding.

For many women, responding to the call of the Goddess, this fulfilment has been found through the Women's Movement, and through allowing a fuller and freer expression of the feminist spirit. The assertion of feminine power within society through developing greater political awareness, and within women's solidarity and consciousness-raising groups, has been vitally important in starting a movement towards social balance. In Western societies, the role of women is slowly increasing in importance, and lunar approaches to life are becoming socially acceptable. We see this in foods, vegetarianism, complementary and holistic medicine, natural living, more aware child-raising and natural childbirth – all involving nurturing of oneself or of others. We also see an increasing female role in politics, business and artistic creativity. The Moon's influence is apparent, too, in the attention now focused on planetary nurturing. Ecological concerns have at last achieved international recognition; we are finally awakening to our potential to destroy or heal the only home we have.

In the more spiritual realms, rebirth has occurred within old fading traditions, and the mysteries of Albion and the Celtic peoples are experiencing a popular resurgence, as many realise that a more pagan world-view fits their preferred perception of life. Both Wicca and modern witchcraft are similarly reinvigorated as the Goddess calls her own back to serve her, and even older shamanic traditions with their emphasis on nature attunement and mediating between levels of reality now have a wide following. Certain aspects of these contemporary needs are looked at in Chapters 8 and 9, especially the potential integration of masculine and feminine principles.

The need to enquire within has exploded within many, and spiritual searches and occult investigations are pursued internationally. The doors to the inner quest have been opened, and meditation paths (especially those of the Western traditions) lead towards the depths of our inner natures and the realms of the Goddess where we can reintegrate our repressed feminine principle and begin to embrace that latent wholeness. Modern psychology, particularly in its Jungian form, teaches us to acknowledge all levels of our being, to honour our feelings and instincts and to release emotional pressures and tensions which limit our personal potential.

This book is an astrological perspective on certain aspects of this reawakening of the Moon Goddess within humanity. Through a greater understanding of our own personal connections to our inner Moon, we can discover ways in which we can integrate the feminine principle. This aids our own self-development but also has a beneficial collective influence too, helping to heal divisions within the collective psyche.

We have a responsibility to invoke the inner Goddess, and to allow her fertilising power to transform ourselves and our world. Through that invocation, we can build channels between the conscious and unconscious mind. Reawakened, the Moon-light shines within the darkness of the unconscious and illumines the paths of the Underworld. Following that way leads to a great healing. Through walking it for ourselves, we share in the task of world healing.

CHAPTER 2

The Mythological Moon

AS IS FITTING FOR A heavenly influence that is so associated with fertility, the Moon has generated a vast array of goddesses and gods which appear as powerful mythological figures in many of the older religious traditions of bygone cultures. The image of the Magna Dea (the Great Mother) has cast her shadow across the world, and it is only in relatively recent centuries that her presence has appeared to wane as the solar influence became dominant in human consciousness. Yet it is often unrecognised that the later solar religions, like Christianity and Islam, have deep roots within previous lunar religions, and that in many cases, the solar traditions, myths and legends are derived from more ancient Moon myths and replace the matriarchal Mother by a patriarchal and masculine Father god-image. In the case of Islam, a major symbol of the religion is the crescent Moon.

The Moon was adopted in ancient times as the heavenly symbol of the feminine principle. She was perceived as the Great Universal Mother, the female aspect of Deity, and she became the mythological source and progenitrix of all ancient cults which were related to issues of growth and fertility. In this sense she became Mother Nature, and was appealed to through worship for the blessing of the crops and to ensure an abundant harvest, because a failure of the food supply could mean starvation and death.

The Goddess was the Divine Nurturer and Nourisher of life, the one who gave form to the seed of life which was implanted in the womb of nature and woman by the Father-God, and so became the patroness of agriculture and of childbirth, whose beneficent presence and light was needed to be invoked as being indispensable for growth to occur. As we know, the Moon influences plant growth, the tides and body fluids, and the sidereal lunar month corresponds to the female menstrual cycle. Observing at least some of these things, the ancients began to perceive the Moon's cycle as reflecting natural phases of fertility, birth, growth and eventual decay and death. The Goddess began to be both a giver of life and a wielder of the destructive powers of nature too, embodying dual light and dark faces within the divine countenance of the Moon.

The crescent Moon symbol is that of the waxing phase and is associated with the cycle of growth and fertility, because it is at that point the Moon had most time to grow, and has been likened in ancient times to the 'swelling of a pregnant woman's womb'. The New Moon (the conjunction of Sun and Moon), proves to be the best time to plant crops, and was considered to be an apt time for 'the copulation of man and woman'. In many older languages, the words for Moon and menstruation are closely linked – *mens* (Latin), which is apparently also linked with *mind* and *mental*: the mind shares the Moon's proclivity for changes.

Moon myths touch extremely archaic traditions and depths within the psyche, and embrace a variety of evocative archetypal themes entering deeply into the mysteries of creation within ourselves and nature. All worship of the Goddess involves a relationship with the less tangible subtler powers and spiritual influences or qualities, explorations of instinctive wisdom, and an attempt to attain an inner at-one-ness with the greater Self. To awaken the light of the inner Moon is to restore the power of Sophia, Queen of Heaven, to unlock that wisdom inherent in the building blocks of life and encoded within our DNA pattern.

It is this inner oneness that lies at the heart of concepts of sacred virgin Moon goddesses that are found in many religious faiths. The word 'virgin' did not have the same connotations in ancient times as it does today; it did not mean a person who had no experience of sexual intercourse, but rather someone autonomous, who submitted only to the real ruler of the inner nature by surrendering to the hidden divinity. Effectively, a virgin was a person who had become transformed by contacting the light of the God or Goddess, Deus Lunus, Dea Luna. The ancient spiritual idea was that the female void was filled by a process of self-fertilisation, symbolised by the conjunction of Sun and Moon, where both Sun and Moon aspects of consciousness worked together in partnership. This concept is again reflected in the theme of the alchemical divine marriage, the *mysterium coniunctio* of the Sun King and Moon Queen, whereby the alchemist achieves the inner union, becoming a complete whole being again within the crucible of his nature. If anything, this is the task facing us individually and collectively as we pass beyond the dualism of the Piscean Age into that of the Aquarian consciousness. This inner union is discussed further in Chapters 8 and 9.

The scope of activity given to the Moon Goddess encompasses a triple influence on Heaven, Earth and the Underworld. Those inner realms of the psyche were often conceived by ancient traditions as the 'underworlds' populated by subjective figure-images, archetypal gods and goddesses and the contents of what we now term the unconscious mind. The Moon Mistress has also been called the Queen of the UnderWorld and of all that lives within the hidden psyche. In this role, she becomes the Gatekeeper to the Unconscious Mind, the Light of the Underworld. In astrological terms she opens the door to the energies of the transpersonal planets through a right-brain attunement to their transformatory influences. Many of the older Moon associations have now been ascribed to the influences of the outer planets. Uranus is now seen as the planet of changes and revolution, of higher intuition, and the narrow dividing line between genius and madness. Neptune is perceived in terms of universal compassion, of imaginative visions, of spiritual sacrifice and unity. And Pluto is now seen as the Lord of the Underworld, where death, rebirth and transformative resurrection are promised.

This connection to the unconscious depths of the human being is also indicated in the legends of the sacred Moon drink of *soma*, which is reputed to have transforming powers, being a drink of the gods which bestows immortality and godlike perceptions. The risk to individuals is that although it may bring ecstasy, universal insight and wisdom, it may bring madness to an unprepared mind. These are the dangers faced by all who become opened to their unconscious mind and the archetypal powers by descending towards those inner caverns and secret lands. In this sense, it is true that to be illumined by the Moon produces a greater clarity of mind, but to be struck by the Moon creates only lunacy.

The Great Mother has been venerated within many world cultures, from the earliest cradles of civilisation in Babylon, Chaldea, Egypt and the Near East, across Europe and Greece,

Rome and the Mediterranean, by the Celtic tribes, within North and South America, Africa, India, China, and Australasia. Her influence has been global, and whilst a study of the many myths associated with the Moon is beyond the scope of this astrological perspective, it will be worth our while to look at several, particularly as they provide an insight into later solar traditions and legends.

BABYLON AND CHALDEA

One of the earliest-known astrological calendars was created by the Babylonians, and this was called *The Houses of the Moon*, based on the lunation cycle, with their twelve monthly periods represented by the twelve signs of the zodiac. Their main Moon goddess was known as Ishtar, and she was perceived as the 'All-Accepting One', indicating a surrender to the will of the universe. The zodiac signs were known as decorating the 'girdle of Ishtar'.

The sacred temples of Ishtar were the precincts of the 'virgin priestesses', also known as the 'joy maidens', and as part of their holy duties, they were required to embody that all-accepting spirit and become non-discriminatory and surrender to the will of their goddess. This became what to modern perception might seem a religious prostitution to men, but to the ancient mind it possessed a much deeper spiritual significance, especially as the priestesses assumed the goddess-form of Ishtar to administer their sacramental task. For the men, this implied the potential of contacting the hidden divine numinous presence (the goddess or anima) within the sexual act, deepening their awareness of the power of the feminine in life. This sacrificial sharing of the *hieros gamos* has still persisted in various forms into several techniques of transformation, either reflected as a union within consciousness, or literally as a union of woman and man. Tantric and sexual magic approaches often involve physical union, as can certain witchcraft rites which evoke the cone of power by the ritual mating of the coven's high priest and high priestess, although these are more often enacted by symbolic ritual drama and by using the associated magical implements. Jungian techniques of individuation and integration and alchemical paths favour the inner subjective union of the King and the Queen, but the original understanding of the need for the 'virgin at-one-ment' goes back to such earlier times.

From Chaldea and Babylon come the goddesses of the Magna Dea of the East, Ishtar, Astarte, Astoreth, Cybele, and Sinn, the Moon God, who will reappear later in Jewish religious myths. In Assyrian Moon legends, 'Sinn Triune' represented the threefold aspects of the Moon and the ruler of their sacred Moon Tree placed in a beautiful garden or grotto which was protected by unicorns and winged lions. This image of the Tree reoccurs in a highly developed form in Jewish Qabalistic paths, as well as an archetypal symbol in many global myths. The holy tree can also be found in the biblical Genesis as the Tree of Knowledge in the garden of Eden, whilst the grotto location implies the Underworld, or roots within the unconscious collective mind. In Chaldea, the Moon was worshipped in the form of a sacred black stone, which later became the Kaaba, the holy shrine of Mecca for the Islamic faith.

EGYPT

Towering over the Egyptian pantheon of gods is Isis, Queen of Heaven, Mother of All Nature, the Silver Shining, Seed Producing, Pregnant Goddess of Time. Isis or Maat represented the Ancient Wisdom for the Egyptians, looking even further back into antiquity towards the legendary Atlantis. Isis was the goddess of fertility, sensual love, magic and sorcery, and the protectress of women in childbirth. She was known as the Mother or Daughter of the Moon, and to the Egyptian priests the Moon was the Mother of the Universe, again associating the Moon with the creation of form for the seeds of life.

Originally, the deity was considered to be androgynous, being referred to as 'My God and My Goddess', although as the solar principle began to be more recognised and the balance began to tip towards masculine and patriarchal attitudes, the nature of the divine pantheons adjusted accordingly. Reflecting this initial androgynous nature of deity Isis and Osiris were goddess and god of the Moon, but as the changes in religious consciousness proceeded to incorporate the solar principle more directly, Osiris became resurrected after death and dismemberment into a Sun god, and by 1700 BC, a trinity had been created of Isis–Moon, Osiris–Sun, and Horus–Hero/Sacrificial Child.

Isis has been associated with the continually changing shape of nature, and this has been symbolised in the image of the 'many-coloured Veil of Isis', which is similar to the Indian concept of the veil of Maya, although this also includes those perceptual and interpretative veils of glamour and illusion (see my *Visionary Dreamer* regarding the Neptune influences on consciousness). In Egyptian magical traditions, Isis was associated with Sirius the Dog Star, and so has cosmic connections.

Animal symbolism has often been associated with the Moon Goddesses, especially the cat, dog and horned animals; even today, the cat is still perceived as a lunar night-animal, and many feel uncomfortable with the feline inscrutability of cats. Isis and Hathor of Egypt were often represented by the symbol of a cow; Cybele by a Lioness, and Artemis of Greece by a Bear. The Minoan Moon Queen, Pasiphae, was the mother of the legendary Holy Bull Child, the Minotaur dwelling in the labyrinth. Kings and Queens who were associated with a Moon lineage often had horned crowns or headdresses, especially in Egyptian, Assyrian and Celtic cultures, where the bull's horns indicated a representative of the horned deity. The horns indicated the phase of the Full Moon, the hound indicated the phase of the dark Moon, and the crescent the phase of the waxing Moon. The Tarot image of the High Priestess has Moon symbolism; she sits embodying the path of equilibrium between the two Qabalistic Pillars of Mercy and Severity, white and black, with the Moon crescent at her feet and wearing a horned headdress.

Hekat, or Hecate was the Egyptian Goddess of Death and Hell, and she was summoned when magical enchantment was required, and one of her titles was the 'Three-Headed Hound of the Moon'. It is Hecate that is invoked when drawing down the magic of the dark side of the Moon. Sacrifices had to be made to Hecate so that the Moon Boat could carry the souls of those who were to be redeemed from the darkness of the UnderWorld. For those who descended into those cavernous depths and returned intact, they retained a sliver of the light of the hidden Moon from the UnderWorld, a light that brought additional wisdom and enlightenment to those on Earth.

GREECE AND ROME

Greek Moon myths passed through a number of phases, but there are several similarities with those of the Egyptian and Babylonian, as in the Triple Goddess of Luna–Hecate–Artemis, repeating the triad of Hathor–Hecate–Isis. The Greeks also called the unified Goddess Eurynome, the source of all things from the earlier Pelasgic creation myths. These three-in-one goddesses were the prototypes for the biblical solar Trinity, although their roots lay in matriarchal cultures and the religions of the divine feminine principle.

Often the Moon goddesses doubled as Earth goddesses too, including Ge or Gaia, Rhea, mother of Zeus, Persephone (the Roman Proserpine), and Demeter (the Roman Ceres). Later developments associated Artemis with the waxing Moon, Aphrodite with the Full Moon, and Hecate again with the waning Moon. Artemis was known as the wild virginal maiden and huntress, the mistress of untamed beasts and the twin Moon sister of Apollo the Sun God. She was the protectress of women's pregnancy and childbirth, and, like the Roman Diana, she ruled nature's fertility, being called the 'opener of the womb'. She accepted offerings from women to enhance their procreative nature and to ensure an easy and safe childbirth and right functioning of their maternal functions. In Asia minor, Artemis was connected with harlotry and wild sexual love, although this may have been confused with the Ishtar-inspired Aphrodite, a temptress and archetypal image of woman's sexuality and ability to arouse passions and lusts. As the goddess of love, she evoked from man his masculinity and also his dependence on her maternal instincts, the dual aspects of woman when expressing her sexual nature.

The theme of virginity continues. The Roman goddess of the hearth, Vesta, was worshipped in a temple in the forum tended by vestal virgin priestesses. Her Greek equivalent was Hestia. 'Home and hearth' are associated astrologically with the Moon. Again we see the Moon linked with women's mysteries and the Cosmic Feminine principle.

Hecate became known as the Crone, the Gatekeeper of the Underworld, to whom the attributes of a 'giver of visions or madness' was made, depending on how the recipient of the lunar insight dealt with the Moon-light. It was only by facing the dark face of Hecate that progress could be made to discover the treasures of the Underworld, or that escape could be made from those underground caves. The triple Moon nature was also reflected by the Moirai, the Fates, who were the powers of destiny with knowledge of the past, present and future. This concept also reoccurs with the Islamic Three Daughters of Allah and the Nordic Norns. This suggests the role performed by the astrological Moon's Nodes. The South Node indicates the past, the North Node the future, with the axis of transformation existing in the present.

OLD TESTAMENT

Amongst Jewish and biblical tales there are many derived from older Moon legends and Goddess worship, with several of these often unrecognised as playing foundational roles in the development of those religious teachings. The original nomadic tribe of the Jews came from the great Moon city of Ur in Chaldea, and initially the Moon was worshipped as either god or goddess, with certain races and tribes preferring one to the other. The Jews were more masculine-biased. Originally, the Jehovah of the Old Testament was the Lord of the Moon, whose living symbol was the heavenly Moon, the giver of Life and Death, and the disposer of form and nature in the world. Jehovah was perceived as a fusion of both male and female aspects of divinity, as were the more ancient deities before sexual polarisation became more common.

Mount Sinai was sacred to the Moon, and derived its name from the Babylonian Moon god Sinn, and it was on Sinai that Moses received the tablets of the Law, the Ten Commandments, from the deity of the mountain symbolised as the burning bush. It was at this time that a developing Jewish monotheism began to confront the matriarchal Moon worship. The new prophets like Moses condemned the older religious practices, speaking of the new dispensation that was emerging. The Jewish reverence for the number seven and the concept of the holy seventh sabbath day came from the fourfold division of the twenty-eight-day lunar cycle, so that the seven-day week equated to a quarter phase of the Moon.

The Judaic Ark of the Covenant is a symbol of the Universal Mother, a receptacle carrying the seed of all living things, the germ of life, which evokes the role of the Moon goddesses as preservers through form of the life seed. This Ark image also is found in the legend of Noah's Ark, the ship of life, and is a fusion of Moon–Sea symbolism. It is a vessel of the mysteries, a container of physical, mental, imaginative and spiritual fertility. Arguably, it may be an ancient source of the Grail representing a fusion of planes, where a receptacle is made within the lower human consciousness to receive the fertilisation by spirit; through human form divinity descends into matter. The word 'ark' is derivative of the Hindu word *argha*, which means crescent or arc of a circle, and the word ark implies the Moon boat which has been previously found in Egyptian myths as traversing the UnderWorld; and Noah is a Jewish form of Nuah, a Babylonian Moon goddess. Before the monotheistic Father God emerged into Judaism, the Moon Mother was venerated and her symbol of the Covenant was carried with them across the wilderness years.

Even the Song of Solomon in the Bible contains references to the darker aspects of the Moon Goddess, which reflect the symbolism of the Egyptian Isis and the later Black Madonna images. When the Temple of Solomon was constructed with the aid of the Kings of Tyre, it was primarily for the generation of a great Moon ritual, with extremely precise measurements being used and forms of temple symbolism associated with Qabalistic teachings concerned Yesod and the Moon. The feminine symbolism of pillars surmounted by pomegranates was included in the building, whilst in the inner sanctuary at the heart of the temple was placed the holy Ark of the Covenant.

CHRISTIANITY

The attitudes of the culture into which Jesus Christ was born were already largely patriarchal. These attitudes have greatly influenced Christianity and conditioned the outlook of the Christian priesthood, which has generally excluded women from the role of spiritual mediation. The Roman Catholic Church still prohibits women priests through fear of reintroducing the power of the feminine back into the Church.

However, even Christianity is not immune from the influence of the Moon. The Vatican is built on Mount Vaticanus, an ancient shrine sacred to the worship of the Mother Goddess, and the Catholic Church is called Mother Church. In recent times the influence of Mary, mother of Jesus has been revived, and many Catholics pray to the Virgin in preference to either Jesus or the Father God. The month of May is consecrated to Mary, and this month was originally sacred to the goddesses Maia and Vesta, representatives of Mother Earth who also personified earthly nourishment. Mary is called the Moon of Our Church, Our Moon, Spiritual Moon, Perfect and Eternal Moon, especially within Italian Catholicism, which retains certain powers of the older Roman and Meditteranean Moon religions. For Christians it is the affinity with Mary that can open the doors towards alignment with the Goddess. In the form of Christ there is the embodiment of the unified consciousness and the inner subjective sacred marriage; but this has been too distorted by the emphasis on his physical maleness and by patriarchal attitudes about the 'Son of God' for the average Christian to understand the subtle implications of Christ's divine nature.

One example of this is in the descent of the Holy Spirit in the shape of a dove at the baptism of Jesus by John the Baptist in the River Jordan. The dove was a symbol of the ancient messenger of the Magna Mater, the Great Mother, and She Who Shines For All. By symbolic esoteric interpretation, this implies that Jesus received the Christ spirit through a descent of grace or initiation involving the Goddess, or that he had achieved the integration with his inner Moon or anima, which he proceeded to reveal through his message and gospel of love. The Gnostics believe that the Holy Spirit is that of the Divine Feminine, and that the Christian trinity of Father–Son–Holy Ghost should really replace the Ghost by the Mother image for completeness and accuracy.

Tales of moon gods parallel Christian myths, reflecting legends of death and resurrection. The moon god becomes mortal, living a human life, suffering as humans do, and then dies only to be reborn as the new moon rises. He becomes a god of heaven, descends into the Underworld to succour and give hope and light to all within, serves as a judge of men's souls, and mediates between heaven and earth. He promises that he will return, and through his moon phases he is perpetually renewed and ever-present.

Followers of Judaism, Islam and Christianity still follow old traditions of calculating the dates of their major religious festivals on the basis of Moon cycles, such as Easter being the first Sunday after a particular Full Moon.

THE CELTS AND NORTHERN MYSTERIES

The Northern Celts developed a Moon calendar too, with their seasonal year being the whole Moon cycle, that of twelve moons or monthly lunar periods. An alternate version of the Celtic calendar is that of thirteen lunar months to a year, the 'common law Moon months' which also indicated the right time for all important religious ceremonies, as both solstices and equinoxes became connected to Moon phases and the nearest days to specific new or full moons. One suggestion of a Celtic calendar is that the lunar month spanned from the New Moon to the next, or another may have commenced at the first quarter, six days after the new moon. Today we are unsure of the exact nature of the Celtic lunar calendar.

The Celts had a triple goddess symbol in Brigentis, the three Brigets who have been called the Three Ladies of Britain, and symbolised the phases of the Great Mother Anu or Annis. It was Bride or Briggidda who hung her cloak of night over the rays of the Sun. In the Arthurian legends, King Arthur was taken away mortally wounded by the three queens to Avalon, with the promise of his later return.

The Celtic version of the Judaic Covenant was that of the Cauldron, a source for much sacrificial ceremonial ritual, even to receiving blood from prisoners. This was the sacred Cauldron of the Moon Goddess, the Cauldron of Regeneration, the giver of fertility, love and inspirational wisdom. Brigid, Rhiannon and Ceridwen, form a trinity of goddesses with a symbol of Ceridwen being the Cauldron, associated with the depths of consciousness. The later Grail myths are probably derived from this Moon symbol, and the idea of the Wastelands emerges from the belief that the Moon has entered the Underworld and requires a process of redemptive transformation to occur again before its fertilising spirit can restore the powers of nature back to life. As in Chaldea, the Moon was worshipped in the form of a stone, and in some tales the Grail is described as a stone. Most Grail imagery includes female anima-type figures, and the Grail as a receptacle is a feminine symbol.

The cauldron is later seen as the alchemical crucible in which base metal is transmuted into gold, or where mortal human matter is spiritualised, inspired, transformed and immortalised as the Elixir of Life is distilled.

Moon myths are extensive and only a few of the common concepts can be indicated here, but it becomes obvious that the ancients honoured the feminine principle much more openly and reverently than we do. The Chariot of the Winged moon flies across time and space. If we choose to ignore it, then it does not mean that its influence fades away; we can only repress its messages down into our individual and collective unconscious mind. Denying the sensitivity and natural wisdom of the sacred feminine is foolish. Men especially need to recognise the presence of the Queen of the Night and to befriend and embrace that inner feminine archetype, so that the path to their own integration and wholeness can be discerned. Women need to reassert their own inner connections to the Goddess, as well as embracing their inner masculine archetype. For humanity, this requires the conscious entering of the realm of the Moon, a re-awakening. Working with an understanding of individual Moon patterns as indicated by astrology is one route to achieve greater understanding and clarity.

The Astrological Moon

THE MOON AND SUN ARE known as the two luminaries or lights. They symbolise the major archetypal principles of the Divine Feminine and the Divine Masculine, which are responsible for the creation of the dualistic universe. They dominate the Earth and give rise to the potential for life on its surface. The Moon has the task of reflecting solar light and purpose to Earth, symbolising the relatedness that exists throughout the solar system.

At the time of birth it is the Moon pattern that is initially absorbed and activated, due to that fundamental contact with the physical mother and the original feeling response of the child to the external world. This is the first imprint, and will set the tone for the remainder of the life. Such psychotherapy techniques as Primal Therapy and Rebirthing attempt to deal with the traumas that can occur during the passage and emergence into individual life.

The Moon's role develops from the first breath and continues amidst all past experiences and the present allowing it to function as a mediator. Through that lens of the Moon, the past can be contacted and explored. Whilst it may be a lost unknown land, it is also the seed-bed for our present reality and self-image. The inner lunar mindscape is a land of contrasts and contradictions, but learning how to map its most prominent features can prove invaluable for personal integration.

Entering the deepest recesses of our nature opens us to experience the personal and collective unconscious areas of our being. We are looking into our roots, our deepest connections to family heredity, ancestors, race, even towards our individual DNA patterns – into whatever contributes to making us as we are now. Each one of us is a living embodiment of the accumulated evolutionary development of mankind; each of us contributes towards the unfolding potential of that intrinsic pattern. Each experience that we have is stored away in our memory for personal use, and at the same time it contributes to the reservoir of collective instinctual wisdom to which we all have access.

Through repetitive experience and behaviour, the Moon reflects the creation of instinctive modes of reaction, revealing our subconscious predisposition and conditioned reflexes in the form of apparently spontaneous responses to situations. We create many types of automatic and mechanical reaction patterns on every level of our being, physical, emotional and mental, and life eventually takes on a shape dictated by habit alone. These build in those psychological barriers, structures and parameters that are essentially protective in nature, designed to shield us from the shock of experiences for which we are unprepared. This is why confrontations with the violence of warfare can cause such psychological trauma in many who have been born into relatively peaceful environments; whilst in others, their innate instinctive survival patterns become reactivated under the stresses, and their feeling functions close down, leaving them more prepared to deal with the barbarity and inhumanity of the battlefield.

The Moon exerts a pull towards the past, towards the conscious mind's domination by sentimentality, nostalgia and an attraction towards established social attitudes and values. It is a reflection of the past contained within each individual living in the present, and if misapplied it can become a trap which diverts attention from the current life experience. As a mediator between past and present, the Moon serves as a principle of rhythmic integration, dealing with messages from the instincts of body, feelings and mind. Our lunar-assimilated experiences from the past serve as guidelines when confronting experiences in the present. The role of memory is vital for a sense of human continuity and identity; without memory, our sense of individual cohesiveness collapses.

Through our Moon roots deep in our own past, which stretch out to our parents, our homes and social environments, the Moon functions by qualities of relatedness. From these roots also arises our image of self, our root feelings about ourselves, a reflected and almost subliminal impression of our actual nature. Due to the nature of these collective roots, we have a tendency towards a psychic inertia that encourages us to become submerged in life experience without struggling to attain individuality and self-consciousness. This is the pull back towards the realms of unconsciousness. This tendency favours a feeling response to life which is closely connected to basic physical sensations, rather than the later developments of mind and efforts at understanding and evaluation of life.

Both the Sun and the Moon serve as the two fundamental polarities within the individual, and have great significance in the formation of the matrix of being from which individuality and personality emerge. They represent the most highly energised and magnetic forces within our psychology, with the influences of the other planets being mediated through their positions and focus. The Sun is associated with *individuality*, and the Moon with *personality*.

The personality is our social face, our mask which is ever-changing and which is the initial response to our experiences and external stimulation. It is through the personality that our individuality is expressed, although due to our tendency towards misidentification, many people make the mistake of regarding that multi-faceted personality as their real self, and in so doing lose their centre in the ever-changing periphery. Self-exploration includes the passage through the personality towards the central individuality (symbolised by the light of the Sun), and so a first step involves working with the depths indicated by the Moon. The ideal is to attain a state where the Sun and Moon are harmonised, so that they co-operate, forming a fixity of purpose and clarity of direction, integrating the divided spheres of the psyche.

As the Sun and Moon are polar opposites, they can be seen as the unity of an axis. The Sun is often viewed as the light of the conscious mind in men, and of the unconscious in women, while with the Moon the situation is reversed. In the contemporary world, this traditional attitude is less embracing in its accuracy. We live in a time when gender barriers are breaking down to some degree, both in physical appearances and in psychological attitudes. Women are not just passive, and men are not just assertive. The early stages of a potential androgynous consciousness are dawning, and many women are actively integrating their own animus through adopting qualities associated with their unconscious Sun, and fusing complement-ary masculine qualities with their feminine ones; and many men are integrating their inner anima and integrating their inner feminine, thus softening and sensitising their own natures and making themselves more receptive and aware. This is the way forward. Both Sun and Moon principles need to be activated, experienced and expressed through every individual for wholeness to occur. This theme will be considered in Chapters 9 and 10.

It is relatively easy to observe the superficial lunar influence operating within us. We can simply watch the changing activity of our responses to daily experience. The Moon acts as a scanning receiver to all the impressions that impinge on our consciousness from the outer world, focusing and selecting those to which we will actually respond consciously. Depending on the nature of our momentary experience and our environment, the Moon helps to protect and guide us in our ways of relating to external stimulations, through the activation of our patterns of habitual behaviour. Our subjective states also relay information which may influence the nature of our emotional reactions, and the nature of our relationships with others, such as partners, friends, colleagues, family, strangers. We establish different patterns of relating, differing degrees of intimacy and closeness. Our emotions are perpetually shifting, rearranging and conveying feeling-information about the well-being of our inner nature. Yet if we choose to identify with this realm of inner emotional flux and reactions to any stimulation, then we are making a mistake in seeing our self in what is merely transient. We may be moulded by our environment and experiences, but we should not be ruled by them. We need to discover that deeper, permanent centre where the roots of the Moon interweave with the rays of the Sun.

Experimenting with a technique such as the Buddhist *vipassana* meditation provides a direct experience of this outer transiency. Just sitting, breathing rhythmically and watching the movement of consciousness and all reactions of physical sensations, can be sufficient to displace the focus of identification from the periphery of our nature, driving it back towards our centre. From that position, we can see our spurious separative self constantly passing by, a phenomenon of the reactions of consciousness.

Within every individual, there are certain issues that are represented by the Moon; indications of how these will be experienced and expressed can be gleaned from the natal chart positions. If the Moon has many challenging aspects, then there may be innate stresses and tensions within the deeper foundations of that individual which require attention and integration. Handling emotions may prove difficult for that person, and the implications are that the earlier upbringing may have been difficult. Some interpretations emphasise 'karmic patterns' on emotional and mental levels that are continuing to be worked through. Whatever type of intrinsic pattern is reflected by the chart, the result can either be advantageous to the expression of natural talents, or alternatively, self-expression can be restricted by barrier-type patterns. Certainly patterns created around feelings of self-image can enhance or inhibit the release of creative energy, as do expectations of success or failure.

The types of issue reflected by the Moon centre on the need for: emotional peace, feelings of belonging, positive self-image, a sense of inner stability and support, domestic and emotional security, self-protection, self-nurturing, feeling wanted by others, social and intimate relationships, family, love and adaptation to the outer world. These themes will be further developed in the analyses of specific Moon positions in natal charts later in this book.

Our relationships come under the aegis of the Moon, especially in so far as they involve nurturing others. One aspect of emotional maturity is displayed in our sense of caring for others. A significant quality of the New Age movement, especially in its more social and political dimensions, is the embracing care and concern for the well-being of the whole human family and life on Earth. Response to our own and others' needs is a sign of development and growing awareness, and the birth of a compassionate spirit.

The Moon can be expressed in two distinct ways. The first remains that of a self-centred perspective, in which self-satisfaction is paramount, and in which possessiveness is often present in relationship, along with the grasping of any affection shown to the individual, fears of loss, and jealousy. In the second mode of expression, the need for relationship and a merging of identity is transformed from either the separative or herd instinct, into that of a greater unity with all life through the expansion of consciousness. By confronting our own Moon, we can learn how to integrate our own needs, then move on to understand the needs of humanity with enhanced tolerance and insight. The challenge is then to fulfil the needs of the human family and achieve a planetary healing. It may be a vast task and almost impossible to conceive any answers, but one thing is certain: unless we take our own part of the world – our selves – and transform that first, then little progress will be made. Moving through that inner lunar landscape is the path towards the source of light, love and power that is our real nature as the spiritual Sun.

THE MOON AND PARENTAL INFLUENCES

In the natal chart, the Moon is considered to symbolise the influence of the mother, and the Sun that of the father; any aspects between them, together with their sign and house positions, will indicate the nature of their relationship and consequent influence on the child. These can be both positive and beneficial, or negative and constraining.

Our mother is our primary connection to the outer world, the source of our life, food, identity, satisfying our needs, and the root of our security by being usually ever-present to fulfil our demands. She protects, comforts and nourishes, and our early life-experience is absorbed within her presence. That original imprint from the mother is one which will remain with us for all our lives. The astrological Moon is perceived as a reflection of the feminine principle in life, so it has also been associated with the image of the physical mother.

It is from these earliest experiences in life that our deepest instinctual and feeling patterns begin to form through our experience of our parents, especially the mother. From the first day, the child absorbs the mental and psychic atmosphere surrounding the parental relationship, as well as registering the vibrations of the mother's inner state and reactions to the child. The child's sense of security is founded on the nature of attention and quality of love it receives during this very dependent and receptive period, and this is carried through into later life. If the mother's love, attention and care are felt to be lacking, the child may grow up viewing life as threatening and disappointing, and with a basically pessimistic outlook.

During our early life, we form patterns of dependency, passivity, relationship, acceptance or denial of feelings, emotions and instincts, self-consciousness, individuality, needs, desires, and abilities to adapt to changing circumstances. These all emerge from our experience of parenting and eventually form the conditioning matrix for later adult personality development, creating either a positive and harmonious inner self-image in tune with instinctual and emotional needs, or a negative self-image which reflects inner divisions and stresses.

The Sun and Moon in our charts show how we initially experienced our parents. This may be based on how things really were or on how it felt to us at the time. This can include perceptions of the type of adult relationship that our parents had; the depth of love or partnership tensions; how the child felt in relating to the parents; what 'messages' were received concerning the roles of father and mother; and how parental attitudes influenced our own emerging personality by encouragement or restrictions. There may be conflicting messages coming to us from parents with different attitudes towards childraising, or one parent may have seemed colder and more distant than the other; the father may become a shadowy figure in early years, or the mother may have withdrawn her care and attention to nurture new children in the family. All of these, and many more influences, help to form our later adult perception and attitudes. The unconscious absorption of such conditioning may be demonstrated in adult life, when within our new family lives we unconsciously repeat our own childhood patterns in dealing with our own children. Our pattern of 'parenting' has been learned from our parents, and to some degree is liable to operate even if it may contradict conscious ideals and progressive attitudes.

The perceived experience of the mother may be indicated by the position of the Moon, in sign, house, aspects, and this can also reveal how those tendencies operate within the personal natal chart. The inner life of the mother may also be suggested through this perspective. Similarly, the father is reflected by the Sun in the chart. The signs on the cusps of the 4th and 10th houses denote the parental influences and may indicate ways in which self-parenting can be achieved in later life, healing the tensions of earlier influences by giving oneself the right kind of inner nurturing. Challenging Moon aspects indicate that the ghosts of the past, family traditions, and established patterns are unduly powerful, and are preventing progress.

The Moon in a woman's chart signifies the image of mothering and womanhood with which she is likely to identify, and on which she is likely to model her own behaviour. In men's charts, the Moon represents the inner feminine image, the anima, or the type of woman to whom he will be especially attracted, and who promises ultimate emotional fulfilment and nourishment to his spirit.

The Moon can be analysed on several different levels. It can reveal its presence through the individual psychology, as a personal pattern of behaviour, and yet it also indicates the parental figures and their relationship. Within our own nature, the Sun sits in the conscious mind, embodying those tendencies that are more obviously recognisable; the Moon hides in the darkness of our subconscious mind, manipulating and directing us by pulling the threads of deeper personality patterns, those which we no longer even recognise as existing, and which were formed during the early months of life. Our torchlight needs to shine inwards to these hidden roots, because it is through understanding them that we can come to feel more inwardly secure and stable, and at ease with the potency of our emotional natures.

SELF-NURTURING

The concept of self-nurturing derives from the psychological need to become independent of our parents and to become capable of providing for ourselves whatever 'nourishment' we required to satisfy all our personality needs and develop as individuals. The necessary understanding of our own unique needs and nature will be aided by a study of the Moon's sign, house and aspects. Working with these astrological indications will help to rebalance the Moon's effects and energies, so that they become more positive and contribute to our well-being.

It is our parents' role to guide us towards social adaptation and integration, to instil socially acceptable attitudes, behaviour, values and beliefs in their children, a process that is reinforced by education or religious teachings. Most parents have dreams of their children's future lives and success, and will attempt to guide them in certain directions.

Many adults live in ways that just reflect these parental dream patterns, moving through life as if acting out a predetermined role. Our lives become predictable and conformist, and often feel deeply unsatisfying for reasons that seem hard to grasp. We may have everything that society portrays as desirable, and yet it may still fail to satisfy. Something has gone wrong somewhere; we become dependent on the outer world, and that can be a fragile dependency. We make choices to change our outer world when fulfilment is lacking, change partners, jobs, houses in an attempt to find that sense of contentment.

What we have lost, or have never even known, is the ability to look within, to discover ways to nurture ourselves and be less dependent on the outer world, and to realise that if we feel integrated we appreciate our lives more. We have experienced part of the nurturing process, that of external bonding and parental relationship, and we need to learn the process of inner unification, and that of parenting our own internal child. The Moon, when operating through this perspective, can be imagined as a demanding child, jumping up and down to gain attention in an attempt to have its needs satisfied. Perhaps through being repeatedly ignored, an emotional temper tantrum may result, which eventually subsides into repressed anger and feelings of rejection.

Self-nurturing is a process of freeing ourselves from patterns of inhibition and restriction in order to move towards a psychological maturity. Through self-exploration, we can begin to determine the nature of these patterns, accept and recognise them, and then choose to transform those which have a negative influence on our adult life. It is not easy and requires a radical change in the nature of our self-perception and often in life-style too. It is challenging to break free of the restraints of the past so that the present and future can be faced with greater self-determination and awareness; but it is a step towards liberation and a more intense exploration of life as that feeling nature is released from those inner prisons.

THE INTEGRATED POSITIVE MOON

As the Moon symbolises our ability to adapt to change, understanding our habitual response patterns is important so that we can be aware of those times when they are inappropriate and self-restrictive.

Positive integration is often the result of a loving and nurturing upbringing. The child who feels loved and valued will normally grow up with a positive self-image, feeling at ease with their feeling responses and instinctual behaviour. The result of this is a relatively well-balanced mature adult, capable of dealing with their emotions in a realistic manner, and of relating to others. The ability to empathise with the feelings of others is a valuable one, enhancing all relationships and forging more satisfactory intimate and family bonding.

Relationships are characterised by mutual support, tolerance and understanding, in which an essential trust in each other serves as a foundation for communication. Yet there is still a need for the assertion of personal independence and identity and for the avoidance of undue reliance and dependency on others. Problems can be mutually shared and support offered through friendship, with the understood aim being that of self-supportiveness through personal inner change resolving the challenging and problematic issues. The empathic sensitivity allows unspoken messages to be received, and this can increase the possibility of suitable nurturing being transmitted to others in need. Once friendships are established they are often long-lasting, and loyalty to friends and family is considered a real virtue.

For those with a positive, well-integrated Moon, a stable home life is seen as an essential base from which to operate, and much enjoyment and emotional nourishment is derived from a close and loving family, with domesticity and privacy from the outer world being highly valued and protected. Home is viewed as a sanctuary, a place of protection, rest and recharging of personal energies. But there is not a total dependency on either home or family for emotional happiness and security, since neither can be relied on totally – we must create our own inner security too.

Feelings of trust in life and an optimistic spirit provide firm foundations for a secure sense of personal identity and stability in life. The personality feels properly rooted, and acknowledges the vitalising role that the emotions and feelings perform in the life of the human being, and so respects and honours their messages and impulses. Through acceptance, those feelings become constructive and positive in nature, freely flowing through the individual and rarely becoming blocked and creating stagnant, festering waters. Instincts are valued as offering additional signposts to guide choices and directions, and 'gut feelings' are given due regard in evaluating available options. Personal vulnerability is accepted as inevitable if life is going to be fully embraced, although there will be a sufficient level of self-protection maintained against unnecessary emotional suffering through empathic identification.

Inner needs will be identified and efforts made to satisfy them, due to a recognition that in so doing this fulfils one's whole nature, remaining healthy and feeling good. Yet this is not just a self-centred process occurring: the individual who is capable of self-nurturing becomes more able to nurture others too.

The ability to adapt should be present, so that changes can be successfully made whenever necessary, such as at times when outmoded patterns are creating restrictions in your life path. Removing or transcending such barriers and blockages can free unexpressed emotional vitality, and can have a beneficial effect in other areas of life. This ability to build more constructive habit patterns and responses is a valuable skill to possess, and one that should be applied more regularly. Adapting can create a more flexible self and personality. It is not a sign of weakness but of real strength.

Security needs may be associated with financial stability, and a positive Moon often displays a wise handling of available money and resources to enhance the life-style in a careful and responsible manner. Wasting money is considered to be irresponsible and foolish.

Balanced and healthy eating habits are developed, so that there are none of the emotionally compensating food obsessions associated with a negative Moon. Digestion of physical food is good, as is the digestion of emotional nourishment.

A positive integrated Moon often retains a childlike wonder at the beauty and mystery of the world. There is a joy in life and an open receptivity to its infinite treasures all around us. Intuition and a psychic sensitivity can attune us to appreciate such abundant gifts. The Tree of Life has many fruits, all of which are ours to attune with and eat for our soul food.

THE UNINTEGRATED NEGATIVE MOON

Emotional immaturity and relationship dependency are signs of an unintegrated Moon, which are associated with inner insecurity and lack of personal stability due to an intrinsic distrust of self and others. The lack of integration may be revealed in one of two distinct ways. The first is that of a distorted emotional expression, whereas the second involves repression.

Emotions are likely to be highly sensitised and volatile, change-able in nature and influenced by others' thoughts and feelings, as the personal self-image is dependent on people's attitudes. If the responses from others are critical, negative and uncomplimentary, then the tendency is to feel wounded and rejected, to sink into an emotional morass, and to resort to emotional withdrawal and retreat. When the world becomes too much the automatic reaction is to go off into a private inner sanctuary, to lick one's wounds until the emotions subside. There is emotional vulnerability, difficulty in dealing with emotions, and an inner instability that is hard to resolve.

Relationships may be problematic and a source of conflict and suffering. Emotional needs are especially powerful within relationships, and the tendency is that dependency will dominate. Family life will be a realm through which great love, sympathy, empathy, protectiveness and possessiveness can be displayed, but this may become excessive and detrimental to the freedom and well-being of family members. The role played may be that of a martyr sacrificing all for others, or the expression of love may be far too effusive and restrictive. Dependency may occur, with a reliance on family members to provide the only meaning and purpose in life, so that when children reach adulthood and leave home or partners leave or die, life is suddenly stripped of all meaning and purpose. In such cases, the individual is dependent on others for nurturing, and fails to develop self-nurturing. There can be considerable self-displacement through identifying with partners, which can restrict individuation. There can also be a tendency to attract very nurturing partners who are prepared to take on a parental role in the relationship.

Security is sought in the outer world, through family members, possessions, home, social traditions and established world-views. Much effort is put into creating personal security, and change is perceived with suspicion. Home becomes the protective womb or castle, barriers against the wildness of life; and financial security may be given a high priority, perhaps as a preoccupation or by careful restraint in spending and a preference for amassing savings. Habit patterns are built into the life-style to provide a safe predictability, and a regulated, organised home will be developed, with rules to which all will be expected to conform. Adapting to changes may prove difficult, and will often be resisted unless absolutely necessary.

Inner needs and desires will be motivating factors, although these are likely to fluctuate, and there can be an impulse towards compensatory self-indulgence to appease inner hungers. This can easily manifest in compulsive eating habits, with periodic excesses, especially triggered by emotional discomfort. Connections between health, emotions and food are likely, and traditional Moon ailments may include digestive problems, and those associated with a woman's reproductive system. There may be a preference for female company, particularly of women who are perceived as reflecting the ideal type of nurturing that a mother should provide, although some men may have certain ambiguous complex feelings related to women, feeling uneasy with dependency tendencies, or needs for a 'mother-substitute'.

For many, an unintegrated Moon indicates an emotional unease stemming from the primary mother–child relationship, which later results in an inability to mature fully into independent adult life. Behaviour patterns established during childhood are still active and influential, although they are now serving mainly as limitation and restriction, and could even be displayed as periodic temper tantrums and sulks when personal desires are unfulfilled.

Another expression of an unintegrated Moon involves a more repressive expression, possibly resulting from a deeper denial of childhood emotions and failure of a satisfactory relationship with parents. Again, there is the lack of self-confidence and trust in the world. Emotions are considered to be threatening and are repeatedly denied. Instinctive messages are thrust back into the unconscious mind, where they begin to form a reservoir of stresses and pressures ready to erupt whenever provoked. A lack of empathy and sensitivity to others is present, linked to an excessive degree of self-protection and self-interest, leading to an immoral or amoral stance. An isolated self-centredness persists, although it is not a fulfilling one, and can equally manifest as signs of self-neglect and surrender to the vicissitudes of existence, the individual becoming a piece of human flotsam floating on the tides of life. Personal needs and desires may be essentially denied, and concepts of nurture rejected, as the links to the emotional and feeling nature are disconnected and slowly atrophy. Outstretched hands from others may be ignored, and alienation will occur due to self-imposed withdrawal. The separate self is asserted in an imbalanced manner. The individual refuses to acknowledge dependency and relationship needs, yet is incapable of self-nurturing and integration. Human bonds are tossed away, commitments dismissed and rejected, and intimacy scorned as being unnecessary, as is social responsibility. The inner life is denied, and most attachments to the process of life that others naturally form are seen as irrelevant.

This may appear in some respects to be an individual assertiveness, but it often results from a much deeper passivity and lack of inner roots. It is a partial, self-absorbed personality that has developed, one that is unable to adapt and live in social relationship in a positive and constructive manner. From early childhood to later adult life, a pattern of inner and outer alienation has developed, resulting in the social misfit, lost, cut off from lunar roots, and equally unable to discover and express the solar potential and individuality, except in negative ways. For them, life becomes a downward spiral into the negative darkness, instead of a movement towards the light. Those of us capable of taking the lighted path have the responsibility to make the most of our advantages, for the eventual benefit of humanity and to offer helping hands to those who find themselves on the downward path in society.

THE MOON IN THE ELEMENTS

The element in which the Moon is placed in the chart can also indicate the capacity for self-nurturing as well as habitual patterns of response and reaction to life-experiences. The Moon's element shows the type of experience ('food') that we need in order to feel inwardly nourished; receiving that can give sustenance to the whole personality as the roots of our being are absorbing the right nutrients. Instinctual behaviour patterns are indicated by the element, as well as the type of energy that you use to adjust to changing life-situations and environments.

Moon in Fire (Aries, Leo, Sagittarius) indicates that there is an enthusiastic response to a variety of life-experience, linked to a basically optimistic outlook. The individual is capable of responding fairly fluently to changes, and is often prepared to initiate them whenever life becomes too predictable and familiar. The emphasis on security and stability is less important for the Fire Moon, and often an impatience and lack of planning may create more challenges than were expected. Choices may be made without due consideration, the preference being for impulsive action and the expression of an individualistic and sometimes self-centred will. Challenges are confronted by assertiveness and wilful power; desire and enjoyment are important motivating factors, and their pursuit adds fuel to the fires of enthusiasm. An effort is made to minimise those spheres of life that fail to give deep satisfaction.

This intent on pursuing personal objectives for fulfilment can be perceived as a childlike naivety and self-centredness. The Fire

Moon individual's parents may have been overly permissive, or they may have encouraged an emphasis on self-reliance and independence without a corresponding awareness of relationship to others and the value of their feelings. There may be a lack of sensitivity to the needs of others, due to the preoccupation with personal satisfaction and feelings.

Moon in Earth (Taurus, Virgo, Capricorn) shows a preference for security and stability. The life-style is carefully organised and predictable, and social traditions dominate the attitudes of the personality resulting in a distinct need for social acceptability. Practicality, pragmatism and rootedness are Earth Moon qualities, and the realm of work is given a high priority. Attitudes, beliefs and values are formed by the tangible world and sense perceptions; generally, what cannot be proven in the physical world is dismissed as fantasy. Even though more subtle realms may be glimpsed, they are soon analysed away as passing fancies and illusions, especially by Virgo and Capricorn. Underlying the practical and adaptive abilities is a less secure personality, particularly with regard to feelings, emotions and self-acceptance.

The Virgo and Capricorn types especially have emotional challenges, often being self-condemnatory concerning their own lack of success or perfection. Earlier parental conditioning may have helped to instil a self-critical attitude, the child perhaps having failed to achieve the parents' standards of behaviour or education. There is often a preoccupation with work and career status, with a lot of time and effort being channelled in that direction in order to avoid emotional discomfort and build a higher social profile to enhance self-esteem. Changes are usually resisted and seen as potentially threatening; a fixed life-style is preferred. There may be a need to integrate the emotions more effectively, instead of keeping them at a distance. Yet the Earth Moon can be very helpful to others who are passing through troubled times, as its stability can be very supportive.

The Moon in Air (Gemini, Libra, Aquarius) indicates that feelings and emotions are analysed and intellectualised, so that the individual becomes distanced from the emotional power that was originally there. Feelings are given second place to intellect, leading eventually to their becoming inhibited and repressed. The emotional nature is neglected and effectively denied, or at least filtered through the intellect. Its expression is limited to what is deemed 'suitable', and its raw power is lost.

Part of this tendency may have arisen through parental dis-interest in childhood emotions, a lack of emotional empathy between parent and child. A child in this situation can become emotionally detached, therefore denying or becoming distanced from their own emotional nature. Certainly thoughts need to be expressed to others in order for there to be a sense of social contact and to satisfy the inner need for communication, but the denial of the feeling nature should not be part of that process. Both the needs to communicate on emotional and mental levels – within ourselves and with others – should be equally recognised as vitally important for well-being. Life is generally approached with careful consideration and forethought; in adjusting to new situations, an attempt is made to employ detached objectivity. Healing that gap between emotion and thought may be necessary to achieve an inner tranquillity that is missing in life.

The Moon in Water (Cancer, Scorpio, Pisces) emphasises dealing with and experiencing emotions and feelings. Life is perceived through a filter of emotional intensity, and most of the inner process is directly involved with the integration of emotions, which are felt as the real vitality of life, enriching, stimulating and motivating. Yet Moon in Water can equally manifest in feelings of vulnerability and fear of emotional up-heaval; much will depend on the overall tone of the chart and aspects made. There can be issues related to empathy with the needs and suffering of others. Moon in Water people tend to over-empathise. They need to learn how to distinguish their own feelings from those of others, and to protect themselves from the feelings of others. Moon Pisces, particularly has a tendency to escape through addictions, believing that drugs or alcohol can fill those aching inner needs. Some may confuse their own emotional integration by becoming overly obsessive about their emotional reactions and feeling responses, too oversensitised resulting in a diminishing of their practical efficiency and life adaptations.

Past influences and conditioning will remain highly significant, positively or negatively. Establishing habit patterns is likely, and it is through these that the Water Moon often attempts to adjust to changing situations. Relationships will have roots in emotional affinities, and it is on that level that long-lasting contacts will be forged. The influence of the parents will depend on their affinity with the child's emotional sensitivity, and could be either beneficial or deleterious to the growing child, depending on whether its vulnerability is respected or trampled over.

MOON AND PLANETARY NATAL CHART PLACINGS

When the natal Moon is positioned above the horizon in the chart, and the Sun is below the horizon, this indicates a need to form a personal understanding of the social values and ideals of the collective. These people need to express their own perspective and interpretation and contribute to the awareness of the social group as reflected by the individual. Examples include Meher Baba, Oscar Wilde, John Lennon, Aleister Crowley, Winston Churchill and Prince Charles.

When the natal Moon is positioned below the horizon, and the Sun above, the attempt is made to place personal and individual ideals and values in a broader social and world context, to see how the individual is reflecting the overshadowing needs and urges of the collective. In this case, the contribution made is that of alignment, receptivity and transmission. Examples include: Alice Bailey, Annie Besant, Timothy Leary, Ram Dass, Krishnamurti, Mikhail Gorbachev, Albert Einstein and Hitler.

When both Moon and Sun are placed above the horizon, the appropriate individual response is directed towards collective activity as a participant in the group evolutionary path, which may involve political, cultural or scientific unfoldment inspired by the light of firmly held personal values and ideals. Here, the personal contribution has wider group implications, with the individual serving a collective effort seeking to guide humanity towards a fulfilment of its destiny. Examples include: Sigmund Freud, Gandhi, John F. Kennedy, Kahlil Gibran, Dion Fortune, Rajneesh, Salvador Dali, Pablo Picasso, Queen Elizabeth II, Maria Montessori, Bob Dylan, Martin Luther King and Da Free John.

When both the Moon and Sun are placed below the horizon, the emphasis is placed on the actualisation of personal potential, ideals and ambitions. This is a relatively egotistical placement. There can still be a significant social contribution and influence, but this is more as a by-product than as an intention. Egoic satisfaction, fulfilment and achievement are the main motivating factors, and expressions of self-effacement and sacrifice for the good of the collective are rare. Examples include: Josef Stalin, Richard Nixon.

Taking a birth chart of an individual born at the New Moon stage, immediately after the conjunction, note any planets falling within the space that the Moon will cross as it moves towards its position at the First Quarter. These planets symbolise qualities, talents and tendencies inherited at birth, which should be relatively easy to express and utilise.

If the natal Moon falls between the First Quarter and Full Moon positions, it will cross as it moves towards Full Moon indicate qualities, talents and tendencies that are only partially developed, and which it may be beneficial to work with more consciously.

If the natal Moon falls between the Full and Third Quarter positions, then any planets it will cross as it moves towards the Third Quarter indicate qualities, talents and tendencies which may be highly significant in the expression of personal potential and creativity, perhaps as gifts to benefit the collective group.

If the natal Moon falls between the Third Quarter and New Moon positions, any planets it will cross as it moves towards New Moon indicate the seeds of qualities, talents and tendencies that are still to be released. By discovering them and learning how to release their potential, great progress may be made. The challenge lies in being able to access these energies successfully, and to adjust the inner and outer lives in order to manifest their gifts.

MOON, PHYSIOLOGY AND HEALTH

Within the physical body, the Moon is associated with body fluids, the lymphatic glandular system, synovial fluids (fluids which lubricate joints and tendons, secreted by membranes of joint cavities and tendon sheaths), tear ducts, the stomach/breast area and the internal reproductive system of women – ovaries, uterus and womb. The pancreas gland is linked to the Moon, and this is placed near to the stomach and releases a digestive secretion into the duodenum, and also produces insulin, which is passed directly into the bloodstream. The pancreas helps to regulate the sugar supply made available for conversion into energy. A low blood sugar level affects the body chemistry, causing emotional instability.

The sympathetic nervous system is also Moon-related, and this is the pair of ganglionated nerve trunks placed alongside the vertebral column and connected with nerve fibres which extend to the blood vessels, sweat and salivary glands and the viscera (internal organs of the body, heart, liver, intestines etc.). In a manner which corresponds to its influence on oceanic tides, the Moon influences the flow of bodily fluids, which perpetually move through the body serving to nourish, aid digestive processes, lubricate vital organs, process nutrition and elimination of wastes, and transmit sexual seeds and eggs within the lubricated male and female sexual organs.

Disturbances in the quality and quantity of body fluids can lead to ill health; joint and bone friction; blood circulation problems – heart attacks and strokes – through hardening of the arteries; and women's problems related to ovaries, uterus and vagina or menstruation tensions. Contemporary medicine now recognises the effects of pre-menstrual tension in women, which affects their personalities and emotional moods, as can postnatal depression or the menopause. One traditional influence of the Moon on the human being is that of the Full Moon, when personality disorders are heightened and the 'lunatic' or emotionally disturbed can become extremely agitated.

As the emotions and feeling levels of the individual are liable to tidal fluctuations and regular temporary cycles of change, the Moon is considered to reflect this activity, and science is still investigating the effects that minute changes in body fluids and chemistry can have on the expression and development of personality; learning to regulate these by other chemical means could provide answers to many psychiatric disorders, for example schizophrenia and paranoia.

An afflicted Moon indicates tendencies to experience physical disorders, as well as negative emotions and desires. As the Moon is so connected with the stomach area, most disorders involve that region and problems with the functioning of the organs. Emotional upsets and lack of integration often are reflected in stomach tensions, and food issues, such as compulsive eating or anorexic behaviour, can occur. To ensure that these areas of physical affinity are not placed under excess stress, each individual should integrate the needs of their Moon into their conscious lives; denial can only generate additional problems.

THE MOON SYMBOL

The astrological symbol of the Moon is that of the crescent, the arc, or semicircle. Within certain occult teachings the Moon is viewed as representing the *soul*, linking the *spirit* of the Sun with the material form of the individual and Earth, providing a bridge between the higher vibration of spirit and the lower vibration of matter. As ancient wisdom considers spirit and matter to be two poles of an axis of Universal Life and Consciousness, the mediating role of the Moon–Soul is influential in relating and fusing the polarities. Traditionally, the Moon is perceived as being a receptive vessel, useful in receiving the spiritual solar light from the Sun, stepping its potency down to enable its transmission to the human and earth levels of existence. As reflected in the physical space-age flight to the Moon, we symbolically rise to embrace the Moon–Soul, prior to being capable of expanding into the greater space and spiritual light of the solar realm.

In ancient times, the Moon became associated with the principle of the Mother, and was viewed as the matrix from which all earth life came as a result of the fusing of soli-lunar energies. In modern times, the Moon is perceived as the symbolic repository of the unconscious collective mind, which has obviously been developing over time. Esoteric investigators believe that this repository can be accessed through analyptic memories, by opening to access ancient mystery school teachings, racial or traditional roots or by reincarnational regression, or through 'reading the Akashic Records'. For the individual, the Moon is associated with the personal unconscious mind, where emotions may be rooted and from where behavioural instincts, personality patterns and habitual responses arise.

The unbroken solar circle of the Sun symbolises the unmanifest infinite creative potential, the source of universal energy, life and cosmic seed. The incomplete Moon crescent indicates the restrictions and limitations of the manifested finite existence, the partial circle on the path to becoming whole. It symbolises the dualistic nature of the human being, which is part spirit, part matter, part conscious, part unconscious, and the resulting need for resolution. The unseen half of the arc or semicircle is that of the unrealised spirit or divine consciousness, whilst the other, visible, half is that of human material nature. The interplay produces the phenomenon of personality and the impulse to become the evolutionary progression of the God-Man by completing the circle. In esoteric teachings, when the circle is complete – when the spirit is realised – the Moon has fulfilled its role and is no longer required. The soul has fulfilled its mediating function and now disintegrates, leaving a clear channel along the axis of spirit–matter without the need for the intermediary Moon. In individual terms, this implies the dissolution of any separation between conscious and unconcious levels of mind; the split has been healed, and a transformed consciousness emerges as the sacred marriage of the King and Queen, the Sun and Moon, within the transcendant human being, has been attained.

CHAPTER 4

The Moon and
Planetary Aspects

THE PLANETARY ASPECTS TO THE Moon in the natal chart are highly significant, as they indicate the probable consequences of childhood experiences and parental influences upon the developing and unfolding individual. Such formative effects will play a powerful role in the later adult psychology, especially in the creation of the dominant self-image, levels of self-esteem and personal confidence, and in the sense of emotional well-being. The Moon can indicate our ability to make beneficial use of our earlier conditioning and of the attitudes, beliefs and values we have absorbed. Negatively, it can show how we are limited and bound by failing to move beyond any restrictive childhood conditioning.

The Moon's aspects may indicate that our deeper feelings, emotions and instincts are operating in a repressed or distorted manner, so that our self-expression and self-nurturing abilities are neglected and unfulfilled. The aspects may also reveal the potential for developing a more suitable pattern of conditioning, in which there is an ease of self-expression founded upon an inwardly secure and stable sense of self, allowing an easy flow of feelings and a positive self-image.

When the Moon is in harmonious aspect to other planets, this is an indication that the qualities of those planets should be capable of being beneficially expressed, and should aid successful adjustment to life. There will be an easier release of the energies of those planets through the personality, a spontaneous fluency and natural affinity which accesses the positive dimensions of both the Moon and planets working in co-operative harmony through creativity and self-expression. Working with those planetary tendencies will feel natural and comfortable, and the previous conditioning factors associated with those planets will serve as favourable foundations. A sense of personal security will be connected with those planets, and they will provide an ongoing source of pleasure, satisfaction and fulfilment. The defensive mechanisms of the Moon will not be restrictive in those areas, and it will be the more expansive relating energy that will flow out to others and the world, and this will stimulate a more positive response from others too.

The challenging or stressful aspects indicate areas of negative self-image, of a lack of nurturing, confidence and life-adjustment. With those planets in difficult aspect to the Moon, there may be elements of repression present, caused by personal denials and lack of integration which result in disharmony and inner stress. Emotions and feelings may be emphasised and perhaps contain a fear of allowing them full release; there may be emotional patterns which are no longer suitable and which need to be recognised and replaced. The power of the past may still have a great influence over the personality and conscious mind, so that the self-image is one rooted in the past and is not reflective of the current stage of individual unfoldment. This can have an inhibiting and restrictive effect on self-expression, as past behaviour patterns still speak with the loudest voices, and it is harder to take steps forward when hampered by the chains of the past.

With a negative self-image, it is more difficult to see the options for real change to occur. Feelings of defeat, discomfort, personal insecurity and inadequacy cannot easily be ignored or transcended. Tendencies towards psychological rigidity are common, and are reflected by the qualities of the planets that are stressfully aspected. Unease and touchy reactions can occur when those spheres of life associated with such planets are stimulated, as such experiences remind us of a lack of integration and expression in those areas. Our defence mechanisms are often triggered at such times, the planet aspected offering keys to the likely type of response. Mars may react with anger, temper, bluster and arguments; Mercury may try to defend with·a flow of logic, rationality and justification; the Sun by a wilful assertion of the individual freedom and right to decide; and Saturn may defend by attempting to impose controls, limitations and restrictions on others.

Stressful aspects to the personal planets may be felt to be attacking the roots of personal identity, with a resistance to move beyond familiar patterns of self and life-style in order to explore new spheres of experience, which leaves the Moon pattern dominating the personality instead of fusing with the planetary qualities. This can involve a tendency to retreat towards emotionally secure inner roots to protect the vulnerability that can result from being more open to life and relationships. Often with aspects to the personal planets, there can be a resistance to expressing exactly what is felt in those associated spheres of life; with Venus, there can be a resistance to expressing social and intimate relationships, a reaction against love; with Mars, assertiveness may be hard to express, or suppressed anger may create tensions; with Mercury there may be a fear of intellectual ability, and a lack of confidence in one's opinions. Conflicts are likely in attempts to express those qualities associated with stressfully aspected planets, although they are also a source for great personal development if they can be successfully worked with and transformed.

Moon aspects for men reveal tendencies related to their attitudes and experiences towards women, or the marriage partner; harmonious aspects indicate areas of good contact, whilst stressful ones indicate areas of potential difficulty and conflict. Aspects made to the Sun can show the ways in which responses to love are made; a stronger Moon than the Sun may indicate a tendency towards assuming a more passive, receptive role in intimate relationships; a stronger Sun will indicate a more assertive role, often reflecting a traditional masculine attitude which may lack a Moon sensitivity. Harmonious aspects help feelings of security in the relationship, whilst stressful ones can reveal underlying insecurities and fears of failure and dissatisfaction.

SUN–MOON CONJUNCTION

All Sun–Moon contacts indicate the extent to which the instinctual, emotional and feeling nature – which has been highly influenced and conditioned by childhood experiences and relationships with parents – is integrated with the sense of a unique personal identity and life-direction, forming the essential pattern underlying the personality characteristics.

The conjunction indicates a reasonably well-integrated personality. Your tendency will be towards self-containment and self-sufficiency focused on a feeling of firm identity and a purposeful life-direction. As there will be a fundamental inner harmony between your feelings and will, energy will not be diverted into dealing with inner conflicts and stresses, and this will enable you to concentrate more on following a definite life-path or career.

You will feel comfortable with your temperament and pursuing your aims will begin to absorb most of your time and energy. Success is likely due to the consistent level of motivation and perseverance that you are capable of applying, and that ability of making maximum use of personal and material resources to further your ambitions is a great asset. Wasting time or effort is not your style, as you have a feeling that you are drawn to follow a golden thread of destiny which gives meaning to your life. If the spiritual dimension is your chosen route, then you may feel you have a 'mission', perhaps involving some type of world service.

Taking responsibility for directing your own life is important for you, and you display a self-assured independence of spirit, refusing to accept any unnecessary interference by others and being determined to follow your own light. You may find that working alone, or taking full responsibility for a self-employed business, is preferable to being an employee, so that you gain the full benefits of your efforts. Whilst you may be able to act in a responsible position of authority, there may be a question mark against your style of relating to others. As you tend to be self-absorbed in your own individual reality, you may lack some awareness of others, and this can result in acting in an authoritarian manner, creating a barrier of communication and maintaining a detached role with no concern for how others are reacting to you. Relating to others can be one of your weak points, except on basically superficial social levels, and people may receive the impression that you are not unduly interested in human contact and friendship. They may also note a certain inflexibility about you, which rarely dissolves unless it is for a matter which will actually benefit you; you may be unable or reluctant to compromise for the sake of harmony. You could be described as having an almost innocent self-centredness. Privacy and independence of thought and action remain high priorities for you.

Much of this stance is derived from a need for protectiveness, emanating from the Moon's influence. It isn't that you feel threatened by others; rather, you feel that you should protect your vulnerable emotions. This side of you is often kept hidden, although you recognise just how intense your feeling nature really is, and indeed in many circumstances your choices and decisions are very much influenced by the Moon's promptings. There is a fear that your emotions may be battered by experiences, so at times there can be an avoidance of certain relationships or contentious issues, because your sense of personal well-being is intimately connected to the feeling tone of your emotional nature. You can be emotionally impulsive at times, especially if the balance between the Sun and Moon is swinging to favour the Moon. There can be an alternating pattern, with one planet temporarily becoming dominant, before the balance rectifies itself again.

It is perhaps fortunate that you are able to trust that unity of feelings and will, applying it instinctively and spontaneously to your chosen undertakings and expecting it to lead you towards desired results. This enables you to focus and concentrate your energy, making it more powerful and penetrating.

Being so self-contained, you may lack a capacity for self-reflection for an objective perspective and appraisal of your actions and temperament; you may rarely try to analyse yourself. Your ambitions are often extremely personal in nature, and may not be easily understood by others. What you may need to be careful about is an overemphasis on either Sun or Moon tendencies, perhaps through an excessive preoccupation with career developments, which can amplify the Sun principle in your nature, or by an absorption in the traditional Moon pre-occupations of the domestic family life. A balance is required, or there is the possibility of health problems occurring if one planet becomes consistently dominant, and your emotional and physical well-being can be affected by unbalanced activity, especially if the career/mission consciousness rises to ascendancy. To remedy this, you may need to withdraw into periodic communication with your whole nature, possibly through quiet retreats and meditation to recharge your batteries, and you should ensure that your emotional nature is regularly vitalised by intimate human contact and not left to atrophy through a neglect of its needs. Maintaining a balance should ensure that your aims are achieved as well as keeping you healthy.

SUN–MOON SEXTILE

The sextile indicates that you should feel at peace with your temperament, easily accepting your own nature and experiencing good relationships with others and an ease of communication. Your personality has a consistency which enables you to feel relatively tranquil in the midst of life. You feel comfortable with your feelings, transmitting a sense of enjoyment and goodwill to others and being willing to make any necessary adaptations to your social environment through concession or compromise if you believe that relationships will be improved by doing so. You see such actions as sensible and beneficial, regarding the ability to compromise as a sign of maturity rather than as something which diminishes individual expression.

Your social relationships are characterised by tolerance, consideration and understanding, and these will be appreciated by any co-workers, friends and acquaintances. Your attitude is essentially 'do to others as you would have them do to you', and you recognise the frailties of being human and usually resist the temptation to condemn others. There is an optimism present, together with a belief that through mutual understanding most disagreements can be resolved. There is also a belief in equal opportunity and egalitarianism. This ease in communicating with others often places you in the position of confidante. You are good at listening, and your self-confidence and balanced attitudes help others to see their problems in a clearer perspective. They can sense your genuine concern, and sometimes this alone provides a healing quality for people in need, when a sense of isolation becomes too much and problems seem to grow ever larger.

You often perceive life as an ongoing school of experience, and you try to ensure that you discern whatever messages are contained within your experiences. It seems to you that learning the lesson now eliminates the need to pass through that experience again, and will provide a platform for future progress. The past does not unduly attract you, except as a source of understanding, and you ensure that you are free to move onwards. You'll recognise what you need in order to feel emotionally satisfied, and what you can do to achieve your desires, and you'll try to organise your life to maximise enjoyment, which, after all, is a sensible approach to take.

You probably possess creative talent within you, although you may need some self-discipline in order fully to express such gifts. However, your emotions are harmonised with your will, so provided that there is a resonance with your actions, there should be minimum inner conflict interrupting the achievement of your aims. As your inner intention and energy drive are united, there is likely to be a corresponding response from the outer world, and there will often be people willing to co-operate with you in fulfilling your ambitions. Sometimes though, you may need to prevent your strong will and assertiveness from becoming too dominant and having a negative impact on the sensitivity of others.

You should find that intimate relationships are enjoyable and successful, and that family life is a sphere where you can easily express the free flow of your emotions and remain attuned to your emotional needs. Your earlier childhood and relationship with parents was probably quite good, and you try to duplicate this in your own family home by forming deep and loving family bonds, and by communicating to any children the benefits of your own philosophy of life. Your general level of health and vitality should be good, although this may depend on the maintenance of emotional well-being.

As your inner life is relatively centred, and your emotions are well integrated into your whole nature, there may be a lack of stimulus to grow and change. You may prefer to remain with the comfortable and successful habit patterns you have formed over the years, rather than risk any degree of inner disruption – in the family life. There may be a lack of objectivity in viewing the self, and you may be advised to evaluate things periodically, not to destroy them, but to see if they can be improved on. There are probably still areas of your life that you could improve without undue disturbance, so why not try to do so? Stretching yourself may also prompt you to make fuller use of latent talents; you have a firm base to work from, so you should be able to accept growth challenges without feeling too threatened.

SUN–MOON TRINE

The trine indicates that there will be a positive harmony between conscious will and the instinctual emotional habit pattern. You are likely to feel self-confident and optimistic about fulfilling your potential, aims and ambitions, and you may discover that doors open for you at the right times, or people offer support and help which enables you to move forward; luck may be a factor in your life.

Your experience of early life, parental relationships and childhood social conditioning has generally been favourable. You may well benefit from hereditary influences, possibly by natural talents and gifts. Some of your habitual tendencies may be family traits, although the likelihood is that they are positive and constructive in essence.

In your adult life, you will try to maintain good family relationships, both with your parents and with any family that you are responsible for creating. You tend to relate well to young children, who enjoy your sincere concern, care, understanding and attention.

Similar to those with the sextile, you ensure that you learn from all of your experiences so that lessons do not need to be painfully repeated. As your basic temperament is relaxed and laid-back, however, generating sufficient momentum to achieve some aim can sometimes seem like too much hard work. You may be unwilling to accept the challenge to develop yourself, and due to this fail to realise the latent potential that you actually possess. In fact, you should have considerable natural talents waiting to be personally exploited, and you should become alert to any opportunities that offer the prospect of personal growth and unfoldment, so that your creative drives and ability to unite feelings and will are successfully manifested in your environment.

Self-assertion may need to be focused and concentrated in order for you to make real progress in a career, and although the potential for advancement is present, there may be a question mark against your level of commitment and desire for promotion. Your sensitive good nature may be a liability in any situation where harsh and impersonal business decisions need to be made. Yet you could serve effectively in a position of authority, especially in a job involving personal contact and communication, where your friendliness, sincerity, persuasiveness and understanding of people's motivations could help you to mediate between different levels of employees.

Feeling right with yourself is important to you, and you recognise this as the key to personal health and enjoyment; the free-flowing nature of this Sun–Moon contact helps you to appreciate your strong physical vitality, stamina and ability to recover easily from any temporary illness.

In social situations, you tend to act as a 'bridge' between people, being able to understand and empathise with widely differing types, and through that reconciling aspect of your nature helping people to join together more easily. You are especially attractive to the opposite sex and this can lead you into successful relationships. The main challenge for you is to make full use of this aspect's positive and constructive nature, and not just allow that stable, tranquil and contented nature to cast a soporific spell over you.

SUN–MOON SQUARE

The square occurs at either the first or third quarter phase of the lunar cycle. It tends to indicate the existence of considerable inner stress and tension within the personality, as will is in conflict with deep-rooted feelings, emotions and instincts. The conscious self may be trying to move in a direction which is contrary to the habit patterns, especially those connected with security and protection of self boundaries.

The ongoing struggle is to resolve contradictory inner messages, and is a psychological tendency which may have its roots deep within childhood perceptions of the parental relationship and your own emotional contact with your parents. As the Moon signifies the mother, and the Sun the father in this context, there is the implication that there was a problem in the parental relationship, perhaps incompatibility on some vital level, or a lack of communication which led to a breakdown on some level. This may not have been obvious, existing rather as an underlying current within the domestic psychic atmosphere. There may have been identification with one parent to the exclusion of the other, perhaps because one parent had little time to spend with you. Somehow the inner dynamics have been distorted, resulting in personal frustration and difficulties in harmonising will and feelings.

Unless you take steps to achieve personality integration, you are liable to suffer from emotional insecurity founded on a reluctance to accept the nature of your habitual feeling responses. Inner denial and repression of these is probable, leading to inner tensions and possible personality splits. Yet because these powerful emotions seem to burn within you, you try to control their release through expression into daily life, and because of the pressures that can accumulate you can be argumentative, provocative and belligerent at times.

The danger is that you fall victim to your own powerful desire nature, and are perpetually frustrated through aiming high and failing to appreciate what exists in the present. There can be a restless, searching quality to this aspect which results from that need to resolve deep inner conflicts; the problem is in finding the way to achieve those desires. This need stimulates inner questioning, especially related to personal identity and meaning.

Yet you can often act as your own worst enemy, reacting in ways that diminish the likelihood of success. You may fail to see how you can utilise existing resources to achieve your aims or enhance your enjoyment of life; you may refuse to make necessary compromises; you may consciously devalue your own potential and abilities, eroding self-confidence away; you may clash with others who could otherwise have been supportive to your efforts. These unconscious patterns of unresolved frustrations stem from friction between your conscious will and deeper needs, tending to negate satisfaction of either. Sometimes, as a result of this inner stress, all you feel like doing is being very destructive, liberating the repressed energies by either verbal or physical expressions of bad temper.

The problem facing you is the movement from 'here to there', and the abyss stares you in the face and will not go away. Try as you might, you still cannot cross over to the promised land. Being 'here' feels wrong, and you believe that you should be 'there' but how can you achieve it? The only way to do so it seems is through a radical transformation, so that the 'old you' remains on this side, and the 'new you' appears there to claim your ambition. How may this be done?

The honest answer has to be 'with difficulty' and with much hard work. Your promised land will not be gained without great perseverance and struggle, proving your capabilities, transcending any obstacles on the way. You may need to pursue additional training or study in order to qualify for a specialist skill, or in order to help unfold latent qualities and talents. You may need to apply self-discipline to maintain your efforts, to work determinedly until success is achieved. Relationships may need improving and compromises may be needed to avoid unnecessary conflicts with others resulting from your frustrations. Lessons need to be learned from previous experiences, and applied in daily living. You may need to examine closely what you desire and what you are prepared to do to achieve it, and whether your aims will actually be emotionally satisfying when achieved. Integration between your conscious will and those underlying emotions is vital; the best way to achieve this is to allow the emotions to rise to the surface of your mind, so that you can examine them and so come to understand them, and then attempt to fuse will and emotions via the intellect. Investing great effort should lead towards realising those desires. It is not an easy path, although viewing that inner stress as a motivating factor is at least a positive perception of what personal frustration can provide as a transformative spur.

Otherwise, what options are left to you? Living with personal disharmony; experiencing lack of success and frustration of aims; a restriction of personal potential; problems spilling over into your domestic life, career, social relationships; dissatisfaction in intimate affairs with the opposite sex; interference by domestic responsibilities and duties by limiting your freedom to reach your ambitions, and possible ill health (digestive problems) stimulated by emotional and psychosomatic tensions.

If you accept the challenge of attempting to resolve the conflicts and contradictions of this square, then finding constructive outlets for your powerful energies may help to form your new path. Learn how to observe those disturbing feelings; integrating them into your life instead of ignoring them will help to restore your sense of balance and well-being.

SUN–MOON OPPOSITION

The opposition between the Sun and Moon occurs at the period of the Full Moon, and indicates two main areas of challenge in your life. One involves your social and intimate partnerships, and the degree of adjustment you have to make to the demands of the external world, and the second is concerned with inner tensions arising from conflict between your conscious egoic will and your unconscious mind, feelings and emotions.

You will probably feel internal division, with opposing messages and impulses arising from the differing Sun and Moon tendencies, and this creates stress and confusion as to which inner voice you should follow. You may experience one voice encouraging you to follow an adult career path, and to achieve and make progress (the Sun), and another more instinctual voice (the Moon) trying to make you pay more attention to your emotional needs. Pulled in two directions, one looking towards those individual aims and desires, whilst the other is turned towards the past, security and familiarity, you become unsure of what to do. Your instinctual lunar responses may reject your egoic solar ambitions, the Sun refusing to allow time and attention to satisfy the Moon's need for emotional nourishment, as this does not conform to your self-image of independent maturity.

One consequence of this inner polarisation is that your energy is burnt away by inner friction. This your opportunities for satisfaction, both in solar and lunar spheres of life, may be reduced, you may fail to realise ambitions, and relationships may fail to fulfil your emotional needs. Over time, there develops a pattern of oscillation as your inner balance between Sun and Moon tilts to favour either one or the other; if the balance is regularly in favour of one planet, then the qualities of the other planet are relegated to the unconscious mind. The tendency may be to force the deeper energies of the Moon back down into the personal unconscious, with which they have a natural affinity, but in elevating the Sun many personal emotional needs are denied, and this will eventually create problems of integration when the lunar energies burst through under pressure in later love relationships.

Often, in opposition aspects, part of the planetary polarity which is less expressed and integrated is projected externally onto the world and people, and it is likely that the existence of your inner conflict will be unconsciously transmitted to others, who then serve to reflect back your unintegrated aspect. Stress in the psyche is reflected in relationship difficulties, and this is likely to be an ongoing challenge for you to resolve, and may spill over into domestic, financial, romantic and marital situations. Continual tension may create ill health and deplete your vitality, and one sign of this may be the experience of restlessness, nervous agitation and psychosomatic illnesses. Changes of moods and emotional responses may occur, ranging from self-confident exhilaration and sense of purpose, to deep depression, feelings of being unloved and loss of individual meaning. These may be triggered by movement within your inner Sun–Moon polarity, particularly when either planet is stimulated by transit.

This unstable energy flow can be noted at time when you commence a project with great enthusiasm, only to lose interest as your energy level wanes. Scattered and uncompleted schemes, projects and ideas may litter your life. Relationships could follow a similar pattern, starting as 'the love of your life' and then collapsing into an unsatisfactory withdrawal as feelings change and disillusionment sets in.

Underlying your relationships and creating difficulties are your deep lunar needs and desires. You tend to hold an image of a loving partner being able to satisfy all your needs, even needs that you often deny or choose not to acknowledge, someone in whom you can almost become lost and rely on totally. These are probably reflections of previous childhood patterns in which your parents proved unable to satisfy your needs; now you search for another adult to do so. For you, a partner has to be a lover, friend and companion, capable of sustaining you, healing your conflicts, tendering to your needs, and offering clear directions in life. There are dependency needs entangled in this pattern, needs of belonging which temporary short-lived affairs will fail to satisfy. You hope to find someone who either takes charge of things, or helps you to develop your own potential; somehow you feel inadequate to do this on your own.

Your difficulty in this is a tendency to project your inner stresses onto your close relationships, with phases of dissension, confrontation and argument occurring as a means of releasing energies. You may need to develop compromise, learning how to give rather than just take. Moderation is one approach to consider: avoid reacting unthinkingly to whatever feeling is temporarily uppermost. Take time to determine what are your most consistent aims in life, make a realistic appraisal of your qualities, talents and potentials, and try to discover how the dictates of Sun and Moon needs can be united and integrated into a common path. Break out of that subjective prison, and take responsibility for your situation, whatever obstacles stand in your way.

Whilst part of this personality pattern may stem from a childhood in which you perceived your parents as offering you two sets of opposing messages, or perhaps lost one of them due to divorce or death, it is your adult responsibility to transcend this difficulty rather than perpetuate it. Integrating the principles of Sun and Moon in your psyche may not be easy, and a careful balance of listening and honouring both voices need to be achieved, but discovering a way to do this may be essential to your well-being, and may emerge after a period when life temporarily seems meaningless. A change in consciousness and integrating those deeper and ignored Moon needs can be achieved, if you generate the will to do so. Pursuing humanistic self-therapy techniques designed to liberate repressed feelings and individual desires/needs may be appropriate at such a stage, and looking towards psychosynthesis, gestalt, encounter and co-counselling may be beneficial.

MERCURY–MOON CONJUNCTION

All Moon–Mercury planetary contacts are concerned with the internal relationship and dynamics of the Moon's instinctual, feeling and emotional tendencies with the analytical, lower mind and communicative abilities reflected by the position of Mercury in the chart. Within each individual, this can imply the type of inner relationship between the more unconscious foundations of the personality and the separative conscious mind and ego.

The close conjunction of Moon and Mercury suggests a relatively open channel between your unconscious mind and your rational mind; exactly how well this relationship works may vary, with both the strengths and weaknesses of each planet being displayed over the years. Much will depend on which sign and element the conjunction is in. If it is in Water or Earth, the Moon will probably be the most influential; if in Air or Fire, then Mercury is likely to be the stronger partner, at least in your conscious experience.

It is probable that if the Moon is dominant and acting from a deeper level of the personality and aligned with the unconscious mind, this will subtly influence the formation of your habitual attitudes, beliefs and life perspective. Your choices will be invisibly influenced by underlying emotional needs, re-emerging as apparently rational decisions, although, if challenged about these decisions, then the rational façade will soon crumble to reveal emotion as the real decision-maker. Another expression of this Moon influence can be the open emotional response and reaction, where rationality is not considered at all and is totally overruled at crucial turning-points by a gut reaction or deciding by the pull of the emotions.

If Mercury is the dominant partner, instead of emotions

affecting clarity and understanding, then your intellectual analysis and over-evaluation of issues may interfere with your instinctive feeling response to decision-making, situations and people. Rationality will be given higher priority, and the possible conflict will then revolve around times when Moon messages are contrary to Mercury messages. A suppression of either Moon or Mercury principles is always possible, and much may depend on the rest of the chart.

Yet potentially the opportunity is present to use these planetary qualities and abilities in a creative and positive manner. These positive qualities can easily shine through relationships and social communication. You are likely to be friendly and sociable, with others finding you easy to relate to, often trusting you enough for them to confide in you, as they recognise your intrinsic sympathetic understanding. You tend to co-operate well with people, especially in work environments, and your personality is flexible and adaptable enough to fit easily into new working partnerships. Confidence in your abilities and knowledge is usually present, and this helps a positive assertiveness that leads to beneficial and constructive results for all concerned. You also recognise your limits, rarely overstretching your abilities and talents to breaking-point, and being able to acknowledge when you need the additional knowledge of others who are more expert than yourself.

Ideally, you want people to perceive you as both intellectual and emotionally sensitive, thus honouring both Mercury and Moon in your nature. You can be a little hypersensitive at times and emotionally touchy, especially if personal remarks are aimed at you, as this tends to activate those defensive postures and attitudes related to the Moon. You are not particularly comfortable with criticism, and will defend yourself either by excessive rationalisation, or with emotionally based denials and personal disagreements. At times, you may register intangible criticisms, being sensitive to the hidden thoughts of others, which can evoke an immediate emotional reaction in you, even though you may not be able to pinpoint any objective reason for it.

The Mercury dimension may appear in intellectual and imaginative abilities, as well as a positive and creative attitude to life's experiences, where you take the position that lessons can be usefully learned from whatever happens, and that 'experience' is truly the best teacher. You can benefit from formal study as you are able to absorb information relatively easily, but the ideal type of study is one which also involves a positive emotional response, so that the Moon is also included. Favouring a more Mercurial, intellectual or abstracted type of study may create an imbalance. You may perceive life as offering a multitude of fascinating avenues of enquiry. It is a 'growth attitude' which leads to positive and creative change, and helps you to adapt to whatever changes in circumstances are presented to you. The main challenge which may face you is that of consistently uniting the Moon and Mercury qualities so that co-operation results and not conflict. You may need to distinguish clearly between opposing internal messages, so that you can see which are those associated with the Moon, those habitual security, instinctual and emotional patterns, and those which the Mercury-influenced logical mind is presenting. These messages can be either complementary or conflicting, and evaluating exactly what is occurring at such times demands considerable perspicacity and self-understanding, but real success will only come when the partnership is in harmony.

Family life and private domesticity will be important to you, both as a retreat allowing you to attune to certain Moon characteristics, for example, self-nurturing, security needs, daily habit patterns and life ordering, and as a safe environment within which to express your strong emotions. You are likely to have a natural affinity with young children, and could become a good parent. Certainly you will devote much energy and attention to ensuring that your roots and foundations in life are secure and harmonious.

MERCURY–MOON SEXTILE

With the sextile, the qualities of Mercury often predominate, as this aspect is associated with the mind, information, understanding and communication.

The Moon's foundations in the personality are usually well established and not disruptive or unduly intrusive. The Moon's qualities are usually expressed in ways which only enhance the Mercury qualities, which should be easily demonstrated by you. Information and knowledge will be especially appealing, and there will be an almost insatiable curiosity and need to explore as widely as possible. For you, the world is like an immense library of information, your mind lighting up with interest as every new volume comes into view. Both memory and comprehension are likely to be above average, thus creating a well-stocked intellect.

You could well be the perpetual student, loving to explore each topic to the greatest possible depth, and becoming an expert in a limited sphere of knowledge. Alternatively, you could have a dilettantish tendency, leading you to taste many varieties of knowledge but rarely exploring any of them too deeply.

You are probably motivated by a need to be socially useful and to contribute to the community. To help achieve this, you hope to discover ways through which you can put your thoughts into action, so transforming that mental ability into practical results. The sense of value and pleasure that this can give you often serves as an encouragement to increase your level of knowledge. The issue of right direction may arise in this context, and it may be that you decide to become involved within civic and social groups, pooling your assets and abilities with those of others to achieve group aims. Generally, you will look at your ideas as sources for practical expression and possibly personal profit too, as you will probably possess an effective business and organisational ability which could be successfully exploited.

You are likely to be an effective communicator, conveying your ideas and presenting them in a clear and persuasive manner, being both articulate and literate, entertaining and interesting. This can manifest in activities related to writing and lecturing, and can be beneficial in social communication, especially in those spheres which bring you into contact with larger groups of people. This can broaden your sphere of influence, and increase the number of friendships in your life; your personality should be flexible and tolerant enough to be able to relate to many types of people. There is the likelihood that you will possess an innate sensitivity to the thoughts and feelings of others, almost acting like a psychic intuition, but operating through a deep Moon attunement of sensitivity and emotional rapport. This can act as an 'early warning system', telling you when people are not as genuine as they superficially appear, and you should learn to trust these inner sensations and feelings whenever they arise.

This sensitivity enhances your tact and diplomacy, whether in social contexts or within the family. Others can recognise your thoughtful and caring nature, and provided that you do not become obsessive about manifesting your ideas, you should be able to co-operate and harmonise well with partners and family. Fortunately, your emotions rarely enter into direct conflict with your mind and ideas, and usually work together in tandem, so that positive and optimistic attitudes and plans can easily flow outwards. This emotional and mental accord minimises the distractions of internal conflicts, and enables the resolution of any problems to be achieved more smoothly.

The Moon's emotional warmth and protective concern is very nourishing to family members and partners, and your domestic life is likely to be well organised, with close communications. Home will be important, but social involvement outside the home will be equally so, especially as the source for applying those ideas which have been inwardly generated. Both your emotions and mind will be acknowledged as having valid messages, and neither should move out of balance through overemphasis, as each will be given suitable priority in the appropriate circumstances. Intimate partnerships within marriage or love affairs will tend to involve a high level of communication and sharing, with both partners' modes of experience and expression enriching both lives, as well as contributing to the likely success of each other's aims.

You will be attracted to people who are intelligent, optimistic and able to exploit innate talents, especially those who conceive ambitions and then proceed to achieve them – although if there are two people chasing dreams and goals then conflict may occur if paths begin to diverge rather than running parallel.

MERCURY–MOON TRINE

The trine offers the opportunity to reconcile the Moon's instinctual and emotional energies with the mental and communicative energies of Mercury. You should experience few direct conflicts between emotional and mental messages. There will be a channel between the conscious and unconscious levels of your personality, yet these should not often pull you in different directions or create psychological difficulties.

Underlying your reactions to life experiences will be an emotional–feeling evaluation, and this will underpin the Mercurial type of intellect that you are likely to display. Generally, you approach life with a relatively open heart and mind, and you perceive all experience as contributing to your own development. Even though your Moon nature may resist life's sometimes harsh lessons, you can see the potential good that can emerge from phases of difficulty. This, together with a heightened sensitivity, helps you to acquire considerable insight and knowledge, particularly in relation to the interconnectedness of information.

This provides a new foundation for ongoing personal creativity and self-expression.

You are inspired by a desire to use your natural talents and abilities for the benefit of society. You display a united head and heart. Your clear-sightedness and common sense reflect a progressive and optimistic outlook which is not excessively idealistic or blind to the realities of life. You recognise that all is not either light or darkness, but that much of life exists in the shadows in between. Rather than dwell on the negative, you turn your face towards positive future possibilities, trying to ensure that hard-won lessons from previous experience are applied in dealing with present realities. Experiences from the past serve as stepping stones taking you progressively onward.

In social and intimate family relationships, you will be appreciated for the level of sympathy and understanding that you display. You have genuine concern and compassion for others, and a love of fairness and equality of opportunity. You are often willing to help others less fortunate than yourself, or who are passing through traumatic times of life disruption. Whilst inwardly acknowledging your own problems and weaknesses, you tend to keep them to yourself, dealing with them privately and trying to resolve any emotional unease through an objective, rational approach. Emotional anxieties are usually kept private; in sharing and helping others, your previous experiences and lessons may be deliberately shared if they can serve to illuminate and support, but you are not the type to unload any current difficulties onto the shoulders of others.

Reason and logic are strong components in your personality, although these will be coloured by your own instinctive emotional evaluations of people, situations and circumstances, forming a uniquely individual and personal viewpoint. With a good memory and ability to apply your knowledge in positive and constructive ways, there may be business talents there waiting to be exploited, and these could be effectively released through the modern communications media, perhaps involving your fluency of speech, literary skills and communication abilities.

MERCURY–MOON SQUARE

The square aspect between the Moon and Mercury indicates inner tension, stress and frustration, and a need for a radical inner adaptation that will rebalance these two conflicting energies. Conscious change is required to overcome conflict between the conscious mind and established lunar habit patterns.

The most likely imbalance is an unconscious domination of the rational conscious mind by the Moon, with attempts at clear decision-making, judgements and objective evaluation being influenced by emotionally charged deep-seated attitudes. Unconscious attitudes and value patterns, possibly absorbed during early childhood or from parents, can condition present-day choices, with isues of the past still dominating your current life.

Simply put, head and heart can be in constant conflict within you, decisions being made according to which has the upper hand at any given time. This can vary, like a pendulum movement, and may also be related to the sign, house and element that each planet is in. It may be that one planet predominates and the other becomes repressed. If Mercury is dominant then the Moon can sink deeper into the unconscious mind, more subtly and pervasively influencing your life from that hidden position. The emotional coloration may be more noticeable to yourself than to others. If it is Mercury that is repressed, your choices may be heavily influenced by emotions, instinctive needs and habitual responses, and are often security-based. Sometimes you may find that in attempting to restore inner balance, Mercury begins to rationalise your feelings and emotions excessively. If this is allowed to persist, you will begin to deny the validity of emotions and feelings, and in so doing repress your Moon sensitivity, creating another imbalance.

The inner tension reflects insecurity and self-doubt, creating highly nervous activity, prompted by the lack of harmony between the conscious and unconscious levels of mind. Sometimes this can manifest as psychosomatic illness, especially nervous illness, digestive problems and diseases related to the bodily fluids. Another problem could lie in an excessive self-absorption which results in self-centredness and separative ways of living and expression. You may tend to rely on fixed attitudes and beliefs to provide a sense of inner security and stability, but these can create interpersonal difficulties if they clash with others. Whenever someone else's opinion differs from yours, you tend to react with aggressive defensiveness, without really considering the other person's point of view. You hate any suggestion from others that you may be wrong; it makes you feel insecure. Your response, therefore, is often defiant and compulsively assertive. Paranoid feelings often accompany this reaction, and you can be very emotionally touchy, often triggering off misunderstandings and breakdowns in communication.

With strangers you always feel insecure and on the defensive; even with closer friends, acquaintances and family this pattern persists, although with less belligerence. Yet even in the family home you react against having to change to accommodate others. Self-centredly you believe that they should change to suit you; the fact that they may not want to is apparently of little concern to you.

Yet you can often communicate quite well with those with whom you can feel safe, often expressing a touching if slightly immature and sentimental emotionality about such relationships. Your hidden dependency on such intimates in your life may not always be realised or acknowledged. Such relationships would improve if you began to be less self-preoccupied, seeing the needs of others to be as important as your own, and an opportunity for you to give out to others what you are so busy taking for yourself.

Sometimes you can become obsessive about your own needs and concerns, and rarely perceive that this represents a state of immaturity and lack of integration. Your attention needs to be turned outwards, so that you realise that other people have needs and difficulties too, and that through mutual support all can benefit and have a more enjoyable life.

You may attempt to avoid inner change by obsessions with trivia or in continual chatter, both of which create unsatisfactory interpersonal relationships and waste energy instead of using it positively to change those internal stresses through understanding.

Mercury is often repressed by a dominant Moon as issues of personal security dominate the life, much like a demanding infant wanting immediate satisfaction. Because of this, rationality and objectivity can be lacking, and this shows in signs of immaturity and a lack of real self-understanding, and through a surfeit of emotional bias. Sometimes the line you draw between reality and illusion, fact and fiction, has blurred edges, and you can often be full of unresolved questions, uncertain of what you really think and feel about issues, or people, even though you defend whatever thoughts you are presenting. Relaxing those inner contracted knots will eventually prove beneficial to you, and help to release previously unexpressed positive and constructive energies within yourself and your relationships. Frustrations and conflicts will dissolve if you direct energy into taking the path of conscious growth and self-development.

MERCURY–MOON OPPOSITION

With the opposition, the friction between Moon and Mercury results in emotions, instincts and feelings pulling in one direction, and rationality, logic and the conscious mind going in an opposite direction. This inner disharmony is then reflected through projection into the external world, influencing the nature of your relationships. Whilst this opposition remains unacknowledged and unresolved within you, then conflicts in relationships will persist. Decision-making can prove difficult, and you may have a tendency to rely on others deciding for you, as you cannot determine which path to follow – the instinctual/emotional or the rational. Inner unity, when both messages coincide, is a rare experience for you.

This can stultify your actions and choices in life, distorting your perceptions and judgement. Confusion often results, with regular changes of mind or heart which disrupt relationships. Sometimes in an attempt to break free of an impasse situation you may act impulsively on instinct, with variable results. Equally, your responses can be emotionally biased, devoid of rational evaluation or commonsense consideration. Alternatively, Mercury can dominate, with an extremely cold perception which succeeds mainly in temporarily denying you any emotional feeling at all; choices made from that perspective can fail once the feeling nature wakes up again and decides to react against the situation that Mercury has brought about!

As a consequence of inner confusion, you are often irritated by social life, and inner friction will evoke external friction too by stimulating provocative arguments. You can be insensitive and offensive to others and you may be unaware of a lack of tact and sensitivity in your expression, although you are quick to rise to others who criticise you too personally. Like everyone else, you make mistakes, but you may need to learn to admit it.

Certainly you need more awareness and willingness to compromise in your intimate relationships and partnerships in order for them to be as mutually rewarding as possible. Otherwise, emotional friction and damage is liable to result as conflicts intensify through clashes of attitude and values. Family life can generate considerable agitation and worry, exacerbating inner confusion unless you can resolve certain of these innate conflicts. Nervous emotional excitement can be activated, and this can have health consequences due to a lack of integration and balance. You may be a compulsive talker, although a lack of depth is probable, and increasingly unconscious emotional patterns may distort your perceptions, diminishing your ability for clear thinking and clear communication.

What is required is a greater self-understanding and a better integration of the emotional nature and the rational mind. More awareness of underlying emotional patterns is needed. Rationality, whilst not totally fulfilling on its own, can play a vital role in rebalancing this disharmonious planetary contact. The challenge is to integrate these two opposing messages within yourself, so that it becomes easier to be true to yourself and to your responses to life. Until some success is made in that, then your style of self-expression is liable to be restricted and distorted. Favouring either planet creates conflict; honouring each planet is the route to wholeness, and the key to resolving this psychological imbalance.

VENUS–MOON CONJUNCTION

Moon–Venus contacts involve the instinctual feeling reactions to social and intimate relationships, as well as responses to the nature and quality of the environment through which experience is gained. The conjunction signifies that the habitual behaviour patterns involve sociable and friendly relationships with others, characterised by sensitive awareness and affection.

You will probably enjoy social contact, feeling naturally at ease with others and appreciating the breadth of communication that this can bring, preferring the company of those who are sincere and straightforward in their relating. You dislike social friction and conflict and try to minimise discord between yourself and others, sometimes by being tactful and diplomatic, sometimes through compromising or through a friendliness that helps to diffuse tensions. This tendency may be elevated into a conscious ideal, a belief that life will be improved for all if everyone is more aware and sensitive, and in avoiding gains made only at the expense of others. You easily offer your hand in friendship, expressing human warmth, civility and conscious goodwill. With your type of personality, if the rest of the chart amplifies these tendencies, then you are likely to find success through working with the public in some way.

You usually receive a favourable response from others, and, by stripping away at least part of the superficial veneer that many social contacts have, you can succeed in transmitting your underlying attitudes to others. Shorn of unnecessary pretences, your direct human approach may appear almost too simple to some, who may even feel threatened and suspicious, especially those who prefer to maintain social masks and distance themselves from others. You allow your sensitivity to shine through, and whilst some may not recognise or acknowledge its presence, others will welcome it. Your genuine interest in others helps to build bridges between people, and given that you also have a natural sympathy with, and understanding of, many of the human dilemmas, you are often in a position to help those in need. Yet if you are brusquely rejected at times, you are not always so sure of how to deal with your bruised feelings, as that sensitivity contracts away from the negative response.

Within more intimate relationships the emotional level is highly activated and given priority. Both Moon and Venus will require emotional satisfaction and stimulation, and the quality of a loving relationship is extremely important. It is likely that you will be an attractive person, often socially magnetic, and that with your combination of grace, charm and artistic sensitivity you will receive the interest of many, with the possibility of a variety of relationships occurring unless you marry or settle into a permanent relationship early in life.

There may be a tendency to allow previous family bonds to interfere with a new or developing relationship. The older lunar patterns may still be overly active and the dependency on parents or family members may affect the evolution of your new family unit; the 'mother-in-law syndrome' may be a classic example of this! Venus can exaggerate tendencies towards a self-indulgent preoccupation with satisfying your own needs, with a corresponding disregard for those of your partner. Extra self-discipline may need to be applied to adjust fully within intimate relationships, especially in areas of mutual sharing and experience. There may be occasional attempts at emotional manipulation, both by you and your partner.

Home life is important, providing secure foundations and roots to whatever life-style you are trying to create, and much of your personal enjoyment will arise from domestic pursuits, especially from a comfortable home, sensual clothes, food and material possessions. It will be important for you to build a beautiful environment to live in, and taking full advantage of your abilities for prudent financial management you will tend to devote resources to your home. That artistic sensitivity will perform a role in enhancing your environment.

VENUS–MOON SEXTILE

The sextile is a favourable aspect for domestic and partnership affairs, and it is likely that your intimate relationships will assume a pivotal place in your life. Finding a successful relationship will be a powerful need for you, and much of your earlier adult social contact may be directed towards this aim. This need may emanate from a close and satisfying early family life, which you hope to be able to find again in your own adult relationships. Maintaining close family associations will remain important to you.

Temperamentally, you are likely to have a capacity for sustained relationships, and once your feelings have been committed to someone then rarely will that commitment be broken or the feelings fade and wither away. There seems to be an innate knowledge and understanding of the nature of relationships, and what is necessary to ensure that they persist in a satisfying manner. Communication is vital within your relationships, and the sextile will amplify your ability to express clearly whatever is on your mind or affecting your emotions. You will regard sharing and talking through any individual or relationship difficulties as essential to ensure clarity and mutual understanding. Your genuine loving concern for partners helps to build deep foundations which are secure enough to withstand the storm. Your faith in the strength of mutual love, and your optimism that all will be well, are vital factors in your relationships, and will help to ensure that energy is used creatively rather than being dissipated in anxiety arising from insecurity and lack of faith in the depth of a partner's feelings for you.

Usually you will have a sense of direction in life, and this helps to generate a sense of mutual purpose, provided that you closely include your partner in your plans. You are probably aware of the benefits to be gained in a relationship by discussions and sharing the journey together. Yet you are also willing to compromise or adapt your ways if clashes of will and habit or temperamental patterns begin to disturb equilibrium. Equally, you expect your partner to do likewise if necessary, as you view the relationship as of greater importance than individual assertion. For the benefits of relationship you are always willing to apply your personal qualities, so that your innate resources – intelligence, sensitivity, love and affectionate understanding – are ready to be expressed as often as possible. You'll hate misunderstandings or personal frictions, and will be eager to resolve any that may naturally arise over time, using common sense, reason and mutual concession to heal any contentious situation.

Socially and career-wise, you have considerable confidence in your own abilities and mix easily and fluently with others, preferring to see the good qualities in all you meet. Your imaginative and artistic abilities may prove invaluable to your progress, and it may be advisable to discover a life-path that can make use of these intrinsic talents. Financial acumen is likely as is a full use of whatever resources you possess, although there may be cautious tendencies which prevent you from taking all opportunities, because of a stronger need to ensure the security of your family needs.

Children are likely to play an important role in your life, and you will probably express a natural affinity with them, perhaps seeing them as the foundation stone of your relationship. You may become involved with other people's children too, through groups or organisations which include elements of teaching and sharing. Hating to see unnecessary suffering in life, you may try to share your life-experience, knowledge and understanding with maturing children, hoping that they may learn life's lessons without having to experience the pain of doing so themselves. You recognise that these are the adults of the future, and that for their future to be positive and constructive, they need careful guidance in the present.

VENUS–MOON TRINE

The trine will give you a harmonious and sensitive nature that brings a spirit of reconciliation to your social and intimate relationships. Working in some mediating capacity, or with the general public, may enable this quality to be successfully expressed.

Your assets include a warm, sensitive, sympathetic heart, empathic understanding, imagination, sincerity, an optimistic positive attitude, and a sense of perspective and proportion that heals, calms and aids communication if conflict occurs. You should have the ability to use these well for the benefit of all. With your support and encouragement, many a troubled heart can be soothed. You can be a good listener, resisting the temptation to interfere by imposing your own perspective. You listen with an open heart and mind, perhaps helping the other to gain a deeper understanding of their problem by proposing key questions that they need to confront in order to progress. You offer straight talking, moving beyond superficiality and evasion to the essence of the problem; some may respond well to this, others may find that type of penetration too unsettling and challenging, and so avoid becoming too involved with you. But your intentions are good, and valid, and you know that you genuinely desire the best for everyone, often spending time transmitting positive and creative energies to others as a consciously supportive action.

You have a positive self-image, and value your own perspective on life. You have a great deal of personal integrity and will avoid compromising it for apparent gain; being true to yourself is given high priority. Your rejection of negative thoughts and emotions often makes you useful to others who are more prone to suffer from the vagaries of life. As you probably realise, positive attitudes, thoughts and emotions generate positivity, whilst negative ones generate only negativity. Essentially, attitudes create individual life-experiences.

There is likely to be some artistic and imaginative ability, and creativity could be usefully pursued as a means of self-expression or professionally, especially in areas like art, music, acting, singing or craftwork.

Love, domesticity and family are important to you, and you will derive much benefit from ensuring that your intimate relationships are honest, positive and optimistic. Emotional satisfaction is highly valued, and you need to feel convinced that your emotional commitment to a lover will not be abused or your trust betrayed. Having children will attract, and will ensure your family interest and care through natural understanding of their embryonic personalities and problems. You will have a protective family instinct, and will keep your home life and relationship private, sharing only what you choose to with outsiders.

VENUS–MOON SQUARE

This indicates that there are inner stresses and tensions related to your social and intimate relationships, and that the battlefield will be within your emotional involvements.

These emotions will feel extremely powerful, and you may fear losing control over them, so there is a habitual pattern of partial defeat and repression through a tendency to avoid the type of relationship that may stimulate emotional activity. Yet at the same time, you need emotional involvement and intensity of feeling. With your emotions and feelings being polarised, you often prefer to back away from real commitment, rejecting the obligations that may be incurred.

These patterns of behaviour can be seen in a starker light when commitment is required in personal intimate relationships, because you refuse to acknowledge the depth of your feelings, and your deep-seated fears begin to rise. These can include fear of loss of freedom, of the power someone else has over your emotions, and of passing through the transformative fires of love. Once someone begins to impose their needs, demands and will on you, their expectations of your predictable behaviour often trigger a rebellious attitude within you. Your insecurity and fears make you express a contrary attitude, which can create conflict within your relationships just at the point when real progress could be made.

Your reactionary drive towards independence and rejection of any signs of possessive behaviour or demands for your exclusive loyalty will tend to shatter any potentially restrictive relationship. Whilst there may be valid grounds for rejecting such tendencies within relationships, your reaction is mainly a response to inner fears and unresolved issues, and so tends to be more negative in essence, resulting in heartbreak and disillusionment for yourself and others, and enforcing an increasingly bitter and cynical view of the nature of intimate affairs.

Other patterns of behaviour associated with this square aspect include self-indulgence and sensuality, with tendencies to become involved with indiscriminate affairs and unsuitable partners as a consequence of a lack of self-understanding coupled with a deep need for relationships. Often, your attempts at breaking free of threatening restrictions only propel you into other, equally unsatisfying relationships. If you begin to express a more passive response to your relationship stresses – instead of taking the active and dominating role – then you may experience others taking advantage of your initial trust, manipulating your emotions and needs, and using you as a support and foil for their own emotional tensions and confusions.

Sometimes, your own emotions blind you to seeing the real feelings of a partner, until a situation occurs in which, to your surprise, you realise that their feelings are not as powerful as yours. This tendency towards illusions also spills over into your social relationships; you often misinterpret the honesty and sincerity of others and your understanding of their motives is lacking so that judgements are seriously affected. Yet this springs from your own lack of self-knowledge; getting to know yourself better you will come to understand others better too, and this will enable you to avoid unsuitable relationships. By analysing the types of people that you are commonly attracted towards and the resulting types of relationship, you can expose your hidden needs and behaviour patterns and so become more aware of those unconscious choices that you tend to make.

It may be that at some stage in your life you will need to withdraw a little in order to gain this perspective, especially if you are becoming trapped in a repetitive whirl of failed relationships. The needs are still urgent and pressing, but a transformation of attitudes through greater self-understanding may be necessary. Certain patterns operating in you are probably derived from childhood experiences and conditioning. The relationship with your parents may have been less than satisfactory, especially in the sphere of emotions, which is why you may now have such ambivalent and contradictory emotional patterns of need and denial when commitment is expected. There may even be feelings of guilt and non-acceptance of your own emotions. A withdrawal from relationship commitment could stem from a similar withdrawal of a parent towards you during childhood; you may now unconsciously seek to punish that parent by rejecting those who try to get close to you.

Your choice of partner is extremely important and the key to relationship success, but this choice depends on self-knowledge, so that both parties are complementary and in essential harmony with each other. Your early choices are likely to be unwise,

and these partnerships will probably run into troubled waters
due to those inner confusions and unresolved issues. New
perspectives on yourself and your needs may be achieved through
a transformative period of relative isolation from relationships, so
that the patterns are dissolved through understanding, and so
that insight, emotional maturity and greater independence can
be gained. Personal therapy counselling or courses in relating
could prove pivotal to future progress. The main obstacle to
relationship joy and sustaining a love affair is often your own
secret patterns; transcend them and a new world of satisfying
experience can open for you.

VENUS–MOON OPPOSITION

This opposition indicates that a major source of dissatisfaction
will lie within the sphere of social relationships. There may
be blockages in your dealings with others and you may feel
emotionally uneasy in social company. This pattern may stem
from a childhood in which you felt unloved, misunderstood and
rejected by your parents, especially your mother.

The opposition implies a psychological projection of personally
unresolved issues onto people and the external world, so that
there is the opportunity to experience these reflected back at
you; your tensions and stresses are embodied by others and
demonstrated in the nature of your relationships with them. You
have a tendency to feel unloved, and this insecurity is projected
onto others and interferes with relationships as a negative
self-image which is communicated in subtle ways to others,
who may sense that you are hiding something and therefore
begin to doubt your sincerity. The resulting distancing within
relationships then amplifies your own negative feelings and fears
of being disliked, and the cycle perpetuates itself. Others may find
it hard to relax around you, or feel inclined to oppose or reject you,
misunderstanding your attempts at contact and communication,
feeling suspicious of your intentions and generally keeping you
at arm's length.

Because these vitalising and harmonising feelings are blocked
in you they fail to reach out into your social relationships, so
people may perceive you as cold, unfriendly or distant, and
find it too much effort to spend time and energy slowly getting
to know you and opening you up. Your apparent reserve and

disregard for social involvement works against you; it isn't what you really want, it's just that inner inhibitions are too active to allow you movement across those barriers whenever you want, or to allow others to cross towards you. Your attempts to share and communicate are erratic, often superficial and lack a recognisable warmth. Even when you are admiring someone's achievements or making gestures of appreciation, there can be an unconvincing feeling in your delivery, as though you are going through socially acceptable motions but lacking any heart in it. As you know, this isn't the truth, but the inability to communicate your sensitive emotional nature to others gives a misleading impression of your character.

You may make compensatory attempts to avoid confronting any sense of emotional unfulfilment, and these can include a preoccupation with income, material possessions and comforts. These may give you a sense of identity, and of self-worth, as well as reflecting Venusian tendencies towards sensuality and luxury. Sexual activity without any deep emotional involvement may attract if opportunities present themselves, possibly to gain some sense of security and attention from others as well as for pleasure. Overeating or denial through anorexia may also act as compensatory actions. A passive stance may be taken in relationships, so that rejections caused by another's displeasure or conflicts created by your assertion are minimised.

Despite your efforts, social friction will persist and often erupt through the emotions, causing crises of adjustment until you succeed in resolving those inner tendencies and understand that, despite your need for closeness, you are pushing people away. Those inner barriers need dismantling, and to move beyond your inhibiting patterns you will need to take some risks and overcome that need for an imprisoning sense of security. Be open to contact, be more friendly and less distant, share yourself more easily, drop expectations about people, be less judgemental, and try to relate on a more intellectual level rather than just emotionally, because your emotions still need some cleansing and healing before their agitatory vibration becomes more settled. Learn how to co-operate better by making effective adjustments and concessions, and the likelihood is that over time the quality of your relationships will improve, enabling those blocked emotional energies to be safely released as you open yourself to a new type of contact with people and the environment. Then you may discover that you possess something of great value which can be shared with others for the benefit of the community. If you can make the transition, then perhaps you can help others who are having difficulty in social relating; at least when you meet those whom you recognise as being in a similar position, then you can offer the hand of friendship across the great divide, helping them to come out of their shell of insecurity.

MARS–MOON CONJUNCTION

Moon–Mars contacts involve the internal psychological relationship between those deeply rooted instinctual and emotional patterns with the ability to act in a decisive manner, by generating a consistent will capable of succeeding in personal aims.

The conjunction indicates that you will experience extremely strong emotions and feelings. These tend to colour your perceptions and decision-making and their intensity may often feel uncomfortable, almost frightening at times, especially in situations of passion or confrontation. You are aware that unleashing these energies often results in expressions of temper, emotional outbursts and anger, and this almost belligerent disagreement with others is really a means of self-defence. Being emotionally touchy to others' reactions and experiencing an underlying anxiety can create a mental state which makes you imagine that others criticise or plot against you. Even before there is any proof, you are ready to retaliate.

Until a deeper integration and understanding of these energies occurs within you, then contentious social and intimate relationships may continue. Those erratic and volatile emotions help to stimulate inner agitation, and this friction spills over into your exchanges with others. Whilst you do desire to form better relationships, there are often problems in spheres of co-operation and trust, at work and in intimate partnerships. You are both attracted and repulsed by emotional intimacy, often unable to deal easily with those feelings that arise from deep within, due to a degree of emotional immaturity, and others may sense those raging feelings and shy away from closer contact. Rejection strikes into your deepest core. Reacting against the pain, you often hit out verbally with unkind words designed to damage and wound, or throw childish temper tantrums when your needs are denied. You are liable to brood on any rejection, often slandering the perpetrator to others for a long time afterwards. Being seen to be losing is an erosion of your fragile self-esteem.

Essentially, one of your major problems is excessive self-focusing; wrapped within your private emotional world, you fail to recognise that others too have needs, that they are also sensitive and have emotions to deal with. Your world is too egocentric and revolves around your own desires, expecting others to serve you rather than welcoming mutual sharing, and often rejecting any attempts at compromise that are made. Being unaware of these tendencies is no excuse; failing to acknowledge that others have an equal sensitivity is a denial of reality. If you react against criticism, then so do other people react to criticism from you.

This apparently negative portrayal of Moon–Mars conjunctions can, however, be transformed by you into a more positive approach. Much depends on an honest appraisal of your relationships, and on dealing with your own inner difficulties, especially your tendency to take out any emotional frustrations on others close to you, which tends to make these relationships fail to satisfy and later collapse. These feelings can be channelled towards more positive aims designed to bring about constructive action. If you consciously attempt, even for a short period of time, to project yourself into the position of others and to imagine how life must seem from their perspective, by seeing through their eyes, feeling through their heart, then your egocentric world may be transformed and your sympathy and latent understanding awakened.

The Moon and Mars can work successfully together, once certain inner adjustments are achieved, and feelings of personal anguish and frustration are reduced by developing an awareness of the needs of others. Then it is probable that you will discover a new meaning and purpose to life. There can be a crusading spirit about this energy, with its powerful, assertive Martian quality. It can generate persistence and eventual success, and could stimulate a real transformation of your life.

MARS–MOON SEXTILE

The sextile and trine are probably the easiest Mars–Moon aspects to deal with, although even the sextile can pose difficulties in the personal juggling of powerful emotions with the impulses of energetic action and desire. Often you will try to impose a degree of mental control over your volatile feelings. This is because previous experience has shown you that there is a volcano lurking in your depths which has the potential to erupt in a powerfully aggressive and destructive manner if your emotions have been provoked or when you have been under prolonged stress. Your temper can flare up at times, and if emotional pressure is building inside you, then you can become argumentative just for an excuse to release some of the dammed energy; yet once the energy has flowed out and the pressure diminishes, you feel much better – the question is, how much damage have you done?

Whilst the Martian energies try to lead you towards spontaneous and impulsive actions, the protective Moon instincts tend to pull you back sufficiently to ensure time to think and to evaluate your decisions; this prevents you taking rash actions which may have detrimental consequences. Usually though, both the directions of your feelings and those of willed action synchronise well, co-operating to make your aims achievable. That temporary lunar block on impulsive action and ensuring that you think before leaping is a great asset.

There is likely to be some ability with financial matters, and an attraction towards enterprise and commercial schemes through recognising opportunities when they arise. Mars increases your self-confidence, providing courage and personal initiative to help you take full advantage of situations, and offering that abundant energy to join with emotional desires to help you complete your objectives. As you feel confident and secure, you relish life's challenges and even occasional failure does not diminish your faith in your abilities. You take a philosophical 'can't win them all' view which helps you to win more often than not. Co-operation with others is one of your strong points, and work concerning close relationships with co-workers or the public can prove successful, especially as your enthusiasm is transmitted to others and everyone becomes keen to participate on common projects.

Your friendly nature helps social communication, and you try to maintain decent relationships with all, attempting to resolve any disagreements by your willingness to discuss them openly and by keeping them in perspective. If all else fails, you will at least settle for an agreement to differ, and you try to ensure that if stalemate is reached then doors are still left open for future negotiation. You probably recognise that you have a tendency to react emotionally at first, and that this can colour your perceptions of others and ideas, so you try to minimise this by taking time to think things through, and, if still in doubt, prefer to give others the benefit of any remaining doubts. Rarely do you seek conflict, preferring to control those inner pressures that can develop at times through your emotional vulnerability. This is something that you have learned through life-experiences, and then translated into a growing maturity, understanding and integration.

You generally enjoy and appreciate life, giving a high priority to your domestic and family life, seeing home as providing a relaxed sanctuary and your more intimate relationships as channels through which your strong emotions can safely flow in positive and constructive ways.

MARS–MOON TRINE

The trine indicates that the energies of Moon and Mars are potentially reconciled and resolved within the personal psyche, and that the more problematic nature of these planetary dynamics should be much less evident than with the conjunction and the challenging square and opposition.

Whilst the level of feelings and emotions will be intense and powerful, you will have confidence in your ability to handle them; they act more as a vitalising source of energy that you can tap rather than an inner ocean threatening to swamp you. You find that by applying your will you can channel your energies into creative and imaginative pursuits, enhancing either personal interests or your career. You rarely waste your attention or energies on frivolous matters; instead you focus on issues and projects that are important to you, and through concentrated effort ensure that the eventual results are positive. Your emotional balance is communicated to others, and your social and intimate relationships benefit from your open and welcoming spirit. You accept the need for compromise and adjustment for the sake of more harmonious relationships, as in all social contact, and with your non-threatening temperament and outstretched hand you are able to develop a wide range of acquaintances and friends. You have regard for the common humanity of all, displaying tolerance, sympathy and understanding of people's frailties, as well as a realism in your expectations that prevents you from suffering undue disillusionment. Usually your perceptions are accurate and realistic, and knowing that people can pass through times of stress and confusion means that you rarely condemn or criticise others through insensitive comment and attitude.

However, you are not gullible, and will steer away from those who actually take advantage of others or selfishly abuse their feelings. You share yourself easily with those who are able to benefit from your company and support, appreciating the qualities of others and allowing for the inevitable weaknesses that will also be displayed. Whilst you are well balanced in both public and personal relationships, you prefer to maintain your independence too, especially in protecting a degree of privacy; you may become touchy if anyone crosses the demarcation lines that you have secretly drawn. This is indicative of the lunar tendency to establish instinctual patterns and protective barriers. If you ever believe that your natural rights are being infringed in any situation then you will rise to fight the oppression, or clearly express your anger at whoever is making such encroachments on your territory. Such actions by you may surprise anyone who hasn't seen this aspect to your nature in action before.

When challenges arise in your life, you tend to take a positive attitude towards them, applying yourself to doing the best you can, although not worrying unduly if failure eventually occurs; your self-image is too firm for that to shake you too much. Although obviously there will be disappointments, you take a philosophical approach to life, shrug your shoulders and carry on. This attitude is particularly useful if you apply your talents to the business sphere, where, if you act on instincts, your enterprising nature can lead to great success.

MARS–MOON SQUARE

The square aspect indicates that there will be inner tensions and frustrations related to your expression of feelings and your active will, and that conflict may occur when you are attempting to apply your will in ways that do not fully engage your emotional and instinctual needs. It is these internal stresses that often prevent your relationships and career being fully satisfying or successful. Emotional volatility is likely, and you may be prone to periodic temper outbursts as that inner pressure overflows in provocative situations.

Your inability to control your pent-up emotions, coupled with a tendency towards paranoia, keeps those emotions in a state of ongoing turmoil which can manifest in an argumentative and confrontational manner. Sometimes you seem to relish arguments as a source of self-assertion, although they are often more a means of releasing inhibited energy than a real exchange of different viewpoints. In fact, your tendency to dismiss others' beliefs and opinions without careful, respectful consideration, with a style of dismissal which can descend to open abuse and verbal attack, succeeds mainly in alienating people and distracting you from following your own path. Eventually there is a distinct diminution of support and help from others.

If the contentious side of your temperament becomes increasingly dominant, then psychosomatic health disorders may be one consequence stimulated either by the stress of interpersonal conflict or by the repression of your anger. Problems of the intestines and stomach areas are possible, perhaps stimulating the formation of ulcers. You need to learn how to release these feelings constructively, or at least harmlessly, perhaps by exploring methods of relaxation or meditation, and by gradually understanding your emotional complexity through forms of self-help techniques.

You can be too self-centred, intent on pursuing your own way irrespective of the impact it may have on others close to you. Sometimes you try to use your Martian energies almost like a bludgeon to gain your way, refusing to make essential adjustments or compromise with others, demanding that they fit in with your desires and needs whilst denying any validity to their own. You may need to realise that 'give and take' establishes a more appropriate balance and movement of energies within relationships; you might have expectations of what you need from others, but equally, they will demand some contribution from you.

Often your instincts and emotional needs will clash with your will for action, and you may feel very confused regarding what you should be choosing. This inability to know which way to turn will increase that sense of frustration, and anyone attempting to offer help is likely to be rejected as interfering; you prefer to tread an independent path, even if it is a solitary one.

Fear of possible threats coming from others tends to stimulate your defensive instincts, and this unease is likely to be an undercurrent running through your life, even though it is mainly unfounded. It is often your own belligerence and ill temper that arouse the ire of others and make your social relationships complex and unsatisfactory. You need to develop a sense of self-esteem based on an appreciation of your own nature rather than on the degree to which you can make others submit to you when challenged; that type of aggressive tactic to achieve a spurious sense of superiority gains mainly enemies rather than friends. This is especially true in a career environment which is likely to be unfulfilling, and where pressures and self-imposed tensions from that sphere have a direct influence on the rest of your life and relationships.

Despite your innate emotional vulnerability and sensitivity, your attitudes may still remain immature and unintegrated; as a consequence of your own inner problem, your awareness and sensitivity to others is diminished. Others should be perceived as enriching your life rather than posing hidden threats. You should concentrate more on co-operation and less on inappropriate competition. You need to develop compromise and trust, as well as a new perception of your own nature which includes the reality of others. Acknowledge these inner stresses, but learn how to find constructive channels for the energies to move out through, instead of allowing them to contaminate other areas of your life and relationships by negative frustrations. Self-discipline may be required to achieve this, and a refusal to indulge in unnecessary argumentative behaviour. Drugs and alcohol should be avoided, as they may further agitate your emotions, stirring them into greater volatility.

Domestic and intimate relationship problems are likely unless greater understanding and maturity are gained. Men may try to be too forceful and aggressive with women, playing a 'macho' role without much understanding and sensitivity to the female temperament, oppressing through asserting raw power without sympathy and identifying with the Mars energy and denying the Moon. Women may passively respond to a more dominant partner, and in the process deny personal instincts and emotions, consigning them to the unconscious, where they will fester and gain hidden power, waiting for the right time to be unleashed to destroy an imprisoning life-style.

MARS–MOON OPPOSITION

The opposition aspect projects inner tensions and unresolved issues into social relationships, and it is likely that this sphere will prove to be problematic in your life, and a periodic scene for crises or turning-points. You will probably use relationships as an area for releasing inner pressures, through arguments, dissension, provocation and antagonism, taking advantage of even trivial issues to turn them into energy-filled confrontations and clashes. This will obviously affect your career prospects and your domestic life, and those rebellious feelings will always be stimulated by any attempt to impose another's will on you through authority or criticism. Anyone crossing that line and irritating your feelings is liable to be confronted by an extremely obstinate and stubborn character. Co-workers will soon lose patience with an emotionally erratic colleague, who can suddenly become aggressive in the face of criticism or personal comment, and people will learn to withdraw from contact with you if you behave in this way.

You feel uneasy and uncomfortable with your unintegrated nature, and, similarly, others may find you hard to understand. That ongoing difficulty with your lunar nature working in harmony with the assertive and active Martian energy needs to be resolved. Sometimes the polarity favours one of the planets, and if it is temporarily Mars, then you are liable to display impulsive behaviour, taking sudden decisions and actions which may be quite irrational, foolish and lacking in forethought. Yet equally, such actions may project you out from a static situation. Expressing the Moon energy may leave you self-protective and cautious, remaining fixed to the status quo and afraid to move beyond familiar boundaries and behaviour patterns. The challenge is to unite these energies into a complementary expression, honouring each as equally valid and necessary.

Part of this aggressive and assertive nature may stem from your relationship with your mother. There may have been a denial of your childlike feelings and a lack of real contact, or you may have been made to submit to an oppressive regime of duty and behaviour at home. In adult life you refuse to submit easily to this again, yet you reflect the pattern by attempting to impose your will on others. Attempting to gain emotional superiority, you may try to be too assertive in that desire to become a leader and not a follower. This often results in a distorted picture of your nature, both for yourself and for others, as you fall into the trap of attempting to be 'number one', behaving in a way which is cold, arrogant and aggressively assertive. You hate others resisting your will, and when this happens you respond with a personal attack. Sometimes such an antagonistic stance may succeed, but eventually its costs far exceed those of other more moderate approaches.

Yet often your personality can appear attractive to many, and there is certainly a vitality about your nature that can intrigue some, even though it is a distorted expression of the planetary energies. Choosing companions, both friends and lovers, is one area where your weaknesses may appear, as you are often attracted to people who turn out to be unsuitable characters with equally volatile emotional difficulties. Intimate relationships may be limited to physical expression, or be entered into for material reasons, as there is often a repression of the emotional and subtler dimensions of interpersonal contact. Sustaining such relationships is difficult as time passes, once initial attractions fade.

There can be an attraction towards promises of excitement which can lead you into dubious areas of life, where the 'excitement' may not prove to be especially beneficial; much depends on your choice of fellow travellers, as the stresses of this aspect can lead to dissipation and a loss of opportunities if efforts are not made to reconcile conflicting tendencies. In a similar way, you may fail to fulfil promises made to others through a shift in your internal planetary polarity, and commitment and responsible behaviour may not be your strongest assets.

Routine life-styles and partnerships may fail to satisfy, and reactions against such patterns may lead to nervous tension, creating those psychosomatic illnesses which are associated with the digestive functions.

Realising that others exist and are entitled to an equality of respect can help to moderate your overbearing tendencies, and seeing that they too have a sensitive feeling nature can enhance mutual understanding. Through greater self-control, you may gain a sense of clarity regarding your relationships. Accepting the need to live harmoniously within a greater society can help to readjust your sense of proportion, enabling you to realise that you can contribute to the well-being of all, instead of merely indulging in alienated antagonism. Transforming this side of your nature will result in considerable personal benefits for you, as well as generating a growing sense of self-esteem and peace of mind. Reaching that will also divest your repressed emotions of that quality of stressful agitation, and without their hidden contamination of your perception you will discover a clarity of thought and decisive action that can be used to your advantage.

JUPITER–MOON CONJUNCTION

With the conjunction, your essential feeling response will be aligned with people and your environment; this will tend to make you very socially aware and most of your attention will be focused in that direction. This involves an expansion of your self into the outer world, and your major concern will be the well-being of society and those around you.

You will have an innate faith in the goodness of the universe and your fellow man, and you will try to transmit a positive and creative view of life to others, for their benefit and for the benefit of society as a whole.

At a deep inner level you feel a connectedness with your environment, and realise the powerful influence that the quality of the environment can have on your sense of well-being, positively or negatively. Equally, you realise that you can make a difference in the world too, and will look for ways through which you can express your caring nature. Your feelings reach out to people and are touched by those who are in genuine need of support, help and care. Seeing those who are deprived or disadvantaged opens your heart and stimulates your mind to conceive ways in which you can offer assistance. Looking through sympathetic and compassionate eyes, you feel that much can be done to make social welfare more effective, and you may believe that you have certain answers or solutions to social challenges.

You may sometimes respond to social suffering with excessive emotionalism, but this is preferable to not responding at all. These emotional reactions may need to be tempered by a more pragmatic and detached approach though, or else you may become too personally involved and affected to offer effective help. The impulse rising within you is that of world service, your feelings being more fulfilled by giving than by receiving, and you rely on that sense of inner strength and unity with life.

You may become involved with various socially concerned groups, those which have a progressive vision of the potential of humanity, or those devoted to meeting the present needs of the disadvantaged. Supporting the work of international charities may appeal, or you may decide to work within existing established social groups, such as the churches, or educational or political organisations. Medicine or law may also attract. The strength of your convictions may give you an almost missionary zeal, and you may tend towards compulsive service in a futile attempt to change the world single-handedly. This tendency may need to be balanced, and over-enthusiasm curbed, if only to protect your own health and stability. You need to pace yourself to ensure your continued social contribution. Times of rest and personal relaxation to renew your batteries are essential too, and a necessary part of your own self-healing. Steady perseverance will reap greater results than a sudden burning out in a flash of excessive activity. Changing the world is a long-term project! Spending time with your own family and contributing to their development is equally valid, and you will feel deep emotional attachments to your home life, aiming to inculcate a social awareness in your children and friends too.

JUPITER–MOON SEXTILE

With the sextile, you will have both an emotional and intellectual response to your environment, although the natural bias may be towards mental activity and stimulation. This is a beneficial combination to have, both personally and socially. Life is fascinating to you, and one of the main driving forces in your personality is your insatiable curiosity, which will result in your absorbing considerable quantities of information. This gives you a broad perspective on the complexities of contemporary society, and encourages you to make some form of positive contribution to improve the quality of life.

Having such an aware and active intellect, you may be attracted to careers which reflect the value of mind and the application of intellect to existing knowledge and problem-solving. These may include medicine, law, education, finance, religion, welfare and charity organisations. There may be a flair for business, for spotting expanding social trends and marketing appropriate products to satisfy consumer needs and desires.

Your social relationships are usually satisfying and varied, and you seem to possess an intrinsic understanding of people which you use in your contacts, and which can also benefit career or business dealings. You have a sociable and friendly spirit which perceives people's potential and helps them to uncover it, whilst also acknowledging their present reality and motivations. In your own life, you are probably reasonably clear about your own path and intentions, maintaining a confident, optimistic and positive attitude which helps to manifest your aims. You look forward to ever greater success, prosperity and fulfilment, rarely looking backwards unless it is to derive a beneficial lesson from previous experiences.

If you choose to pursue self-understanding, through religion, science, meditation and techniques of self-help, then it is likely to have great benefits for you, enhancing meaning, purpose and direction in your life and showing you ways through which you can apply your potential more effectively. Underlying your intellect there are likely to be religious feelings, and a social and moral idealism fuelled by sympathy and compassion.

Imagination will be active in you, and connected to your innate understanding of people your intellectual abilities may generate a creative potential waiting to be released. This may be literary in nature, or involve the spoken word, and what you express may be valuable to others, due to the insights that you try to communicate. This may be centred on 'the ray of hope' of the Jupiter vibration, which transmits optimism, positivity and support towards others in need. Sharing yourself in such a way may become part of your life-path, helping others to resolve their problems and then to unfold their own latent potential. You will have a generous, accepting nature, refusing to condemn when people are just being human. People may come to look to you for guidance.

You will want an emotionally satisfying home life, and will devote considerable attention to building a comfortable environment and relationship to enjoy. You need fulfilling and deep emotional ties, and will look for a suitable partner to share daily life with, one with whom there can be a sequential personal development which will enrich each other's lives.

JUPITER–MOON TRINE

You will probably have optimistic, positive attitudes which contribute to your sense of well-being and are communicated through relationships with others. As your energies flow easily, you find that making contact with others is natural and exhilarating, with expansion in your life coming from releasing your abundant enthusiasms into the world. You may be oversensitive to environmental influences or to negative reactions from people, but you have a natural resilience and prefer to work through any personal problems as soon as possible, rarely allowing them to spoil your enjoyment of life for long. You prefer a simple, uncomplicated life-style, replete with satisfaction and will not tolerate negative intrusions of any kind.

Compassion for all, generosity and an altruistic, humanistic spirit will be present, and these may lead you towards social involvement, perhaps as a result of feelings of moral and civic duty. Associated with this may be deep-rooted religious idealism, especially of the kind that might be inspired by the Christian parable of the Good Samaritan. You will feel a sense of social responsibility, and will support attempts to improve the quality of life for those disadvantaged in any way; for you, the strength of a society is in the level of support, care and attention that it gives to those in need, rather than penalising them for being less able than others.

There is likely to be creative and imaginative potential in you, which you should develop. Even if it only manifests in spare-time interests, perhaps artistic or literary, but its enriching contribution to both your own and others' lives may be significant. For some, taking this potential step-by-step may lead to it becoming a life-purpose and career in itself.

Friends may find your self-assurance supportive and strengthening, and you may become an adviser and confidante for them. Provided it does not turn into a parasitic dependency, then your advice may prove beneficial to others, helping them to confront and resolve their challenging problems. However, you may need to distinguish between those times when people actually use your advice and support to transform their difficulties, and when they just transfer part of the burden to you, without making efforts to resolve the problem. The parable of the seeds falling on stony ground may be appropriate here. To achieve the best use of your talents and abilities, you may need to determine a clearly defined focus for them, rather than allowing them to be dissipated in several directions at once.

In your intimate relationships, you will look for partners of a high calibre and quality, people with whom you can experience a deep and meaningful relationship, intellectually and emotionally fulfilling, and who are also following their own individual path in life to unfold their own potential. You prefer partners to be self-aware, possessing self-understanding and maturity, and you are less attracted towards those who will bring chaos and confusion into your life, diverting you from your chosen direction. You prefer peace and relative harmony, because providing that you do not sink into lethargic stagnation, that is the best base from which to work. Once your emotions are committed, you will be highly faithful and devoted to your partner, always looking for ways in which the relationship can be improved and stimulated. Family and home life is important to you, and much joy will come from this source.

JUPITER–MOON SQUARE

The square indicates that you may have difficulty in uniting your sensitive feeling and emotional nature with your personal impulse to expand and unfold your innate potential; the two sets of inner messages either conflict or fail to conjoin, thus diminishing the clarity of your intention and motivation. For example, you may well possess some creative ability, yet fail to express this in any tangible form through not making sufficient effort to develop it. You tend to react against most types of hard work, and can display a lazy, apathetic attitude at times, especially if you have little interest in the work to be done. Underlying this is a belief that you should have an easy life with few worries, allowing you to be self-indulgent; part of this may have arisen from your relationships with parents who served and indulged you, or made you feel special, and encouraged a belief that the world would take care of you.

You will react to the world through a powerful emotional filter, which will condition your perceptions and evaluations of your experiences. There will be less intellectual analysis or evaluation made, as your instinctive emotional responses will be given the highest level of validation. Taking such an approach may not always work to your advantage, and over time you may begin to realise that relying on emotional responses alone may prejudice your decisions, often leading you in unsuitable directions which might have been avoided if a more rational approach had been taken. As emotions can wax and wane, consistency may be lacking in your attitudes and relationships; greater stability is required for maturity. Tendencies towards impulsive emotional decision-making need to be superseded by deliberate planning;

a rush to satisfy immediate desires may be regretted in the long term.

You may need to learn greater realism, both in respect of people and the material world. Sometimes your optimism and emotional projections are too extreme, your feelings being amplified into 'the greatest love of all time'. In addition, genuine feelings of generosity may leave you bankrupt, perhaps through extravagance, lending to the wrong people, or just a lack of financial acumen. Be extremely careful not to overestimate business prospects. You may benefit from receiving expert financial advice, although even here considerable discrimination is needed to avoid choosing the wrong type of adviser.

Your intimate and social relationships may be erratic at times, as you can vary between outward-going moods and internal preoccupation, depending on the relative fluctuating strengths of either Jupiter or the Moon. You have an independent spirit and you may often feel that you do not really need much social contact, and so your friendships may become characterised by infrequent contact, indifference and fickleness at times. You'll do your own thing, whether it's with complete enthusiasm and commitment however temporary, or with apathy and disinterest. These fluctuating tendencies can be rectified and transformed if you seriously choose to work on them. Self-determination and concentrated application is the path to take, once you have actually settled on a suitable direction to follow, one which offers the potential for greater meaning and purpose.

It is likely that in your earlier life you were not overly ambitious, preferring freedom, acting with little responsibility and moving in and out of situations and relationships as it pleased you; directed by your inner emotional pendulum. This could have been a phase of wandering and exploration, lacking any distinct aim. This phase may continue with varying emphasis and degree until you confront the need for responsibility in life, perhaps discovered through settling into marriage, financial commitments and the raising of a family.

Having to 'shape up' may shock you into several realisations. You may begin to make greater efforts to make your life stimulating, to prevent it becoming staid and restrictive, and the need for planning and organisation may help you to see how that can make life flow more smoothly, with less conflict and fewer ups and downs. Social awareness may deepen, as you become less self-preoccupied, and tendencies towards extravagant fantasies become modified by the recognition of the limitations of real life. When reality intrudes, illusions should dissipate; if they persist, then reality is being ignored.

As maturity deepens, you may begin to move in new social directions, clarifying your awakening awareness and sensitivity, and releasing previously inhibited talents. Social concern and activity may begin to replace the desire for emotional freedom, and you may begin to work in ways designed to benefit those who are socially deprived.

If you come to this route through religious or political paths, then you may need to be wary of that tendency towards imbalance in attitudes which may still persist there. Your emotional power may be channelled into zealous proselytising; you may become obsessive about your newly chosen path and lose sight of a realistic perspective in the wake of your enthusiasm. Learn how to moderate any such tendency, and allow others the freedom of their own ways through life, or else you may find increased clashes with parents, friends and social traditions.

JUPITER–MOON OPPOSITION

One of the major personal difficulties with the opposition is the unease caused by a lack of self-confidence, especially with your abilities and individual worth. This seepage of energy into self-doubt tends to diminish your actual level of achievement, forming a vicious circle that needs to be broken. Emotionally, you feel unable to evaluate your own abilities or creative efforts; they are too close to you, too peculiarly intimate to your nature and well-being. Yet such creative potential is present within you if you are willing to take the risk to release it through you; you need to feel supported by others to do so, and will feel more empowered and believe in your talent when it is recognised by others whose opinions you respect.

You tend to protect your vulnerable, sensitive feelings, although you are likely to discover that most of the pain in your life comes from your relationships with people. This can include friction with parents, either during childhood or in later life; unsuccessful love affairs and romances; being taken advantage of by unscrupulous colleagues or friends; and having disputes in your own family home, such as with children. You will prefer to evade emotional confrontation from any source, although evasion often exacerbates the eventual and inevitable conflict in such situations. You prefer to think well of everybody, giving them the benefit of any doubt and relying on mutual trust; unfortunately, deception is common. Your evaluation of character can often be misguided or lacking perception, and discrimination is not your strongest asset.

Giving to others is your natural form of expression, prompted either by sincere and genuine feelings, or by a desire to gain the affection of others; but there are many 'takers' in the world waiting to exploit people like you, and you may need to guard against making snap emotional commitments and decisions until time has passed and experience shows that the person is honest and genuine. Your generosity may need to be limited to those who can appreciate and value such gestures.

You may discover a suitable outlet for your social feelings and concern by working for people's welfare; your sense of civic responsibility is well developed, and you may see such community activity as the moral duty of a responsible citizen. Certainly, working for the good of society will fulfil you in many ways, and reassure you as to your own worth. Care and sincere concern is vitally needed by many in every society, and there can never be enough impersonal love released through world service to heal all who suffer, and who will do so for many decades still to come. Because of your own self-doubts, you can empathise with those who are socially deprived, and through possible contact with them can encourage them to lift their own sights higher and to help unfold their potential; in fact, your help is also helping yourself to grow and expand, creating mutual benefit through mutual interdependence.

You may need to be wary of a tendency towards restlessness, which can disturb your inner state and relationships with others. Whenever you feel a period of restlessness and dissatisfaction coming on, you may need to seek new areas of interest and activity, or new sources of emotional nourishment. This may require the unblocking of existing attitudes and values which are forming crystallised habit patterns of behaviour, and which are inhibiting the free-flow of emotional energies; dependency on security patterns tends to restrict, eventually imprisoning you in repetitive behaviour, and this self-imprisonment should always be avoided.

SATURN–MOON CONJUNCTION

The Saturn–Moon combination is not a particularly harmonious one, and in all of these contacts the lunar nature of the individual is affected, often detrimentally.

With this aspect, you are likely to express a sombre, self-restrained and conservative type of personality. There can be a lack of spontaneity and enthusiasm in the way you relate socially, an emotional defensiveness and reserve. Thus you can find it difficult to express yourself in company. You may be apprehensive about social contact and life in general. You may lack faith in life, tending towards a pessimistic world-view, and this negative and restricting attitude will also inhibit the expression of your own potential.

Your self-esteem is diminished by this dominating attitude, which acts like a shadow falling across your relationships and experiences. One source of this may lie in your childhood and early social conditioning. It may have been that your earlier childhood experiences were negatively influenced by family discipline, which may have manifested either through parental authority, or through religious, political or social beliefs strongly imposed; perhaps there were family upheavals, and discord, or there may have been a strong feeling that you were not really wanted or loved by your parents – whether or not this was actually true. The residue of this is a fear of emotional expression, to others and even to yourself, and your need for protection of your sensitivity has become associated with 'negative experiences'. In adult life, there may be one parent towards whom you still feel resentment, deeply contradictory attitudes and powerful emotions.

There will be unease in emotional integration; it is a level of your nature that remains uncomfortable and relatively immature, and will spill over into your efforts to create adult relationships, which may be difficult to develop beyond the early stages. A lack of self-confidence, and an inner reluctance to make your feelings vulnerable to another tends to make you withdraw back into those negative behaviour patterns when the possibility of a close relationship arises. You need to open yourself more to relationship, to take the chances of rejection in order to move towards the greater likelihood of success; to learn to trust in others and to begin breaking out of that self-imposed prison. Obviously, making suitable choices in relationships is a key factor, and you may need to be cautious here.

Learning how to dissolve the binding ties of the past is necessary; you will probably be emotionally attached to memories and material possessions, perhaps nostalgic or sentimental, even though your childhood life may not have been especially satisfying. Liberating yourself from the chains of the past will be a great relief and release for you; it may not be easy, yet it could hold the keys to a bright new future. You may be surprised at just how much past experiences and conditioning have affected your adult personality; looking for ways through which you can heal and integrate your inner child would be extremely beneficial and transformative.

Achieving such a step forward could enable you to improve the quality of your relationships. The potential is there for you to enjoy mature contacts with other essentially serious and thoughtful partners, where there is a maturity and depth to the relationship and a progressive emotional unfoldment as the sharing increases across every level, physical, emotional, mental and spiritual. If this happens, then you will experience the dawning of a positive and optimistic outlook within you, as you release the weight of the past by redirecting your emotional energy into more suitable patterns. Others may encourage you to move forward, and if they do so, then accept their support. You just need a little encouragement and convincing of your self-worth.

You are likely to progress in your career due to that ability to focus your attention within a defined sphere of operation, especially in earlier adulthood, whilst your emotions are controlled and are probably repressed to some degree. You have a tendency to insulate your emotions into a separate compartment locked away, although you will need your sensitivity to others' feelings if you are in a management position. Normally, you will display honesty, impersonality, fairness, competence and efficiency in employment, enjoying positions of authority and responsibility and will expect comparable standards of commitment from others. Areas which may attract include law, medicine, business, politics and education.

SATURN–MOON SEXTILE

With the sextile the relationship between these two planets is easier to deal with, and whilst the underlying emotional restriction will still remain, it is less limiting since the light of the mind will help to dissipate inner darkness, helping you to understand and resolve your emotional conflicts.

Whilst you recognise that you do not have all the answers, you realise that the act of attempting to understand helps to build a bridge, whether within your own nature, or between yourself and others, and so you have learned to listen and be ready to communicate about problems with others for mutual support and benefit. To you 'a problem shared is a problem halved', and you know that by taking a realistic approach to emotional problems there is the likelihood that eventually a constructive solution will emerge. You will still be drawn towards self-help, because you are essentially a serious, reserved and cautious personality, still uneasy with expressing your feeling nature to others, unless they are old and trusted friends and family. Yet others may begin to turn towards you for support, not necessarily because they believe that you have the answers, but because they recognise that you will honour and acknowledge their own emotional pain and confusion, and in that mutual recognition a form of supportive healing and acceptance can be transmitted.

Generally, you will try to apply an intelligent approach to life founded on common sense and personal integrity. You will demonstrate efficiency, practicality, pragmatism and order in whatever tasks you undertake, being relied on to perform in an organised attentive manner in accordance with standard procedures. You work well within traditional environments with established working practices to which you are expected to conform. This satisfies the Saturn characteristics. Attractions to law, medicine, politics, management, local government and education are likely. There may be financial skills which you can exploit, especially through business endeavours.

There is an aura of respectibility and realism about you; you are not an ineffective dreamer, and basically you are a reliable member of society with reasonably high standards of behaviour. Your personal integrity is a quality that you will not compromise, even if this means losing opportunities. If everything seems above board, however, you are usually alert enough to take advantage of whatever opportunities arise. Persistence and determination are two of your assets, and you try to apply these in whatever task you set for yourself. You are reasonably ambitious, although not obsessively so, and will probably make steady progress anyway.

You are attracted towards self-development, study and learning, enjoying increasing your knowledge and understanding, and although you may limit this to specific interest areas, you can develop considerable specialist knowledge if you so choose. This can then be shared with others through teaching in some way, as you have an ability to communicate your knowledge in an effective manner.

You will prefer friends and partners who like you, are intelligent, serious-minded and thoughtful. Close friendships and trust are important for you, so you will form a small, select band of confidantes around you based also on emotional bonds, mutual care and concern. For a permanent partner, you will want someone with whom you can relate deeply on every level, building a whole relationship which enables mutual unfoldment to occur naturally over time, and where the presence of the other creates mutual benefit and a creative interdependence.

You may need to ensure that you do not deny your feelings, instincts and emotions, especially at times when your mental preoccupation is more emphasised and active. Feelings are an important level of your nature which is weaker and vulnerable, and you may need to check that you are not ignoring its messages. Cleansing those emotions, liberating those feelings, and listening to those instincts are vital actions to take; learn how to express them in the security of your intimate and close relationships, and trust their guidance too.

SATURN–MOON TRINE

The trine offers the potential to resolve these two disparate planetary energies, and it is likely that you will feel a more positive and optimistic attitude than is common with the other aspects between these planets. You should express a stability in your personality and in developing a suitable life-style, demonstrating a practical and resourceful nature, and being reliable and persevering in fulfilling whatever duties and obligations you have incurred over time, whether domestic and family ones, or through career, social and civic responsibilities.

Your personality will be centred on a cautious and conservative perspective, valuing social rules and regulations, and trying to adhere to them. You will possess considerable self-discipline and sense of adult responsibility, together with a great respect for social structures and traditions. You may view experimentation and proposals to change social establishments with unease and suspicious concern, preferring to stay with tried and tested ways. However, you do also recognise the virtue of change in renewal, and will support change if you believe that it will have a beneficial effect; change for change's sake you will view with distaste.

Building firm foundations in life is seen to be important; part of this may have emerged from consciously benefiting from stability and permanence during a childhood in which your ongoing development felt safe due to that sensation of secure environmental structures around you, and the comforting presence of your parents. You realise that the successful erection of anything depends on right foundations being made, and that following this pattern will ensure success in your endeavours, whether in business, career, marriage or family life. It is possible that you may benefit from inheritance, perhaps business or through some type of institutional involvement.

You will apply a shrewd, pragmatic common sense to your affairs, preferring either self-employment or a position of authority and responsibility, where opportunities to express your potential are more readily available. There is creative ability present in you, although this may be directed along socially traditional channels, business or career. The spheres of law, medicine, engineering, politics, management and education may attract. You will tend to be a good worker, believing that in order to gain the benefits you need to commit your efforts to the task before you.

It will be rare for you to be emotionally demonstrative, and at times your attitudes may seem quite austere and privately withdrawn. Emotionally, you will remain in control and reasonably stable, and your feelings will be displayed honestly and in a straightforward manner, so that others know what you think and feel about things. Emotional manipulation and distorting complexities are anathema to you, and you may react strongly against anyone playing emotional games with others. Friendships are founded on mutual compatibility, trust and faith in genuine care and support for each other, although each has to be a relatively independent type of personality and secure in their own self-esteem; you are not so keen on the dependent temperaments whose emotional vacillations and confusion may activate that level of emotional unease that can lurk deep within you.

You are usually cautious in making decisions that involve an emotional factor, taking time to evaluate your feelings and intuition, knowing that they have valid messages to convey and also recognising that you may not have been listening to them enough. Once you are certain, then you commit yourself, especially in a marriage or partnership context, and you will tend to expect a similar level of clarity and commitment from your partner too. Maturity and emotional stability are necessary in a partner, and you will dislike emotional changeability; if you find the right partner, then much of your creativity will flow into the relationship so that it develops and progresses to mutual benefit.

SATURN–MOON SQUARE

With the square, there may be limitations on your opportunities and experiences created by unresolved and unintegrated emotional patterns. The source of this may lie in emotional attachments to the past, to memories, experiences and earlier relationships. You find it difficult to break free from the past, and your past life will strongly condition your present choices and attitudes.

The likelihood is that you may have grown up with a negative self-image, one which effectively diminishes sufficient self-confidence and also perpetuates restrictive world-views. Part of this may have been derived from experiences in childhood which disturbed and unsettled you, against which you erected barriers to protect your feelings being more damaged. You may have believed that you were not loved by your parents, or you may have been left with just one parent through separation, divorce or death. Issues of emotional dependency may have arisen, and a mother or father complex may have formed, making it difficult for you to cut the parental umbilical cord as you became adult. Taking some time and investigating the roots of your childhood inhibitions may shed considerable light on aspects of your adult life.

Your life perspective may tend towards pessimism, linked to a diminution of physical and emotional vitality, moodiness, melancholic dissatisfaction, and depression. Lacking confidence in yourself, or seeing the world as a harsh, loveless place, you may develop a bitterness and cynicism, and prefer to isolate yourself from deeper involvement, especially in relationships. You may feel that there is a barrier between you and others, making contact and communication difficult to achieve.

Family ties bind you. This could mean that you are older than the majority when you leave home to become independent; or you have the onerous duty of caring for an elderly parent. Or your own family life may turn into an imprisoning environment in some way, perhaps through children, economic hardship or social isolation. You are very sensitive to the complexities of family relationships, and despite your own emotional difficulties, will hate to cause anyone else emotional distress. Yet these ties limit you, and will continue to tighten until you take your life into your own hands.

You may feel uneasy with intimate relationships and try to avoid such involvements, fearing that you will not be able to cope or that what you imagine to be your inadequacies will be exposed. Feeling unloved, how could anyone feel love for you? That attitude turns into a vicious, self-defeating circle, and you may become socially awkward and excessively shy. Dissolving such inner barriers and protective emotional mechanisms is essential, both to liberate yourself from those negative conditioning patterns and to free your repressed emotional energies to vitalise the inner wasteland that you have been creating.

You are maintaining these inner tensions and frustrations by refusing to release those patterns of behaviour established during childhood. It is your choice if you wish to continue limiting your life, but it is not inevitable; limitations are only imaginary parameters that we draw around ourselves as a barrier, and can be erased or expanded. Your creativity is blocked by emotional repression, and if that was dissolved and the energies redirected towards positive and constructive channels, then much could be achieved. Finding additional interests and stimulation would lighten your load and show you that the world has much more to offer if only you let it. Becoming involved with children could show you new ways to see things; their enthusiasm and sense of wonder could be transmitted to you. With contemporary self-help techniques, visualisations, meditations and affirmations, and other ways to release blocked energies available, you can transform your life so that you face the future with positivity and optimism.

SATURN–MOON OPPOSITION

The opposition indicates the likelihood that there will be restrictions and limitations derived from other people or environmental pressures, and that difficulties may be experienced in your relationships.

Childhood experiences, perceptions and parental or social conditioning will have made their mark on you, and duty, obligation and responsibility will hold a high priority for you. These are perceived as qualities expressed by the socially mature individual, but instead of naturally developing as a result of real maturation, they have been imposed upon you, probably during childhood before you were really able to deal with them. In effect, parental pressure or environmental circumstances may have forced you to 'act grown up' before you were really ready, fulfilling those social demands as an expression of conformity and discipline. Internally, you may have felt strong reactions against the absorption of rigid behaviour patterns and constraining attitudes, and may have perceived your parents as lacking love or understanding for you.

Life presents a vista of duty and obligation; it is seen as a serious affair in which it is all-important to 'do the right thing', even if it means going against your feelings, instincts and emotions . . . or so it seems to you. So the result is a controlling of your childhood feelings, exuberance and enthusiasm, times of childhood play and 'silliness', of acting out imaginative fantasies, of refusing to conform.

By adult life, this may have resulted in phases of emotional moodiness, bleak depressions and negativity, emotional inflexibility, phases of stagnation, and fears of people, experiences and situations. This is symptomatic of emotions forced into your unconscious mind. Sensing this repression, others may avoid close contact with you, as they guess that your social stiffness inhibits relationships, and as your vibration is that of a loner, they may feel uncomfortable.

This negative tendency becomes restrictive and limiting to you, as opportunities are lost through refusing to take chances, or relationships denied through feelings of social unease. If you can redirect your attitudes in a more positive and constructive direction, then things will begin to open up. Making such a shift is likely to prove difficult, yet if achieved, it will be highly rewarding.

Becoming clear about a life-direction is important, so that you can apply your energies in a definite plan to achieve certain personal goals. Whilst you have that 'duty and obligation' program running in you, you can also be antagonistic towards authority figures, such as employers or managers, especially if they happen to provoke your feelings, or touch on any point of emotional sensitivity. This is another sign of that emotional repression and ambivalence coming through. If you choose not to branch out into self-employment, then work related to medicine, research, social welfare, community service, law or government may attract you.

Relationships may prove problematic. You find it hard to let down that emotional drawbridge to let others in, and hard to express your feelings too. Sometimes embryonic relationships are destroyed by you allowing previous relationship experiences to interfere, by your prejudging people according to past disillusionments and so preventing deeper contacts from developing as a means of self-protection. You may be attracted to older partners or those who appear to display a maturity that you believe you lack, and need to be careful here of becoming too dependent on them. You may fall deeply in love with someone who displays an affection for you, which could leave you vulnerable through unlocking the padlocked doors to your emotions which could come flooding out. Such experiences could prove most uncomfortable and traumatic, yet releasing those emotions is the only healthy route to follow. If a relationship develops, then you may become less defensive, and your hidden potential may begin to blossom with a loving partner.

Children may help to unfold you even more, providing a relationship into which you can pour your loving concern, and so begin to feel more at ease in expressing that aspect of your nature, although you may find that family obligations can create limitations as well. A more balanced approach to fulfilling responsibilities in a more relaxed, emotionally responsive manner is required, and much depends on a transformation in your attitudes and feeling behaviour patterns. If achieved, limitations dissolve as emotional stresses are released, and a new feeling of liberation takes its place. With emotional freedom comes the dismantling of the barriers prohibiting creativity and imagination to flourish, and taking these progressive steps may reveal untold depths to abilities that have remained dormant in your life.

For the Moon aspects with the transpersonal planets, please refer to the interpretations in my books. *Phoenix Rising* (Moon–Pluto), *Revolutionary Spirit* (Moon–Uranus), and *Visionary Dreamer* (Moon–Neptune).

CHAPTER 5

The Moon in the Natal Houses

THE NATAL HOUSE POSITION OF the Moon signifies an area of life through which the individual may move without full awareness, reflecting patterns of behaviour that lie within their unconscious mind which are stimulated to active expression by repetitive daily habits and routines. There is often a lack of objectivity regarding this area, although closer examination may reveal the nature of patterns formed in the past by early parental and social educative influences.

In some cases these influences may have been constructive and beneficial, in tune with the developing personality, whereas other influences may have been negative and destructive in essence, restricting, limiting and inhibiting a natural opening of that unfolding personality. In later attempts to evaluate childhood influences, the enquiring adult may explore the implications of the astrological Moon. Thus it may be discerned how and in what ways their nature has been shaped by external influences.

The power of social tradition is considerable, and most societies have their own class structure, whether it is openly expressed or not. Whilst in England, the class structure is less defined now and more diffused, it is still present and the attitudes that will be inculcated within children born to a prosperous 'upper-class' family will still be quite different to those born to a family with traditional working-class roots. The spread of a middle class does at least ensure that more children stand to benefit from social mobility and advantages. People born into ethnic minorities tend to receive mixed imprints, from the ethnic family root tradition and from the external society, which can increase the possibility of identity confusion between remaining true to the ethnic culture and adapting to the wider society in which the personal life will be lived.

In addition to parental and social influences, the Moon's natal house position may indicate inherited personality tendencies, gifts and natural talents. For those who have a belief in reincarnation and the perpetuation of the separate individual personality, there may be discernible patterns that could be attributed to past lives and which arise as instinctual expressions or goals. What does seem more definite, however, is that emotional habit patterns reflected by the Moon are aspects of life which have been especially conditioned in childhood, and which can only be changed through consistent effort to expand one's awareness. Natural talents emerging from this house position may often appear to operate to great effect, supported by a tendency towards repetitive practice, which hones them to perfection, and by opportunities occurring to enable those talents to be used.

For instance, Moon in the 2nd house may indicate a person focused on materialism and possessions, security and acquisitions, with a belief that emotional peace and stability can be gained through the accumulation of wealth, equipped by early conditioning to pursue this path successfully in later adult life. Moon in the 6th house, could indicate a workaholic, or someone dedicated to serving others, perhaps a committed medical expert whose preoccupation with health becomes a constructive channel to work through, and reflects adult or religious conditioning to live an altruistic life of service to humanity.

Deep personal needs for nourishment and nourishing others can be signified by the Moon position. The individual will need to feel right and that they belong in that house, otherwise there will be inner stress; the Moon's needs are vitally important and should not be denied, or else damage to the personal sensitivity and distortion of those inner Moon messages will occur. The individual needs to acknowledge and express those feelings and emotions, so that self-healing and integration occur, instead of attempts at denial which serve only to fragment the psyche. The Moon demands a firm foundation from which to operate, and will generate feelings of unease until that is achieved.

The inner Moon is a point from which the individual opens to the reality of others, as well as a connection between the personal and collective unconscious mind, although this contact often exists mainly as a sensitive feeling response to people. Issues of personal security are often associated with the natal house and its sphere of expression, and it may be used as an area of private retreat and withdrawal from the pressures of life. It may also be an area where tendencies of conformity are displayed so that the person adapts to his social grouping and prefers to blend into the crowd rather than stand apart. In that sphere, some may attempt to repeat parental roles, not just within their own family, but with others too, especially by displaying a mothering function of support, care and nourishment.

As the Moon has a nature of cyclic phases, the natal Moon position may also exhibit this tendency of fluctuation and change, and the individual response to its presence in the whole chart may vary and move through repetitive patterns similar to the lunation cycle. The Moon will not act statically or absolutely predictably; moods will emerge and disappear, feelings and emotions related to that particular dimension of life may flow erratically, and the individual perception may change subtly from time to time, especially if existing active childhood patterns are stimulated and the individual attempts to reassert his stability through childlike defensive mechanisms. There may be feelings of impending threat to that sphere of life, especially if there are challenging aspects to the Moon from Uranus, Neptune and Pluto, which tend to dissolve false illusions of security and stability in favour of new experience and the potential for inner development.

MOON IN THE 1ST HOUSE

In this position, your perception of self and of other people and the environment will be strongly influenced by your feeling responses, emotional reactions and instincts. Life will be experienced and interpreted in emotional terms, and your actions and decisions will be very much influenced by emotional biases and instinctive feelings.

With such a subjective response to life, you may lack the ability to understand those with a different focus to their nature. This may lead to mutual misunderstandings and difficult relationships with those who relate to life through other perspectives, such as those who evaluate their experiences more intellectually.

You will have a sensitive and receptive lunar-type personality, with a tendency to vacillate between distinct temperamental phases. Internal 'waxing and waning' will lead to a moodiness and changeability that both you and others find disconcerting, especially where issues of emotional relationship or commitments to aims are involved. Finding a clear direction in life may prove difficult, as you will be preoccupied with satisfying your emotional needs, and so may feel obliged to follow the paths of those on whom you rely for emotional nurturing.

Your attitudes and values are highly influenced by others: you tend to reflect back what they want to see. This may have developed during childhood. You probably felt a deep need for the approval of your parents, especially your mother, therefore acting in such a way as to live out what others projected onto you. In so doing, you may have built a life-style that reflects the wishes of others rather than fulfilling your personal needs. Recognising your own needs, desires and ambitions might not be easy, yet it may be essential in order to break ties of negative dependency, or within relationships where you have to deny your own deeper feelings in order to satisfy someone else.

It is these same lunar qualities, however, help to form a sense of emotional connectedness with people. This sensitivity can be close to a psychic or mediumistic receptivity at times, with 'messages' being received from people or the environment. You may feel a special emotional empathy with some, and will have considerable sympathy for those experiencing emotional pain, but may have to guard against too deep an empathic, emotional involvement with others. People with problems may find you very supportive, although a dispassionate, objective counselling is not your style, due to that inability to distance yourself from the feeling level, which can distort your perception of others' needs.

MOON IN THE 2ND HOUSE

Material and financial security, together with a stable life-style, will be essential to you. The foundation for this will be in the establishment of a loving family home, and achieving this will be a major desire and preoccupation for you. The Moon is exalted in Taurus, associated with this house, and it is therefore no surprise that you prefer a settled existence in which steps are taken to ensure that unsettling influences are kept to a minimum. Money is important in this respect to protect against financial concerns and pressures, although it is unlikely to be absolutely secure due to the Moon's fluctuating nature. If the Moon is placed in a fixed sign, then your financial situation may be more stable than if it is placed in a mutable sign.

You see your home life as a castle guarding you against the storms of life. Sitting there, surrounded by family, material possessions and comfort, you feel a sense of solidity, emotional security and well-being. If anything threatens this, you feel extremely vulnerable as your stable identity has been displaced. Much of your feeling life has been projected onto your family and possessions, and they become the centre of your life. Losing a favoured possession becomes emotionally damaging, reminding you that life cannot be controlled and that instability lurks around every corner, pointing out the impossibility of erecting inviolable barriers. If allowed to become too powerful, this need for emotional security can become claustrophobic and suffocating to loved ones, and leaves you too vulnerable to the actions and choices of others.

These needs may have developed during a childhood in which you felt protected and nurtured by your parents, so that you wish to recreate that feeling in adult life. You may have received social or parental attitudes related to the need for security and stability in life, beliefs in the value of maintaining the status quo, or in the pursuit of financial prosperity as an essential adult objective. Certainly such attitudes and values have influenced your adult behaviour.

If you can develop some flexibility within these security needs, and try to rely less on other people or possessions to fulfil them, then a more sensible balance can be achieved, one that is less prone to being shattered by unexpected experiences. That sense of emotional well-being should be sought within your own nature, through integration of your feelings and dependency needs, and through self-nurturing, not in the external world.

There may be an attraction towards mankind's history and heritage, or family traditions, which could be used either for personal interest or for business purposes. You may have an instinctive talent for understanding the market-place, using your affinity with material possessions and comfort to sense what consumer products people need or might be persuaded to desire, and this could be effectively exploited in business for your own future prosperity.

MOON IN THE 3RD HOUSE

In this position, the Moon will influence communication and thought-patterns by emotional colouring, so that underlying attitudes and beliefs are emotionally biased. This is revealed when attempts at rational decision-making flounder because the decision has already been made by the dominating feeling response, or in intellectual disagreements when rational thought dissolves into a passionate and emotional defence of a particular point of view.

One area of difficulty may lie in establishing consistent patterns of thought or even concentration, as the Moon's fluctuating nature may lead to changeability and lack of persistence and application Routine and repetition is found to be boring, and there may be a need for regular changes in mental stimulation to satisfy the needs of a real curiosity for knowledge. Information is felt to contribute to your security, as the more you know about the world and about people, the safer you feel. Absorbing knowledge will be a task that attracts you throughout life, and, associated with a retentive memory and imaginative abilities, may provide a rich source of opportunity. This is especially true if you continue to unfold your talents for written and verbal communication. As your mind has a tendency to fantasise and day-dream, this could be focused for creative expression.

Your environment and relationships will perform a very in-fluential role in your life, due to the absorbent and reflective lunar nature of your personality. Whilst you may be capable of adapting to various types of environment and relationship, it is through a process of reflection and remoulding your nature to accommodate changes. This can be through receiving the world-views of those closest to you, adopting them as your own and then reflecting them back out again. The demarcation lines between yourself and intimates dissolve, and your thoughts and attitudes become indistinguishable from those of others who are the major influences on you at that time. You may imaginatively project yourself into others, so that you instinctively sense whatever they are feeling or thinking. This derives from an emotional need to feel connected in life, both through discovering knowledge and empathic relationship.

Your experience of life is conditioned by the state of your feelings, emotions and instincts at any given time; these deep-seated emotional complexes are the source of decision-making, even though you may try to disguise this logically. If your life is not satisfying and fulfilling, or decisions, aims and relationships are failing, then you may be advised to explore deeper into yourself, in order to gain clarity regarding the types of emotional bias which are secretly running your life. Establishing the underlying roots of your attitudes may help you make wiser future decisions; transforming negative complexes is likely to release considerable blocked energy when healing has occurred. Holding on to negativity can only bring unhappiness; moving towards a positive outlook will enhance life. Learn how to observe and listen to yourself in communication and relationship; signs of your inner needs will be there for you to realise. Recognising them is the essential first step towards being able to fulfil them.

MOON IN THE 4TH HOUSE

The Moon is dignified in the 4th house and there are connections to Cancer which is ruled by the Moon. Of special emotional significance for you will be home and family life, and the anchoring of your personality roots within the domestic environment so that you feel stable and secure. There is a similarity with the 2nd house, although here it is the family experience dominating rather than the material environment.

To feel emotional security, well-being and peace with yourself, you require a satisfying family life, and you are prepared to devote considerable effort to building one; it is probably the most meaningful sphere in your life. Having a vitalised, positive and loving home is your dream, and if this is achieved, then your world-view will be correspondingly positive and constructive; however, if you are having difficulties in your family life, then your whole outlook suffers. Creating a safe family and home structure to act as a sanctuary from the insecurities of life is a vital task for you; you love to retreat back into the protective embrace of the family.

Your earlier childhood experiences are likely to have been very formative influences on your personality, and your relationship with your parents has contributed to your adult needs for nurturing and security. Aspects made to the natal Moon are significant, as they will indicate the likelihood of harmony in the childhood home; challenging aspects may suggest environmental disruptions, or a lack of harmony with a parent, particularly your mother. It may be that you preferred your father, or that his influence has proven to be more influential in your later development. In adult life, this may affect the type of intimate relationships that you prefer, in that a woman may look for a strong father-figure type, or a man may look for a partner capable of performing a mothering role.

You may feel uneasy about the foundations of your personality, spending time looking backwards instead of forwards, reliving the past as an experience of known security. Ties to parents may still be important in your adult life, in a physical sense and by the influencing of inner attitudes and needs. You are not always comfortable about your feelings, and those which fail to fit into your ideal life-style may be denied and repressed. Sensitivity to the quality of your environment and to people around you will influence your moods, so awareness may be needed to register your reactions to certain people or places.

If you are unable to create or experience your ideal home and family, then you may feel lost in life, with your identity feeling unanchored through a lack of foundations. A need to belong is urgently felt, and if unfulfilled can lead to great insecurity. During such periods, those conditioning patterns derived from your childhood may become extremely active in determining your choices. It can be a potentially positive step to realise the nature of them, so that when the situation has stabilised in the future such needs can be taken into account, enabling appropriate nurturing to occur.

MOON IN THE 5TH HOUSE

In this house, the lunar expression and requirements will manifest through the spheres of creativity, love affairs, children and pleasure. Romances may play a pivotal role in your life direction, and you are likely to experience emotional fluctuation related to love affairs, possibly relating to your own emotional instabilities and changeable nature. This is especially likely when your Moon has challenging aspects, as these can diminish clarity regarding your feelings and deeper needs. There may be an element of parental interference in your romances, perhaps not in an objective sense, but through inner attitudes, values and beliefs that you have absorbed during childhood development, or through living in the psychic atmosphere of their own intimate relationship.

Those sometimes unrecognised inner needs will influence the nature of your adult relationships, possibly arising as imaginative desires, or in the idealising of a partner. Emotional dependency will probably be projected onto any lover, and becoming reliant in such a way may leave you vulnerable to later disappointment and suffering if the relationship fails, or your partner proves to be less reliable and trustworthy than you believed.

The role of children is highlighted, and you will greatly enjoy their company, and it is probable that your creativity in this area will be potentially fecund; having a large family is likely, or at least a family structure that becomes highly demanding of time and attention. In your own parenting, you may repeat parental patterns absorbed during your childhood.

Artistic creative talents are probably present, although their realisation may require a determined focus; if undeveloped, they may remain latent, which would be regrettable, especially as expressing them would contribute to your sense of well-being. It could also be through this route that you become known to the public.

You have a well-developed self-confidence, often seeing yourself as possessing a 'lucky streak', and this can lead you towards impulsive speculative adventures in business, the stock market or gambling. Such activities can generate excitement, especially if progress and good fortune are made early on, although their roller-coaster of a ride may tax emotional stability and financial security.

MOON IN THE 6TH HOUSE

In this position, the Moon will be active in influencing the spheres of health and employment, and you are likely to find that unfulfilled feelings and emotional needs have a detrimental effect. Diminishing physical vitality and psychosomatic bodily symptoms may occur through unresolved emotional tensions and stresses, and the quality of your health will fluctuate depending on the quality of your emotional life. When your outlook is positive, your health will be good; when you have a negative perception, then a loss of vitality will occur. If you persist in maintaining a dissatisfied outlook, then hypochondria and physical symptoms will increase. Obsessions with health, diet and appearance may develop if unchecked, and if this occurs then you are moving away from a natural body balance and failing to listen to inner messages telling you how to keep your energy flowing freely between the levels of your being.

It is on the emotional level that the short-circuiting is actually occurring, and you may need to take remedial action to transform the tendency of moods and anxieties that are building up. Challenging aspects to the natal Moon may indicate the type of stress liable to be problematic. If depressions become regular, then you may need to spend time in self-therapy and personal exploration, trying to become objective about the roots of such feelings, and discovering ways in which you can begin to release and resolve some of the pent-up stresses. Altering diet and becoming more conscious of the body–emotion–mind inter-relationship is important to create well-being.

Work will be affected by your emotional states, and will often prove to be an unsatisfactory sphere of your life, unless you are fortunate in entering a type of employment that can fulfil your need for real emotional involvement. Pursuing a career alone will not fulfil unless it satisfies that emotional need too. A Moon placed in a mutable sign may indicate employment changes, and a fixed Moon may indicate a stuck position which could be equally unsatisfactory, although you do have a preference for continuity and repetitive life-style/work patterns in daily life. For you, a sense of security is found in the familiar and the predictable. Confrontation with strangers and new experiences stimulates feelings of unease and fear, as you cannot rely on repetitive responses to deal with the situations.

Service or vocational activities may prove to fulfil certain inner needs related to nurturing others. If this route became your main employment then you could find it more fulfilling and personally beneficial; any tendency to obsession with your own emotions and health would be diverted into caring for others, and you are likely to possess good practical abilities and an affinity with healing. You enjoy feeling wanted by others and being of some use, receiving stimulation from the sense of interpersonal connectedness that comes from working directly with others. Looking towards such a direction may be the road to greater meaning, purpose and integration in your life.

MOON IN THE 7TH HOUSE

It is within the sphere of relationships and partnerships that the Moon is active, and this implies that underlying needs and feelings will be influential in determining the nature and quality of such relationships.

Security and well-being are sought in the nurturing given by a partner, and a belief that security lies in togetherness and companionship encourages you to search for a fulfilling intimate contact. There is the danger that this need will override other valid considerations in the choice of a partner, such as real compatibility. Or else the relationship may become unbalanced through one partner being dependant on, or dominated by, the other. Wanting to 'belong' to someone is not a suitable base for an evolving relationship. Nobody is a possession, and wanting to be one may make you vulnerable to abuse and exploitation.

You need to look clearly at your deeper needs; just what do you want in a partner? Do you even recognise what your underlying needs actually are? What nurturing do you need to receive from another? What can you offer to a partner, and is that what they need? Are you looking for a surrogate mother or father, capable of protecting your hidden child nature, and making all the important choices for you? Do you adjust your own will, emotions, feelings, desires in order to accommodate those of a partner? Is your identity dependent on that partner, and could it stand alone? Is your focus on satisfying your partner, even at the expense of your own needs?

You will be very emotionally sensitive to others, and if unprotected this could be detrimental to your own emotional stability. As you are liable to emotional fluctuation anyway, through moodiness, inconsistency of feelings and restless impulses, additional external influences can only exacerbate this tendency. Yet you will continue to look for emotional sustenance through relationships, as you believe that the search is necessary to discover one which becomes emotionally nurturing. Resolving the dependency need and learning how to honour your own needs as being equally important in a balanced relationship may prove to be keys for future success.

MOON IN THE 8TH HOUSE

This indicates that the Moon will be connected to extremely powerful energies, within the individual and the collective, related to issues of sexuality, death and magical regeneration, subjects which evoke strong responses from people and which carry certain connotations of social taboo and unease.

Your emotions and feelings are likely to be amplified by your unconscious mind, and so can erupt with great intensity and passion if provoked. You may register the presence of inner pressures which need to be released, and these may take the form of sexual and sensual desires which appear to provide the means through which you can gain emotional satisfaction. The experience of sex will be of considerable importance to you, and many of your needs will revolve around intimate relationships. There may be a tendency to experience phases of compulsive or obsessive behaviour, especially if your emotions become attached to a lover and begin to get a little out of control.

The subtler and more intangible dimensions of life will be attractive to you, and you may choose to explore the mystical, spiritual and magical teachings of humanity. Spiritualism and channelling may appeal, and you may take steps to experience the reality of these dimensions for yourself, and experiences of ESP may be likely in some form as you proceed to unfold that latent psyschic ability.

You may be sensitive to registering those hidden underlying feelings and motivations in people, or environmental atmospheres. Even during your childhood this ability may have enabled you to sense the inner lives of your parents, revealing to you that all was not always as it seemed. Such sensitivity is not always an advantage, and this may have helped form some of your underlying feelings and may need further resolution and integration. It is possible that childhood experiences of death or sex may have been an influence on you too, opening a door into adult life which you may not have been fully prepared to confront at that age.

Adult relationships may provide some challenges, especially if the Moon has stressful aspects, which can indicate anxieties if relationships fail. Yet you are able to co-operate and adapt well within relationships, often being very supportive in helping a partner to develop and unfold their own potential. Your ability to modify your own behaviour patterns for the sake of harmony with a partner can have mixed results, depending on whether or not you are repressing your own feelings, needs and desires. Through such partnerships, your financial situation is highlighted, and this could come through inheritances or joint business ventures, or could imply financial struggles if the relationship collapses.

This 8th house is one of transformation and rebirth, and this is likely to occur on the emotional level; crises may stimulate an unavoidable transformation, but these are to be viewed as ultimately beneficial. Within any negative phases, look for the positive potential that can be reached through them. Hidden deep within the darkness is the ever-shining light waiting for your arrival. It is a purification and cleansing of your deeper emotions, feelings and instincts that is required, and when this is achieved, a healing harmony will arise.

MOON IN THE 9TH HOUSE

This implies a need for a mental paradigm, a world-view or personal philosophy through which the world can be perceived, experienced, interpreted and understood. This is an internal structure which helps to provide a sense of security and stability. You may have been conditioned by belief structures during your childhood, perhaps from religious, political, social or parental sources. You will have deep emotional connections to this conditioning, and any attacks made on it by others will tend to be met by an immediate emotional defence, as your convictions are rooted in your feelings rather than being derived from any stringent intellectual analysis. In a religious sense, faith takes the place of reason. This emotional identification with your beliefs prohibits real discussion, and may restrict your ability to progress into a deeper understanding due to those mental barriers being present. A narrow-minded and dogmatic attitude may emerge at times, especially when there are challenging aspects to the Moon.

However, you do recognise the importance of clear values for the individual and family life, and as this is the house of the higher mind, you may be able to move beyond earlier limitations into a higher expression of these tendencies. This demands imagination, inspiration and intuition. With these, you may be able to stretch beyond the parameters of traditional beliefs into your own experiences, perhaps through meditative contemplation and a personal spiritual quest for greater meaning and purpose in life. As your approach is feeling-based, you may discover that you can make progress by working with symbols and images which evoke a feeling response and stimulate your imagination. This may be more effective than a more rational approach. You may in this way feel inner presences and subtler energy vibrations, and you may discover a latent talent for prophecy.

If you evolve your own personal paradigm, then your life will change accordingly. Travel may become prominent, and the concept of journeys emphasised, although whether in the outer or inner worlds remains to be seen. Much depends on how you develop your spiritual path. You must, however, guard against escapist tendencies. The spiritual path is never an escape route, it includes and embraces every aspect of human existence and is never exclusive in nature. It may be that your eventual insights and understanding can be used to benefit others, and you may act as a way-shower pointing out roads to follow, or lighting the way like the Hermit in the Tarot. But all this may depend on moving beyond the level of conditioning absorbed during your childhood, and on transcending those inner and outer barriers that limit your progress.

MOON IN THE 10TH HOUSE

This position of the Moon indicates that needs for public recognition, status and success are emphasised, and that high expectations are influential motivating forces operating within you and determining many of your eventual choices and decisions.

The root of this may lie in your childhood experiences; it is likely that your parents held high ambitions for your future development, realistically or not. This may be related to your social class and to parental aspirations. You may have received projections of parental wish-fulfilment, especially from your mother, who may have wanted you to achieve or experience something that she was unable to reach. It may be that the life you have been living is a reflection of your parents' desires rather than your own, and one way of establishing this is by checking to see if your life-style feels satisfying. If it does not, then take a look at your basic attitudes and motivations, and try to determine whether they are actually yours or have been unconsciously absorbed from others.

You still look for approval from others, as if you are a child wanting to be reassured by your parents; in so doing, you conform to others' expectations of you, and may deny your own feelings and instincts, and surrender your freedom. If you achieve social approval, then you feel more secure and have a sense of belonging; you need to feel wanted and safe, and may gravitate towards careers which have a high social profile or status. Becoming an authority in some sphere attracts you, and having others relying on you has great appeal, as this gives you an opportunity for caring and nurturing in a professional context.

You are extremely concerned about what others think of you, and by trying to ensure their good opinion you mould your persona to fit a consensus social image appropriate to your role. If taken to extremes, this can create severe repression of characteristics that fail to match that image, leading to personality splits, and this should definitely be avoided. You need greater self-awareness, so that you recognise your own deeper needs, and you need to take time to fulfil these; the results will be extremely beneficial. Self-denial is just a route towards personal fragmentation, and is a foolish course which sows the seeds of your own downfall. You need to accept and love yourself and be less dependent on the transient opinions of others; living through your own light is much more revealing than living through reflected light.

MOON IN THE 11TH HOUSE

Your sense of well-being depends very much on your social relationships, family, friends and involvements with group and organisational activities. These offer that vital sense of belonging, and provide you with stability and security. Such group associations will both reflect and influence your attitudes, values, beliefs and opinions, and will have a powerful impact on your social experience, as you will tend to modify your own perception in order to conform to the prevailing group ethos.

You can be quite impressionable and easily swayed by the opinions of others, especially when hoping to become part of a group or to maintain friendships. Through becoming reliant on the good opinion of others, you may fail to express your own thoughts and feelings for fear of being rejected by the group. You need to develop greater courage in your own convictions and not be so easily influenced by what other people think is right for you. You must ensure that you become clearer as to your own path, and become less emotionally reliant on others.

You can become emotionally possessive about friends and acquaintances, and may take it as a personal slight if one disappears from your life, for whatever reason. If your Moon is in a fixed sign, the tendency will be to maintain longlasting friendships, perhaps centred around a small select grouping of personal friends; if it is in a mutable sign, your own changeability may be reflected in having a variety of shorter-lived contacts and acquaintances, with less ongoing deeper friendships. The role of women in social relationships is likely to prove highly influential, whether it is through personal relationships or friendships, or through business contacts.

Clarity concerning your long-term aims and ambitions may be lacking, and due to those changeable moods you may find that perseverance and determination are not two of your prime qualities. You need encouragement from others in order to apply yourself consistently, and this can be one of the inner motivators that also attracts you towards group activities. By group commitment, you place yourself in a situation where demands may be made of you, and this can help you to achieve more than you would do on your own. It is wiser to choose groups you can relate to positively on a deep emotional level, as you have a need for this sort of relationship in itself, added to which it will help you to express your own potential.

If you displace your emotions into adherence to a group, you may upset your own internal balance, and occasional spells of solitude may be needed in order for you to reconnect to your emotions. Otherwise, you may begin to lose touch with your deeper emotions, and to lose that ability for self-nurturing which is so vital for everyone.

MOON IN THE 12TH HOUSE

The Moon in the 12th house may pose a variety of personal difficulties with oversensitive emotions and feelings. There are close connections made to the unconscious mind, and this will influence your moods and sense of well-being. It may be that there are unresolved experiences derived from your childhood and parental relationship that have made a powerful impact on you, especially those involving your mother. The approval of your parents may still play an important role in your adult life, either in that your life-style reflects their desires for you, so that you follow a path initially indicated by them, or in that you rebel against their attempted influence by pursuing an alternate route designed to display your independence. Look at your relationship with your parents and see how it has affected your life, and to what extent it now influences your choices and decisions. This may not be easy, as the roots of some of these patterns may lie deep within your unconscious mind; but if the shadows of your parents still loom large in your life, then much benefit could be gleaned from such an exploration. Your mother's role is especially pivotal in this situation.

You will often feel very vulnerable to life, sensitive to others and empathic to their inner suffering. You will often attempt to veil this heightened feeling nature from others, and may keep much of it from your own attention too, by control and emotional denial. You may fear that allowing it full expression would make it too powerful to contain, and this can also lead to a fear of emotional intimacy and relationship. As a form of protection you lock yourself away, refusing to open and embrace the totality of life. You may feel uncomfortable dealing with feelings, fearing expressing them to others and revealing that vulnerability. You may erect barrier of shyness or create around you an atmosphere of distance and disinterest in social relating. Your own identity boundaries can be extremely diffused, lacking a stable and distinct inner core that you can feel secure within. Your tendency is to feel inwardly open to the presence of others, failing to establish your own personal identity, and often you will be reacting to the influence of others instead of to your own inner movements. Psychic and intuitive perceptions are likely, and you will be highly sensitive to the unspoken and intangible realms of life; the nature and quality of your environment is important, and will influence your feelings of well-being.

You may experience some difficulties in successfully coping with the demands of daily living; city life may be particularly challenging and stressful. There is a tendency for you to withdraw into the privacy and seclusion of your home as a personal sanctuary and retreat from the world, and also to relax into the vibrancy of your inner life, which often appears more attractive to you than tasting the fruits of the outer world. This can be used positively or negatively. It can become a world of evasion, fantasy, delusions, neuroses, if the emanations from the unconscious are not resolved through a cleansing self-healing, and which may eventually precipitate a descent into forms of mental imbalance. Or, used positively, it can become a source of great inner wealth. Dreams may become prolific and meaningful, new ways of living may be intuited, and you may become a channel for inner guides, becoming able to unlock the doors to an inner storehouse of wisdom through a contact with your spiritual self.

You may well experience some type of inner crisis, created by the clash of inner and outer energies, between inner messages and impulses and the necessity of coping with daily life. This could be triggered by any transiting planets (especially Saturn, Uranus, Neptune and Pluto) moving through the 12th house towards the Ascendant. The need is to ensure that there is a positive conclusion to such experiences, that they lead to greater integration rather than disintegration. There is a need for an inner healing which through releasing unresolved patterns and blockages of energy will cleanse you of the accretions of the past, and enable you to face the future with a renewed confidence and personal stability.

CHAPTER 6

The Moon in the Natal Signs

PROBABLY THE MOST IMPORTANT POINT about the Moon's sign is that it can indicate what the individual needs to experience and absorb in order to feel good about himself and develop a sense of security and fulfilment. The Moon sign also indicates how we express our nurturing instinct – how we make others feel good. The key actions are experiencing, absorption and expression. If these are consciously aligned in harmony with those deeper patterns of the unconscious layers of mind which are reflected by the individual Moon natal sign. The expression of the Moon through the specific sign should also take into account the natal house position, so that the area most affected can be noted and evaluated. For instance, Moon in Leo in the 1st house may demand a powerful public demonstration of the individual existence and identity, feeling a sense of belonging through public recognition. Therefore those with this placement are self-assertive in achieving such a position.

The sign can indicate the style of immediate emotional-feeling response to experiences, based on conditioned attitudes and belief structures to which the individual has become emotionally attached. Responses to others can be gleaned through this Moon sign or elemental position, and the nature of relationships, domestic life and exchanges with women or the mother can be sensed. Patterns of dominating attitudes can be discerned which colour emotional reactions to everyday life. For instance, Moon in Pisces may indicate a very sensitive type, tending to passivity and avoidance of conflict, preferring to withdraw into the security of a private inner dream world; feelings of defensiveness, emotional vulnerability, changeability and great needs for love and dependency may be prominent. Place this in the 1st house, and there may be problems with self-assertion and a reaction against being in the public eye, unless being loved by the public overcomes natural shyness. The quality and type of individual emotional response is indicated by the sign of the natal Moon. Moon in Aquarius, for example may indicate a more mental type of emotional need, more individual and eccentric in type, a little colder, more detached and independent.

In more esoteric evaluations the tendency is to perceive the Moon as representing the accumulation of past-life personalities and repetitive patterns that act as a weight restricting the emergence of soul consciousness, as an inhibitory physical form that limits experience and which counterbalances any impulse for spiritual growth, favouring past patterns and inertia. In this sense, the sign of the Moon represents what should be transcended through alignment with the new higher purpose, and indicates the battlefield of the current life where conflicts between the magnetic pull of the soul clash with the inertia of the personality level and which are reflected more fully in the positions of the nodal Moon axis.

When the Moon is placed in a cardinal sign (Aries, Cancer, Libra or Capricorn) the individual's habitual approach to situations is through direct action, making things happen in the physical world; the focus is on the present, and on fulfilling needs and desires now rather than having to wait. This impatience can be displayed in a lack of consideration or awareness regarding the feelings of others. The instinctive reaction to life is that of action, and the individual will not spend too much time in decision-making; even the moody Cancerian is aware enough of their needs and desires, and their emotional depth and complexity rarely stands in their way once their desires are activated.

When the Moon is placed in a fixed sign (Taurus, Leo, Scorpio or Aquarius) the habitual approach is through emotional reactions and responses. The habit pattern revolves around a desire to repeat experiences that have stimulated the emotions – which were satisfying, exciting, fulfilling, intense or pleasurable. This impulse to develop a pleasing life-pattern tends to project from the present into ensuring a similar satisfying experience in the future. The need for direction and purpose will be felt, and aims will be pursued single-mindedly. Attitudes, beliefs and values will reflect underlying habitual emotional responses, and can display inflexibility and resistance to change or opposition. Through persistence, the individual will attempt to persuade others to agree with their viewpoint. Attitudes tend to polarise into either/or situations, black or white, leaving little scope to encompass alternative opinions. Once the world-view is developed, it tends to remain fixed.

When the Moon is placed in a mutable sign (Gemini, Virgo, Sagittarius or Pisces) mental reactions and responses are emphasised. Yet this pattern has a mutability inherent in it; experiences are re-evaluated and re-integrated in terms of a 'life philosophy', often derived from favourite and influential systems of belief or theories which intrigue and have a personal resonance. This mental filter conditions the individual world-view and is often concerned with attempts to make some sense out of the mystery of life; the conceptual and intellectual dimension of life is often preferable to the full reality. Theories may be attractive, as are mental games, although adherence to the reality of such theories may distort the actual living experience. Morals, ethics, scientific objectivism, religion, superstition and social traditional behaviour are all types of belief system that can govern the types of repetitive patterns displayed by mutable types. It is an adopted world-view that has been previously developed in the past that usually conditions the individual's present experience and habitual life-style.

MOON IN ARIES (CARDINAL SIGN)

The Moon does not find it easy to be placed in the active sign of Aries, and you will discover that a tranquil life-style is not to your taste nor can you settle into mundane complacency and routine behaviour patterns. You will prefer to launch yourself into the experience of life, following spontaneous impulses to action which you hope will lead to exciting experiences and which give you the feeling of life coursing through your body. You will be ambitious, seeking out challenges and ways in which you can assert your own unique nature and individuality before other people; your aim is to become number one, standing out from the crowd.

There is an independent spirit within you, and whilst you may disguise deep feelings of personal insecurity, you are determined to follow your own chosen path of action, irrespective of whether you are proven to be correct or incorrect in your decision-making.

You tend to react against well-intentioned advice from others, trusting in your own light, and even tending to act in a contrary manner as a form of self-assertion at times. Eventually, close friends and family will realise that this is your way, and will just let you get on with doing what you intend to do anyway!

There are certain contradictory tendencies within you, and most of these relate to a probable denial of the Moon nature and a favouring of the Aries qualities. One example of this is the changeability of your moods, emotions and feelings, and a lack of consistency on that level, which can often erupt in emotional volatility and impulsive, ill-considered actions. As inner pressures accumulate, you tend to jump into action as a way out of a 'decision log-jam', in the hope that action will prove a resolving factor. It is unusual for you to display adequate forethought and planning, and you are often surprised at the consequences of your actions. This can be due to self-centred, Arien naivety or innocence, although it still doesn't enable you to evade any negative repercussions and wrong moves in the game plan of life.

You can be overly sensitive to the reactions of others, yet this does not dissuade you from your headlong course; it only irritates and slows your forward rushing movement for a few moments of self-doubt, which you then proceed to ignore because entertaining such thoughts may open up an area of your nature (the lunar realm) that you prefer to forget. If really pushed, you try to dominate through self-assertion and fixed attitudes, and there may be occasional outbursts of temper if someone is effectively presenting a viable argument against your own decision.

To balance out this planetary relationship and your own inner unmet needs, adjustments may be required. Feelings and emotions have to be acknowledged and accepted; evasion only forces them into the unconscious mind to agitate and fester. As an integral part of your need for self-assertion, you need to learn that these feelings are a vital facet of your nature requiring release and nourishment too, and that a probable attempt at emotional self-sufficiency will only dry the well-spring of emotional vitality and feeling responses to life. Due to this uneasiness with your deeper lunar needs, you may display some resistance to intimacy in relationships; not physical or mental intimacy, but the emotional communion and empathy that can occur through mutual love.

Yet it is the movement in this direction that will open the doors to greater fulfilment and satisfaction, once you become less insistent and defensive about your Arien need for independence and freedom. Self-expression is very important, but you need to respect your feelings and emotional needs and take steps to satisfy them, instead of choosing only to respond to impulses to action and novelty. A deeper integration into your individual foundations and physical reality is needed; once the connection is established to the Moon roots and a flow of fulfilling experiences is developed through relationships and self-nurturing, then the need for compulsive activity will diminish and give way to a state of balance.

MOON IN TAURUS (FIXED SIGN)

The Moon is in exaltation in the sign of Taurus, and this will be displayed in a heightening of the Taurus and Moon patterns of behaviour within you. The concept of *roots* will be extremely important to you, and you will need to feel secure, and have a predictable, routine life-style in order to feel a sense of well-being. Change is viewed with open unease, and reactions against it being forced on you will be strong. As you tend to rely on established values and standards of behaviour, you will tend to embody the dominating customs of your society and peer group. Those who seek to bring radical change to this static social pattern are seen as threats, and because your own sense of identity is so attuned to this social collective consciousness, your attitudes are traditionally conservative and uphold the status quo. Your peace of mind comes through routine; coherency and consistency are important qualities. You hate to have your habits disturbed, and are very resistant to having to make changes at all; indeed, you find it extremely challenging to alter your inner patterns.

You tend to hold materialistic and pragmatic views, relying on the tangible aspects of life and evaluating things through that perspective; there may be a tendency to dismiss certain artistic or intellectual styles of expression as being too abstract, and you feel uncomfortable with the more subtle, intuitive types of feeling, as they hint rather than giving you clear messages. Financial security is seen as essential to your emotional peace, and you should have good financial skills to support your desires for a physically comfortable living environment. Once attained, that enjoyment of sensuality and luxury may make you a little apathetic and lazy, and you may need to be prodded into new activities and projects by others, although once you have been galvanised into action, your commitment and persistence should ensure success.

Intimate relationships are important for your emotional well-being, and these have to be well founded, secure and reliable for you to feel content. Your energies are applied towards creating permanence in life; a comfortable home, economic security, stable employment, marriage, family and barriers to fend away any threats to this stability.

Within your inner life, the same tendency exists; there may be a denial and repression of any impulses or feelings that cannot be easily categorised and fitted into the life-pattern. It is also likely that you will try to ensure that your emotions remain under control; volatility is seen as highly threatening, and you will not want anyone around you who displays regular emotional changes, moods and unpredictability – it reminds you that you cannot control everything.

Underlying these tendencies is the probability that you feel personally insecure, having doubts about your self-worth and abilities, with fears of letting go and inability to cope without known familiar patterns. Such external supports include the family circle, dependency, food addictions, money and status. Whilst you freely give support and physical affection to your family, you may also treat them in a possessive manner, and their important role in building your security buffers should not be underemphasised.

You may need to become more flexible in both an inner and an outer sense. Your security is really very fragile and vulnerable, and is liable to be threatened by the vicissitudes of life. More self-sufficiency and faith in yourself would help. You need to become confident in the strength of your own individuality and in your ability to exploit talents and personal resources. Habit patterns should not be perceived as inviolable, and greater flexibility should ideally be built into them, as a risk-free life is virtually impossible, and at any rate would preclude the possibility of growth. Possessive tendencies may need to be curbed, as do patterns of personal rigidity, which only inhibit experience and expression. Slowly, those barriers need to be dismantled, feelings accepted and expressed, and a willingness to acknowledge the reality of other non-physical dimensions of life developed. Focusing on security needs will begin to repress your feeling responses and negatively condition your world-view with fears and anxieties. Learning how to satisfy your deeper needs and how to relax into enjoyment will release your higher personal qualities and characteristics, unfolding your potential.

MOON IN GEMINI (MUTABLE SIGN)

You will feel a need for mental stimulation, verbal communication and a variety of types of relationship. The satisfaction of an alert curiosity and a desire to know will be a high priority, and your intellectual life will be a continuing sequence of fascinations, areas of human knowledge that have attracted your interest for a period of time. Whilst over time you may become superficially acquainted with a great many subjects, you may have no real expertise or wisdom in any particular subject. But the Gemini influence is like the activities of a magpie, accumulation is the game played, and this may partly satisfy the Moon's need for acquisitiveness. Displaying that fund of information will be enjoyable for you, and you will hope that others will find it impressive and respect you more.

Mental stimulation enlivens your life, although with the Gemini restlessness and changeability of the Moon, your interest in most subjects will wax and then wane, only to be reawakened by the next exciting set of ideas. Indeed, words, ideas, conceptual structures of symbolism, may be especially attractive, and in these you can almost become lost; the danger may lie in the trap of misrepresentation, where you focus on the pointing finger instead of what it is pointing towards. . .

It is likely that you will favour the Gemini dimension of this astrological relationship, and there are benefits to be gained from following this tendency. Mental development through training and constant use can help you to respond to a highly stimulating environment, and any knowledge acquired can always have a potentially practical application; rational analysis can be used for decision-making, and a higher quality of communication may be achieved when the intellect is brought fully into play.

Yet there are also the more negative aspects of Gemini, and the probability that in emphasising the characteristics of Gemini, the influence of the Moon is given less expression and acknowledgement. The negative attributes of an unbalanced Gemini Moon can include a lack of mental consistency due to a tendency to be swayed by every passing influence that comes along. Ideas and projects are suddenly dropped due to more exciting ones coming over the horizon. Sustaining your interest and completing things may be a weak spot, both intellectually and in relationships. You insist on a freedom to change, and tend to apply this by looking for variety and diversity, even to being fickle with lovers and friends. You may find it difficult to remain committed to any idea or person for long, and restlessness and a tendency to become easily bored do not help to create stability.

The influence and needs of the Moon are probably denied to some degree and yet will still filter through into your life irrespective of attempts to block them. Your emotions are change-able and represent an unintegrated realm of your nature, one that you prefer not to have to deal with too often. Their subtle influence often distorts your reasoning faculty – even without your conscious realisation – and helps to form your judgements, decisions and personal values, even if you do garb these in apparently rational disguises; begin to scratch the surface of some of your defensive arguments and you will observe that there is a deep emotional and feeling colouring to them, and that what you are really protecting is your Moon pattern.

With Moon in Gemini you may also attempt to rationalise your feelings away, reducing the level of direct feeling or covering the messages from that aspect of your being – avoidance tactics. Ignoring the deeper instinctual and feeling needs can lead to compulsive and negative Gemini-type behaviour; continual talking, continual absorption of information, a whirl of non-stop superficial social activity, and a scattering and dissipation of personal energies.

If this is occurring, then there may be deep inner patterns which are conveying messages of confusion regarding the validity of your feelings and instincts, and a lack of self-confidence in the demands and needs of your physical and emotional natures. Your mind has become overly dominating, and is out of harmony with the other levels of your whole self. To begin to redress this imbalance, you may need to cease such a wide diversity of activities and interests, and at least temporarily begin to re-centre yourself, and stop displacing your identity into external interests or social environments. Relationships need to be transformed so that you are free to experience and express whatever you really feel. You need to concentrate on quality of personal communication and deeper communion with a more select, intimate group of friends and family. Essentially, you may need to re-evoke the Moon in yourself, integrate your denied feelings and allow them expression. The intellectual activity is not to be used as a substitute for personal feelings. You need to acknowledge your repressed instinctual feelings and emotional needs, to fuse your personality together into a harmonious whole, rather than believe that you can find fulfilment by ignoring your inner promptings. These needs are an integral part of you too and should be accepted into consciousness.

MOON IN CANCER (CARDINAL SIGN)

The Moon rules Cancer, and this will emphasise the degree of emotional intensity and depth that you experience, and the likelihood is that your earlier childhood conditioning will act powerfully on your patterns of adult behaviour. There will be strong connections to your parents and your current domestic or family life. Your foundations lie in emotional depths, so you have a great need to feel secure and stable within anything that involves your emotions and feelings. Relationships need to be stable, trustworthy and relatively predictable, in actuality as well as in appearance, because you possess a degree of psychism which reacts on emotional and feeling levels, so if a partner is unhappy and discontented, even if this is not openly communicated, you will feel it through the subtler senses. Excessive absorption of others' moods and feelings, both positive and negative, will influence your own behaviour and state of well-being; as this will probably enter you through the area of the body including the stomach, solar plexus and heart, you may be advised to protect yourself psychically from all external and unwanted influences.

As most of your life is conditioned by your deep feeling responses and childhood behavioural patterns, you will benefit from greater understanding of them. Look especially towards the influence of your mother upon the formation of your values, attitudes and beliefs. Review any memories of emotional suffering over which you still brood, and look at those emotional wounds that you carry around with you; note how you often overreact to personal comments, how you tend to imagine 'what they think/feel' about you, and look at the fluctuations in the way you relate to people. Observe how you tend to evaluate others through the emotions and intuition; realise how your attitudes, beliefs and values are connected to emotional biases; see the emotional power making your major decisions for you, and how your reactions are all generated by emotions.

You may experience emotional instability, ranging from a denial of needs to emotional possessiveness, dependency and suffocation of intimate partners and family. Accepting the needs of the Moon in Cancer is vital, as they will exist throughout your life. Only an understanding of how they operate within you will limit the compulsive, unconscious nature of much of their activity. With greater clarity, you should be able to perceive the patterns activated within you, but choose how to respond with more consciousness, instead of following those dominating automatic reactions.

You need to love and be loved, to experience a deep level of contact between yourself and your partner or family, and this will strengthen your sense of security. Excessive dependency traits should not be indulged in though, because these will leave you too vulnerable to the inconsistent behaviour of others, and prone to emotional manipulation. The tendency to retreat into an inner shell should be modified, so that it does not prevent your range of social activities and unfoldment of personal potential to a restricted familiar environment; you need faith in yourself in order to move beyond challenging situations and so make new progress, instead of moving within repetitive habitual circles.

MOON IN LEO (FIXED SIGN)

There is a strong sense of individuality with this position, and often a self-contained emotional nature, which nevertheless is attracted towards the emotional gratification of basking in the spotlight of attention, approval and applause. Attention is an emotional fuel to you, and you may tend to display a childish petulance if denied this need, to exhibiting dramatised feelings and over-the-top emotional displays when your demands for suitable attention are ignored by family, friends or colleagues. Your ego and vanity are easily wounded, through high sensitivity to criticism, and you tend to enter moods and brood on any negative comments.

There are probably deep compulsive needs for success and public attention, which may have their roots in childhood, particularly in your relationship with your parents. You seek to assert a belief that your rightful place is at the centre of the universe, like the Sun surrounded by the planets. To some, you may appear to be too confident and assured or forceful, but this is an expression of an intrinsic inner strength, and you are often guided by this inner integrity, responsibility and sense of purposeful direction. The fact that Leo is a fixed sign implies the ability to concentrate the will, and this should be expressed through you once your direction is determined. Your will can be one-pointed, and only bends under considered need instead of being intrinsically flexible and compromising.

You need close, loving and intimate relationships, as you have a deep need to love and to be loved, and in a love relationship there is scope for expressing and receiving admiration and appreciation. Your emotional self-determination, linked with a personal magnetic charm, can make you attractive to others, especially those who are looking either for a stronger partner, or for others equally independent in nature. That stubbornness may cause friction and conflict when wills clash, particularly if you try to dominate a partner or family member, and it is at times like that when a degree of emotional immaturity is often demonstrated. Yet you genuinely want to better yourself, and once the moment has passed and tempers have cooled down, you can identify the emotional button that has been pressed, and resolve that 'next time, I won't rise to that again'. Time will tell.

If the Moon nature has been denied, then signs of compulsive activity may occur, especially self-adulation, hogging the centre stage, ego-inflation, and dominating behaviour towards anyone unable to resist; the 'superiority complex' is one which is often seen in social/employment hierarchies. This is when insecurity lurks beneath the surface, and self-esteem needs to be derived from status or from the attention of others. There is usually a susceptibility to flattery and a need for social approbation.

The potential is to develop a constructive and optimistic approach to life's experiences and the needs of the personality. You may need to create ways in which you satisfy your own needs, rather than being reliant on others, to appreciate and value your own talents and qualities and to accept the totality of your nature. Pay attention to satisfying your own emotional needs and feeling; succeeding in this will reduce your compensatory need to play centre stage, and make you less vulnerable to audience reaction.

MOON IN VIRGO (MUTABLE SIGN)

With Moon in Virgo, you will prefer to develop a life-style that is externally and internally ordered, disciplined and controlled, and you will tend to follow repetitive behaviour patterns which give a feeling of stability in life, even if only through predictability. Whilst you may choose to rationalise such behaviour, or attempt to justify it by referring to religious, philosophical or moral tenets, the underlying impulse behind this self-protection is a fear of chaos, of releasing uncontrollable emotional forces. You refuse to allow yourself full freedom of expression, restricting yourself physically, emotionally and mentally to what you regard as socially acceptable.

As an integral part of this self-structuring, you will be attracted towards intellectual theories and systems of thought which aim to impose meaning, order and coherency on the mysteries of life. Science may be such an approach, or the unfoldment of a logical, rational and objective perspective. The main danger from this is the forming of an excessively rigid mind-set that refuses to accept or allow any world-view other than your own.

It is likely that you will have a perfectionist streak, often associated with a preference for the detail, appearance and minutiae of things. In focusing on the parts, you may often fail to see the whole picture; analysis can be fascinating, but the revelation and meaning lies in the act of synthesis.

You can be too self-critical and unforgiving, chastising yourself for failing to meet your own exacting standards. In addition, applying these to others may cause friction, as not everyone will consider that your priorities and evaluations are valid for them. Your perfectionism may not always be appropriate, and some may find that your attention to detail is irritating and unnecessary. As you will be a conscientious and practical worker, you may be an exacting taskmaster, but your workaholic tendencies and devotion to duty may also stifle your relationships with colleagues at work. Trying to contain life energies within categorisation and efficient order can often strip them of all vitality; predictable and controlled, yes, but of no future value.

It is important to you to feel of use, and you will be one of life's unsung servers due to that quiet, reserved and retiring nature. With your work ethic, you may find it difficult to unwind, and you may become obsessively active in an attempt to feel useful and to avoid facing other aspects of your life. For the same reasons, you may become obsessive about health, diet and hygiene.

Your weak spot is the realm of feelings and emotions locked behind that tight, intellectualised mental grip, and you tend to use your mind as a defence against your feelings, often denying their validity and trying to ignore their inner movements. At worst, you could become almost a dry and sterile personality as a consequence of prolonged repression; and by losing contact with your feelings, instincts and emotions, those Virgoan characteristics would begin to present their negative qualities through your life, affecting all relationships and your own state of mind.

To avoid this, you need to learn how to accept the totality of your nature, not persist in emphasising the mental control and the denial of your physical and instinctual needs. Through self-acceptance, you will be able to expand your tolerance and understanding of others, becoming more flexible and able to experience your human nature to the full. Rigidity of thought and world-view can be dropped, and a new universe of potential will emerge, untainted by your attempts at limitation. Acknowledging your feelings, emotions and instincts and respecting their needs and messages will reap immense personal dividends. Rebalancing your nature will lead to wholeness, and dammed inner energies will freely flow again. Initial stages in this may be painful, and you may feel threatened by slowly dissolving those erected barriers and want to reassemble them again, but if you persist, then you can be reborn, capable of consciously using the beneficial qualities of Virgo in harmony with the self-nurturing needs of your Moon. Self-esteem will naturally grow through personal development, rather than being a fragile construct protected by a variety of inner defences against the encroachment of world and emotions. Learning to trust yourself and the world is the step to make for progress.

MOON IN LIBRA (CARDINAL SIGN)

With Moon in Libra, much of your feeling of self-worth will be tied in with social acceptance and relationships, and your self-perception will often depend on what you believe are others' opinions of you. If others are critical of you, or you are experiencing disharmonious relationships, then your health and vitality are affected, as well as your self-esteem and confidence. Your emotional well-being is dependent on feeling loved, liked, appreciated or admired by others, especially those closest to you, such as colleagues and intimate partners or family. You find it difficult to self-nurture and fulfil your own instinctual needs without having to rely on other people.

Social conditioning, cultural and group attitudes, beliefs and values have a profound influence on you, especially those which have high ideals, and it is often by these standards that you evaluate others; but in holding a judgemental perspective, it also puts you under the pressure of being judged by others too – thus putting your own self-esteem at risk.

There is likely to be an awareness of class and social status, and you may be motivated by desires to improve your social standing, perhaps through association with certain types of people, or by creating an elegant, sophisticated life-style and prosperous home environment. In several ways, you will try to form a life-style that excludes aspects of life that fail to match your standards, trying to protect your sensitivities against the harsher realities of existence. Reflecting the Libra need for a harmonious home environment with charm, elegance and beauty is important for you, and you will enjoy sharing this in congenial social gatherings.

Your need for approval may mean that you follow the group path rather than listening to your own inner promptings or your own personal needs, due to a fear of becoming ostracised or alienated from group acceptance. You need to belong, and this need is projected out onto social groupings, but perhaps the deeper need is that of owning and reflecting your whole nature. In trying to please others and make yourself indispensable you may be repressing areas of your own nature, especially the Moon qualities, resulting in emotional repression and a denial of your own feeling instincts.

In an attempt to minimise disharmony, Libra can tend to evade conflict, whether inner or outer, especially those painful areas of self and life, preferring to ignore or run away from them. This is often the case where the alternative is to face up to the realities of a relationship, where the need is for a direct confrontation designed to resolve developing differences, and for a deeper level of communication to clear the air. As relationship is so vital to the Libra nature, the fear which must be avoided is the fear of being alone; if this exists, then dependency is also present. Sometimes, you may be satisfied just with maintaining surface harmony and appearances, rather than ensuring that a deeper harmony exists in your relationships.

Whilst the Libran tendency is that of mind, intellect and objectivity, the Moon needs must not be ignored. It is essential for you to honour these too, to become self-confident and assured of your own value irrespective of what other people think of you. Your lunar needs must be recognised, accepted, and allowed into your life-style, because in respecting your own needs you will be able to respect the needs of others. Mutual dependency is never as strong as self-responsibility. You need to listen to all of your inner messages, finding your own personal path, rather than just following the overcrowded path of the masses. Being self-assertive does not mean the loss of relationship; indeed, it can bring deeper and more satisfying contacts based on mutual respect for each individual uniqueness. Follow the way indicated by your feelings; do not settle for superficial harmony as the best alternative to disharmony, and look for that depth that offers the potential for real fulfilment; trust the messages of your Moon to guide you to greater integration, and these will give you a sense of well-being and personal harmony that is not reliant on any external supports. Only then will the Libran balance rest in equilibrium between the inner and outer realities.

MOON IN SCORPIO (FIXED SIGN)

The Moon is in its fall in Scorpio. Your emotions will be intense, powerful and volatile, and you will try to keep the lid firmly shut on those potentially seething passions rather than allowing them unrestrained expression. Maintaining emotional control seems essential for you, as you are aware of your vulnerability on that level. You may appear quite cool and collected to others, but they are only seeing the inscrutable Scorpio mask, which rarely slips to reveal the emotional intensity behind the strict control.

In relationships, you will tend to look for passion and intensity, for total involvement with a lover, and you will take your relationships with great seriousness, becoming heavily emotionally committed even though you try to resist surrendering into full intimacy; before you fully realise it, you're hooked. Falling in love is like a descent into your own underworld; fascinating and obsessive, evoking great riches and pleasures when going fine, but exacting great suffering when it fails, leaving your heart (and mind, and soul) in the possession of your lover. You may be able to resist such intensity of experience, but this will be at the cost of denying full involvement in intimacy, and in those efforts to protect or conceal your vulnerable emotions, you inhibit a deeper, more satisfying intimate contact.

Jealousy, possessiveness, obsession, and sexual preoccupation are likely to emanate from the Scorpio energies, and the impulse to discover union will be strong, especially on sexual and emotional levels, where you may look for absorption in the other, or to absorb a partner under your own domination. You take any rejection hard, entering emotional turmoil and confusion, and you often plot revenge, brooding over emotional hurts and holding grudges until time heals the intensity of your betrayed feelings. You may recognise this as a tendency in you, but as to changing or redirecting the powerful energies, that is another matter. Due to insecurity, you may be afraid of losing those you love, and this may lead you to attempt to control them, to ensure that they remain tied to you by one means or another.

If you repress your real feelings, then this energy may emerge in a tendency to manipulate, dictate and dominate, especially through your sexual or financial power, or erupt vengeful behaviour, spite and malice. Powerful unfulfilled needs and desires, vitalised by strong emotions, can lead towards compulsive behaviour in which unconscious instincts begin to direct your life. Wherever your desires are, your emotions are there too, activating them incessantly; satisfying these desires is a way to gain emotional respite, although doing so at the expense of others is not the right way to proceed. Will–desire–emotion is the source of your motivation, and if you can define your objectives, then little can stand between you and success. If that triangle of energies is not fully activated, then you may fail to act decisively and effectively.

You need to understand your inner dynamics, to learn how to accept and handle this volatile emotional powerhouse, so that instead of expending effort on its repression, you learn how to channel it constructively for your own development. Your feelings are inner guiding messages for you, and they should be noted; in your own secret privacy, they should be honoured and steps taken to satisfy their needs. Ignoring them only fans the emotional flames even higher, until there is a real danger that they can ignite an inner conflagration which bursts out causing damage to yourself, your life-style and others near to you.

The path is one of descent into your own depths, seeking to discover that deepest root of your own identity where you can establish trust and secure foundations. Your potential is considerable, but to discover this a transformation may be required, through which your innate resources and qualities can be unfolded. Emotional pain may be the initiating force behind this redirection within you, and an essential component of your inner change will relate to the owning and reintegration of repressed emotions, feelings and instincts. Bringing them back to the surface of consciousness is the first step towards healing them through expressing your own deepest needs for self-nurturing. Focusing at your root centre, you should be able to direct your passionate energies instead of being at their mercy. You will then learn how to harness these energies, holding the reins of knowledge in conscious control, like the Charioteer in the Tarot trump. In understanding yourself, you will be able to meet your own needs, instead of manipulating others into fulfilling them for you, or in other ways relying on others emotionally.

This may not be an easy path to follow, but attempting to do so will offer the potential of great inner riches and stability. Harnessing that emotional power can be the key to achieving your lifetime's dreams, and at least will ensure that you feel at ease and content with your own nature. Self-acceptance brings a deep relaxation which will aid the emergence of more satisfying relationships. You hold the key to your own fulfilment; inserting it into the lock of your own nature and opening the inner door may become the most important action in your life.

MOON IN SAGITTARIUS (MUTABLE SIGN)

With the Moon in Sagittarius, the dominating impulse will be towards freedom – physical, emotional, mental and spiritual. The need for 'freedom *from* . . .' may be easily recognised, but 'freedom *to* . . .' may be unfamiliar. You have a powerful expansionary urge and your need to transcend barriers and boundaries is insistent, although this may work against requirements for commitment and perseverance as an escapist tendency is ever-present when obligations become too oppressive. Part of the expansionary impulse is to exploit personal potential in whatever way is favoured. You may have a particular need to leave your options open, avoiding fixed decisions by an insistence on mobility and freedom of choice. Relationship ties in particular may be resisted.

Intellectualism and idealism are likely to be strong in your nature, as well as futuristic and optimistic attitudes. The need for a distinct belief system with lofty aspirations will be strongly felt. This belief system may not be conventional or traditional – although you may have absorbed one from your earlier social conditioning, but it has to satisfy your idealistic nature. Most beliefs are ambivalent in their actual application to real life, and with your outlook this is likely to be the case, whether the beliefs are expansive and universally tolerant or narrow and sectarian. Looking through the rose-coloured glasses of your own perception, your social beliefs will be heavily influenced by unconscious emotional factors, and may therefore lack objectivity. Sometimes a trusting gullibility may let you down, or involve you in directions that may not be in your own best interests.

You will probably be gregarious, particularly enjoying intellectual exchanges, and will often be very generous to friends and colleagues in a variety of ways. Mutual companionship is important to you; even in intimate relationships this will be a vital component. Understanding of the multiplicity of individual differences may be less evident, and could constitute a blind spot for you. You may fail to recognise individual needs in the same way that you often fail to acknowledge your own. You may gain self-esteem by expressing social influence through your intellect, perhaps garbed in the robes of a teacher. The expansionary impulse may lead you to explore other countries; you may react against being stuck in one physical location, and when you feel trapped may escape by running far away in order to reassert your freedom.

There is considerable self-belief, and you will often feel lucky, and will test this, perhaps by taking gambles in your life, through relationships, career changes, home moves or financial speculations. You may have difficulty, however, in accepting your emotional nature; it is hard to fit it into a belief structure and is unpredictable, and when active it tends to involve you in intimate situations which threaten your freedom and flexibility. You tend to perceive responsibilities and obligations as inimical to your freedom, hearing the warning bells going off whenever anyone crosses over that invisible dividing line, fearing that the prison bars are going to clang shut on you for ever.

So you tend to inhibit and repress emotional involvement, or if you find yourself in situations of emotional relationship tend to start looking for reasons and ways to escape. If inner barriers are continually erected against contacting these disturbing feelings, then the higher Sagittarian qualities may become distorted. You may impose a rigid belief system on your world-view; you may physically seek escape from the situation, running away from commitment to your decisions and people; you may avoid confronting issues by adopting the ostrich position of head in the sand, hoping that the problem will go away; you may avoid emotional issues in a flurry of external activity and mental stimulation. You may dream long-term plans, instead of applying your efforts in the present to achieve them; you may avoid making decisions and defer your actions; you may absorb yourself in idealistic fancies rather than accept the less glamorous reality; or you may amplify your intellect at the expense of your repressed feelings.

A reorientating balance between Moon and Sagittarius energies is needed, so that the higher qualities of each are expressed and the needs of each are equally honoured. Independence and self-responsibility need to be cultivated, so that you do not use an external belief system as a shield against facing the real world and your own unexplored nature. A degree of self-reflection is required so that you perceive and express your instinctual and emotional nature, listening to its whispered messages and subtle movements of feelings which point to your real needs and how you should be satisfying them. These Moon messages can act as an inspirational guide for you, and acknowledging their validity and importance can become a vital step towards self-integration. If you need to retain a world-view then try to form one that is individually suited to your own needs, that incorporates the totality of your being and does not just reflect a dominant part. Maturity for you involves the balancing of personal freedom with the inevitable restrictions and limitations of daily life; exploration can occur wherever you are and in any circumstance, as freedom is a state of mind and not dependent on the external environment. It is an inner realm of freedom that will offer you the deepest sense of a satisfying sanctuary.

MOON IN CAPRICORN (CARDINAL SIGN)

The Moon is in detriment in Capricorn. The emphasis of your inner need is on gaining the approval of others and establishing a position of social status and recognition. This may be through achieving financial or community influence and power, and much of your self-esteem and confidence will be derived from this social relationship. As you have an innate insecurity and doubts regarding your intrinsic personal value, you need recognition and approbation from colleagues and family to help you to begin loving yourself and accepting your nature as it is.

The source of these inner doubts may lie in a childhood perspective of feeling unloved; a perspective that may have been accurate or else unduly coloured by a natural tendency to amplify those times when you felt a lack of loving contact with your parents. There may have been a diminution of open affection and loving care displayed, and the feeling level of the relationship may not have been sufficiently developed, or else emotions may have been kept firmly under control. The result is a lack of ease with that aspect of your nature. Capricorn has a tendency to negate or repress the emotions.

There is likely to be a lack of real trust and faith in life, allied with a reserved, cautious attitude seeing life through a serious perspective, and adopting a more materialistic philosophy with an emphasis on success in the external world. You will try to buttress those feelings of insecurity or inadequacy by gaining social power, strengthening your ego through positions of authority, prestige and influence on the lives of others. You will be ambitious to succeed, both for the status and financial security that can be achieved, and for the sake of self-validation.

You will be a hard worker, perhaps seeing yourself as moving towards some type of personal destiny, and if so, this will concentrate your efforts even more as you may be willing to dedicate yourself to fulfil that mission, even if it has a distinctly personal bias. Work is important to you, and receiving appreciation and recognition is necessary in order for you to feel fulfilled. Following your path may lead to friction with others, especially if you become too egocentric about your purposes, or begin to abuse positions of responsibility. You may lack awareness of the feelings of others, therefore behaving tactlessly. Manipulation and scheming may not always work to your advantage either; you are sensitive to the comments and opinions of others, but fail to apply this same sensitivity to those close to you.

Underlying these tendencies is a need to feel wanted, yet you may express this need in a distorted manner. Your own feelings are often denied and ignored, as they remind you of an aspect of your nature that is not under your control, an area that is an unknown realm for you and which you fear is threatening. You feel weak and vulnerable, afraid of emotional rejection. You prefer to deal with the tangibility of the material world, rather than the shifting flux of those inner emotions, and try to focus your attention on building a solid secure organisational structure around you as a foundation to achieve those compensatory aims.

You need to acknowledge those deeper needs, to develop ways whereby you can nurture yourself through allowing deeper emotional exchanges, and by releasing your feelings instead of blocking them. Containing and repressing them may lead to depression, a sense of meaninglessness, negativity, and self-criticism. You need to take the risk of opening up to the world as you strive to contact that deepest sense of self-validation that does exist beneath your personality tendencies. Security lies within yourself rather than in status or material possessions. People will not love you just because you may have achieved; you will be loved for what you are. Apply yourself to unfolding your own potential, integrate your totality, and develop your own unique path so that it includes the vitality and warmth of genuine human relationship.

MOON IN AQUARIUS (FIXED SIGN)

The Moon in Aquarius indicates that there will be a powerful social awareness influencing you, and that many of your personal needs will be connected to social groups or organisations. There is an attraction towards involvement with socially active groups, although these may be more modern radical pressure-groups rather than established social organisations because of your intrinsic rebellious nature. You find that the idealistic vision and values of such groups is especially appealing, both intellectually and emotionally, and as Aquarius is the sign of group conscious-ness you will at least mentally align yourself with such progressive groups. Yet as you perceive yourself to be highly individual, actually working within groups may not suit you so much, as you are determined to pursue your own iconoclastic approach. You can enjoy the freedom of remaining on the fringes as an observer rather than becoming really involved.

Socially, you like to build a wide network of friends and acquaintances, where there is a breadth of various relationships based on a communality of social and creative interests. You enjoy variety and constant mental stimulation, and often your home-life is turned into a meeting-place for like-minded individuals. The revolution may occur only in your mind, but you do like to reflect the changing world and to express its new perceptions, if only to see the effect they have on people; yet you may become dedicated to a cause or belief, and your attitudes are genuinely held, even if the eventual application may be lacking.

Relating to humanity as a whole is easier for you than relating on a one-to-one basis, especially within intimate contacts. Your emotions are not particularly well-integrated, and sometimes your social whirl serves as an excuse to evade your fear of emotional closeness. You intellectualise your emotions rather than directly experiencing their power and intensity; the feeling level is diverted into a mental examination, otherwise you may feel threatened by their wildness. By demanding emotional freedom in relationship, you are just trying to keep your emotions at a distance, and this can manifest in fears of commitment, even though you may actually need that.

The Moon is not particularly happy in Aquarius. The lunar emotions, instincts and feelings try to break free of that Aquarian impersonality and mental focus, searching for greater closeness and for fulfilment of unacknowledge needs; and the Aquarian energies may stimulate sudden radical changes of life-style as an escape from family responsibilities or emotional suffocation.

The Moon and Aquarius may be brought into deeper harmony if you begin to honour those emotional and instinctual needs, and resist the impulse to make a dash for freedom. Your sympathy with the needs of humanity is genuine, engaging a heart response from you, but this feeling response needs to be liberated throughout all of your own life too. Unfolding your own potential also means working with your whole nature and recognising your emotions and feelings as a vital part of that unique individuality that you value so highly in yourself. Cutting them off makes as much sense as chopping a leg off. Let your natural emotions flow more easily; follow their messages too, instead of just paying attention to your intellect, logic or philosophical belief systems. Otherwise you pollute and damage the personal ecological system of your own nature; and like stagnant water everywhere, it will become poisoned and fetid, distorting your advanced social perceptions and destroying your humanity.

Allowing emotional vitality to flow will also enhance your

intuitive perception and release your natural inventiveness; this may enable you to make a greater contribution to society too, as well as vitalising your own inner realms through improving the quality of your intimate relationships.

MOON IN PISCES (MUTABLE SIGN)

Moon in Pisces indicates that you may be an emotional dreamer, highly sensitive to the tidal vacillations of your feelings and those of others around you. This heightened sensitivity verges on a psychic ability, and you will be open to impressions from the collective emotional psyche, acting almost like a psychic sponge, leaving yourself vulnerable on an unconscious inner level. Without realising it, you often reflect the moods and feelings of those close to you, incorrectly believing that they are your own feelings; you may carry the emotional burdens of many, and this can weigh your own spirit down. Some may take advantage of your self-sacrificial attitude, trying to turn you into a victim or martyr for their own ends, so you may need to guard against this unconscious tendency in you.

Real life is not really to your taste; it can be too harsh and demanding, making too great an impact on your malleable feeling nature and wearing you down through constant emotionally based agitation. There can be a tendency to seek escape through imagination, fantasies and dreams, and through addictions to alcohol, drugs and sexual activity. Prolonged exposure to your private dream-world may make you even less able to deal with the demands of human existence, and much time and effort may be spent in dreaming of a better future rather than actually working towards it.

You will have easy access to your unconscious mind, and this may pose certain problems. Whilst it can enhance your creativity and imagination through channels such as poetry, art and music, this needs to be carefully disciplined and focused. If such channels of expression are not available, then they could be developed, and if you have no way to direct these energies then they will circulate within your own nature. What this implies is that they will further amplify your sensitivity, emotions and feelings, and probably make you more psychologically vulnerable. The danger is one of imbalance, and of stimulating some of the more negative Piscean tendencies. Feelings of guilt and persecution may arise, together with a tendency towards martyrdom, hypochondria, or losing touch with everyday reality, with dreamscapes taking over. The unconscious may flood your personality and swamp it, creating neuroses and psychoses in unintegrated personalities.

But equally, there is a positive dimension to this which can be unfolded through your own choices. There is probably mediumistic ability, which could be developed through the modern technique of 'channelling', whereby inner teachers can be contacted for guidance and support (although discrimination must be applied to ensure that the messages are genuine and reliable). Your feelings and emotions are easily expressed, few blocks exist in you, and you are most familiar with following the messages of these impulses within you, even to the exclusion of any rationality at times! Your natural empathy can be developed into practical aid and support for others, such as through counselling, healing or teaching. Your ideals and dreams of a better world can be made more real by actualising your visions, and by manifesting the spiritual realities into the physical level. Cease any tendencies to live through the vicarious feelings and experiences of others, and reabsorb your projections back into yourself, so that greater integration can proceed instead of allowing disintegration to occur through losing yourself in others. Take a more positive approach to honouring your own feelings, rather than assuming that the feelings of others are more important. Value your empathic contribution to relationships, and appreciate those feelings of intimate closeness that this brings, and learn how to fulfil your need to serve others, not through self-sacrifice, but as a means of empowering them to accept their own emotions and feelings, to show them how to live with them and to gain the benefits of a feeling response to the mysteries of life.

By transcending your tendencies to protect your emotions, perhaps through social shyness, you may learn how to make the fullest advantage from this sensitivity, both in a constructive attitude towards your own emotional dynamics, but also in the compassionate service of others. Your path through life lies through the watery realm of feelings; learning how to navigate those sometimes stormy waters may help you to guide others across their own inner seas.

CHAPTER 7

The Lamp of Night:
The Lunar Phase Cycle

THE CYCLE OF LUNAR PHASES reflects the changing pattern of relationship between the Moon and the Sun, and the modifications in the appearance of the night Moon as perceived from the perspective of Earth.

Many of the astrological concepts and teachings concerning the influence of the lunation cycle derive from the perception of a relationship between the Moon and Sun, whereby an oscillating wave-pattern of 'light transmitted' to Earth by the Moon either increases or reduces according to the particular stage reached in the cycle. This concept then introduces the idea of phases of separating from the 'light source of life' and then returning back to the Sun's power and influence, and parallels religious and esoteric evolutionary doctrines of a fall from paradise and grace – involutionary and incarnatory descent and the loss or diminution of light – and then a slow evolutionary ascent back to the spiritual source of light.

The lunation cycle is connected to the material substance of the human personality, and symbolically serves to demonstrate how the solar life-process is operating within each individual, and how the person can attune to these cyclic rhythms and actualise their transpersonal purpose as shown by the degree and house position of the Sun in their natal chart. Essentially it is a rhythmic pattern which indicates the reality of the solar type and helps inner alignment with the spiritual self. This is why it has been applied in many types of esoteric and religious ritual across different cultures for several thousand years.

The Moon is perceived as mediator of solar light to Earth, stepping its power down like a transformer because humanity is not yet capable of directly absorbing the Sun's energy. This concept is similar to esoteric teachings of the mediating soul between personality and spirit, or the descending ten emanations of the Sephiroth from the God-Light to Earth in the Qabalistic Tree of Life teachings.

Due to a cultural and human preference for separatist thinking, the dyadic polarity of Sun and Moon has often resulted in antagonism, as witnessed by the dominance of either matriarchal or patriarchal social attitudes and perspectives throughout history. Perceiving the dyad as confrontatory is a spiritual misunderstanding, in which the physical form and personality (the creation of the Moon principle) is seen as negative to the positive pole of soul/spirit/solar principle, rather than as complementary and in an inviolable relationship of great evolutionary potential.

The modern humanistic approach reiterates esoteric teachings concerning the sacred marriage of Sun and Moon, the *mysterium coniunctio* of the alchemists (see Chapters 9 and 10), and tries to encourage a much more positive approach to the Sun–Moon polarity, viewing it as a relationship of internal and external union, through which vitalising meaning can be attained by the integrated individual.

To help reach this relationship and the potential to unfold creativity and meaning, a positive attitude should be adopted during the waxing period, so that action taken to grow or become free of restrictions and limitations can have beneficial consequences by the time of the Full Moon. It is then that the Moon is at her most receptive to the seeds of solar light and inspiration, which are then symbolically released through her reflective light to Earth. However, if the waxing phase has not been taken advantage of, or the personality has erected negative and repelling walls against the lunar influences, then the Full Moon may seem to stimulate additional stresses, tensions and inner conflicts.

Positivity during the waxing phase should enhance the prospects for meaning and purpose to be grasped during the waning phase. The light of the Full Moon can reveal a new vision, the potential for renewal and rebirth, and new purpose, if the personality is held in concentrated reflection. The waning phase is the assimilation of new impulses and insights, forming seeds which will form the future path prior to their later release into action during the next waxing period.

PERSONALITY AND THE LUNATION TYPES

The concept of lunation personality types has emerged from the fourfold lunar cycle and the further midpoint division, thus creating a circle composed of eight sections of 45 degrees each. Evaluating the lunar cycle in terms of personality tendencies can offer certain key insights into the means by which individuals are likely to express themselves during life, in that by their type of solar–lunar relationship we may see how they receive, absorb and transmit the light available to them.

New Moon Personality: The Waxing Phase

This is the individual born at the time of the New Moon or within the following 3½ days, with the Moon 0–45 degrees ahead of the Sun.

What characterises this type is the impulse to act in the world, that urge to become involved and make a mark. In certain ways, there is something akin to the state of adolescent consciousness, characterised by self-centredness, subjective inner absorption and innocent naivity. This type often act impulsively without realistic consideration, and this can lead to later difficulties, even if the initial impulse is well motivated. The driving force of the personality is to impose that personal conception upon the world, those desires, needs, ideals, ideas and concepts that are believed to be important and valuable new seeds for future progress. The actual personality may display some contradiction, especially in confusing the projection of unresolved aspects of his own need for self-integration with the actual reality of the world screen on which he is trying to perform his own drama. He is preoccupied with his own life-path, and all perception is absorbed back into that viewpoint, so that he may fail to acknowledge the objective reality and differences of other people, and fail to understand the complexities of the world. His manner of evaluating and dealing with life is very much based on emotionally biased responses, irrespective of how he may attempt to disguise this.

Examples include: Sigmund Freud, Karl Marx, Richard Nixon, Queen Victoria, Osho Rajneesh.

Crescent Personality

This is the individual born with the Moon 45–90 degrees ahead of the Sun. The main characteristic of this type is the impulse for self-assertion founded on self-confidence, and again involves the need to make a personal mark on the world, to influence the collective direction in some way. Yet the keynote of this influence lies in the tendency to challenge the existing established order, and action is directed towards overcoming old inertia and trying to bring through 'new seeds'. This inner sense of being a 'spearhead' for something trying to emerge adds extra impetus to the transcendence of any obstacles, and may demand a transformation from a personal emphasis into one of a collective channel. That is the crucial transition, and some born at the crescent may not succeed in making the full adjustment, reverting back into being oppressed by a lack of momentum and by their own personal difficulties in moving beyond established personal or social structures, thus failing to achieve their potential.

First Quarter Personality

This is the individual born with the Moon 90–135 degrees ahead of the Sun, 7–10½ days after the New Moon.

This type involves will in action, associated with a sense that time is passing while there is still much to be achieved, a sense of urgency and a need to drink deeply of life's rich experiences. There is probably managerial and organisational abilities, together with general leadership potential. The powerful will and sense of personal direction will focus towards ways of either exalting the separate personality in social spheres or creating social structures/organisations which are designed to fulfil future collective needs. There may be personal pleasure at seeing the old order collapsing, and an intensification of a belief in one's own power when the signs of this are appearing. There is an innate rejection of existing ways, and a knowledge that liberating change is vital, although with many possible ways of perceiving how this can be brought about. There can be a more egocentric response with this type, which moves towards social negativity and ruthlessness in applying that powerful will on a collective scale. The examples below indicate the wide variety of ways in which this impulse can be expressed.

Examples: Josef Stalin, Charles de Gaulle, Queen Elizabeth II, Timothy Leary, John Lennon, Alice A. Bailey.

Gibbous Personality

The individual is born when the Moon is 135–180 degrees ahead of the Sun, or a few days before Full Moon.

The tendency towards personal reflection commences now, and this personality type is more introspective and concerned with personal growth and expression rather than action and assertion in the external world, although the impulse of contribution to society is still powerful and, as the examples demonstrate, can manifest in a variety of ways. It is the unfoldment of talents within the personality that characterises this type, and there is likely to be an emphasis on the role of the mind and intellect with its capacity for association, analysis and new synthesis. Often, there is a enquiring nature, searching for understanding and insight, for the revelation that greater light can bring, and for opportunities to share this with the world for future benefit. The life is often highly directed and focused towards individual and specific aims, and this concentrated approach is a key to later success. It is the questioning mind that can open new doors, allowing intuitive glimpses of what can be achieved, or what will come through welcoming human channels.

Examples: Jacob Boehme (mystic), Lord Byron, Isaac Newton, Louis Pasteur, Prince Charles, Aleister Crowley.

Full Moon Personality: The Waning Phase

This is the individual born when the Moon is 180–135 degrees behind the Sun, at Full Moon or within the following 3½ days.

The challenge confronting this type is the absorption of the light in a balanced manner, and the discovery of suitable channels through which it can be released into society. There can be a greater clarity of consciousness and an openness of mind, with a search for personal fulfilment. The self-reflection of this type may shine a light which is either illuminating or blinding. Some may simply retreat into a delusory condition of inner division, unable to integrate the available light. For this individual, integration of the self and the collective is the main directive, and his thinking will be conditioned by concepts of individual and social perfection. Much will depend on how the individual integrates these concepts, whether he can hold a balanced stance and see them slowly unfolding, and then add his contribution to their progress, or whether blinded by the light he rejects anything that misses the ideal level, and in so doing fragments his own nature and distorts the full potential of social development.

Examples: Rudolf Steiner, Krishnamurti, Goethe, Mary Baker Eddy (founder of Christian Science), General Franco, Roberto Assagioli.

Disseminating Personality

The individual is born when the Moon is 135–90 degrees behind the Sun.

As the concept of dissemination implies, what is most important to this personality type is the release and sowing of 'seeds', which are often related to ideas and insights which have made a profound impression on him personally, and which he considers to be of universal or social significance. The mental process for this personality is initially that of assimilation of ideas, attitudes, perceptions, insights, revelations and knowledge, followed by a period of evaluation and synthesis into a new and coherent pattern, which will result in the seed of innovation which can be communicated to others to ensure its future growth. Such individuals are motivated by a desire to teach, to share their world-view with others, thus creating an affinity group through which they can to work. It involves a degree of popularisation, of introducing a greater public to unfamiliar ideas. There can be a tendency to adopt a crusading mantle, and if this impulse is strongly operating through an unintegrated personality or an ego with powerful separatist attitudes, then a negative manifestation can emerge, conditioned by fanaticism, obsessive adherence to a cause, or evocations of the collective emotional level, of which Hitler was a notorious example.

Examples: Adolf Hitler, Benjamin Disraeli, Otto von Bismarck, Richard Wagner, Meher Baba, Ram Dass (Richard Alpert), Winston Churchill, Da Free John.

Third Quarter Personality

This is the individual born as the waning Moon is 90–45 degrees behind the Sun.

What characterises this type is an emphasis on an individual integrity, founded on a personal commitment to an ideal, principle or philosophy which they feel they are responsible for expressing and communicating to the world. This is often associated with future progress. An inner pressure demands that the individual embodies this and demonstrates its importance to the public. For the individual it involves a crisis within their consciousness, prior to attempting to build either a new system of thought, or new organisational structures designed to reflect the inspiring ideal. Risks are taken to promote and strengthen the ideal, and confrontations with existing structures and systems of thought are likely. The personality often feels itself to be alienated from the masses, attuned to fulfilling a secret destiny, for which it is endeavouring to serve as a pioneer. There can be a tendency to seriousness, and a vulnerability to criticism, and the personality may appear to be so focused on the particular life-path that deviation, flexibility or compromise will rarely be allowed. People born at this phase may often have a collective responsibility both to embody and to release 'future seeds' into the ongoing historical drama, and may symbolise through their actions and words the dawning needs of the collective for renewal and transformation, invoking a latent future through becoming a channel in the present.

Examples: Martin Luther, Mohandas Gandhi, George Washington, Lenin, Trotsky, Henry Steel Olcott (co-founder of Theosophical Society), Annie Besant, Dion Fortune, Benito Mussolini, Albert Einstein, George Bernard Shaw, Carl Gustav Jung.

Balsamic Personality

This is the individual born with the Moon 45–0 degrees behind the Sun, within 3½ days before New Moon.

The balsamic personality continues the theme of the third quarter type, and is also future-orientated and less bound by any ties to past traditions. There may be a distinct sense of 'mission' in this type, and an impulse leading towards some type of destined social action, almost as if they are possessed by a power greater than themselves to which they need to give acknowledgement and free access to operate through them. This evokes the transpersonal dimension, with the communication of future visions in the present, creating pathways to follow and aims to inspire. It is working towards the imminent release of new seed-ideas at the New Moon, and there may be an element of personal sacrifice to enable this release to come to fruition. Some may express this as prophets of the future, seeing dawn shadows of the coming world.

Examples: Abraham Lincoln (emancipation of slaves, human rights), Thomas Paine (concepts of modern democracy), Cecil Rhodes (vision of an imperialist African empire), Dane Rudhyar (pioneer of humanistic and transpersonal astrology), Bob Dylan (musical evocation of a spirit of youth), Kahlil Gibran (poet, visionary, author of *The Prophet*).

THE INFLUENCE OF NEW AND FULL MOONS

Contemporary social and scientific analytical research demonstrates that there are noticeable effects on the human being, physically and psychologically, under the influence of the lunation cycle of New and Full Moons. This is related to the fact that at these times the gravitational effects are at their most powerful as the Sun and Moon move into either the conjunction or opposition alignments. In a parallel sense to the contraction and expansion of land masses, or to the oceanic increase and decrease of water quantity at such times, so do we open and expand to the reception of the soli-lunar light, or contract and release seeds when it diminishes.

Scientific enquiry has shown that our body chemistry and internal fluidic systems are affected by the Moon's influence, for example in chemical releases which improve the circulation, or in the body's tendency to bleed more profusely at Full Moon, a phenomenon observed by medical surgeons. We recognise now that changes in the chemical and glandular body secretions are of immense influence on the physical and mental well-being of individuals, and that glandular harmony and right activity is essential to perpetuate adequate health.

As the magnetic field of Earth is affected by the gravitational pull of the Sun–Moon at New and Full Moons, there is an intensification of natural electricity and the atmosphere is charged with more positive ions, which also affects behaviour. Epileptic fits or breathing difficulties caused by asthma attacks may be increased, possibly due to this additional electricity in the human body and the change in atmosphere. Sleep researchers believe that dream activity increases, as unconscious muscular responses to this inner mind stimulation is amplified. Women who follow a more natural menstrual rhythm uninfluenced by modern chemical contraceptions, discover that their ovulatatory cycle tends to synchronise with Moon phases, and that higher chances of fertility can match the major Moon positions of conjunction and opposition. Human needs for expressing relationship can stimulate heightened sexual activities, and psychological tensions are also exacerbated at such times. Instinctual and unconscious drives seem nearer to the surface of the collective mind/emotions, and one negative result of this is the increase in social violence, murder, theft, physical aggression and psychological illness that is often related to the Full Moon period. Acting under the pressure of the alignments of Sun and Moon at conjunction or opposition, the strengths and weaknesses of the human psyche are displayed, and any existing stresses are liable to be exacerbated, as are stresses within relationships which are ready for emotional explosions and the release of pent-up energies.

It can be an interesting experiment for anyone with astrological knowledge to monitor their own Moon influence, to become consciously aligned with observing Moon activity on their bodies, emotions and mind during its cyclic movement. Psychological moods and emotional reactions may be observed to fall into repetitive patterns, and anyone who has a noticeable Moon presence in their natal chart should consider this; it may be a valuable key to possess in unlocking the dynamics of your own inner psyche. Those with either a New or Full Moon personality, several Moon planetary aspects, a strong Water or Earth emphasis, or a high Cancer profile (Cancer on an angle, or several planets in Cancer) may be especially vulnerable to the Moon's influence on their psychological state, often exhibiting pronounced patterns of emotional ebb and flow.

The New Moon

The time of the New Moon can be an appropriate point to initiate new activities, make personal inner reorientations, and take steps towards new directions.

The challenge confronting us at the New Moon is the expression of our nature through activity, primarily an outward movement of ourselves into the environment. This can include glimpsing what we wish to manifest in our lives, the vision that we will pursue, making decisions to change unsatisfactory areas of our lives and make new beginnings. It is a phase of renewal and it is that energy that we can harness to aid our attempts to change.

This energy of renewal reflected by the New Moon will stimulate the area denoted by the house in which it is placed, and especially any planet that it aspects, whether a natal planet or a transiting planet. The energising of the house placing of the New Moon may offer the potential for renewal in that particular sphere of life, whether it is the stimulation of clarified action and decision, or clarified awareness of its significance in the individual life. Certainly there will be an instinctive expression of personal needs, instincts and feelings in the sphere of life indicated by the house placement.

The activation of natal planets by New Moon aspects is especially important; particularly noticeable are the conjunction, square and opposition contacts, when the tendencies, qualities and potentials of the natal planets involved are activated into renewed vitality. This can mean that planet becoming highlighted in the personal psyche, moving to the forefront of consciousness and playing a more influential role relaying messages into the conscious mind or attempting to instigate necessary changes, rebalancing or indicating new directions to evoke its own potential. Such inner activity can begin to display itself a few days before the exact aspect is made, as the transiting New Moon nears the position of the natal planet to make the aspect, and the energies begin to merge and intensify through their fusion, prior to a fuller release through the psyche.

This reawakening of a planet through the influence of the soli-lunar power and the lunation cycle is very significant. The conjunction enables us to make a deep inner connection to the particular planet contacted, and this will release a new impulse which will slowly grow and emerge into consciousness. Noting the times of such conjunctions may enable us to use that planetary energy in beneficial ways; it is a deeply placed power-source within us that we can tap, and if we do so, then we are more likely to experience success in aims associated with that planet.

With conjunction aspects made by lunations (New or Full Moon), the emphasis is placed on the expression or experiencing of that particular planetary energy. For instance, a conjunction with the Sun may stimulate us to act in a more individually decisive manner in the world, to assert our unique nature more effectively, to aim to fulfil latent potential, to attain a higher social profile. A lunation conjunction with natal Moon may make us decide to indulge ourselves more, to spend time and money on things that make us feel good, to ask for more loving and deeper relationships with partners, to decide to stop doing things in life that do not feel right anymore. A conjunction with Jupiter may make us want to expand our boundaries, to explore and investigate life more fully, to gain the sense of the greater whole of which we are a part.

The sextile and trine aspects made by lunations indicate an ease and flowing quality to the planetary energies involved, a time to express and experience the positive potentials of the planet, exploiting their gifts to us. The square indicates inner conflict and tension, especially on deeper instinctual and feeling levels, and reveals the need for internal adjustments whilst offering an opportunity for a renewal of the relationships between the soli-lunar energies and that planet. The opposition may emphasise interpersonal conflicts, through intimate and social relationships, perhaps facing the individual with the consequences of their own inner attitudes and unresolved shadow projections onto the world, and their reflection back at them.

The essential point to be remembered at the New Moon phase is that the cycle is being renewed; it is an opportunity to change, modify, redirect, to clarify personal intentions in relation to the particular planet, house and sign involved. It appears that there is a continuity between decisions taken at one New Moon being followed through into activity taken at consecutive New Moons until that particular impulse has run its natural course.

Full Moon

The Full Moon is the time for reflection and receptivity to the soli-lunar channel which is opened. At this time, Sun and Moon are in opposition near the same degree of opposite signs, and the Moon's reflected light is at its greatest. The Moon appears equal to the Sun, and their joint gravitational effect is maximised.

In recently developed spiritual practices, working with the Full Moon cycle has become popularised (see Chapter 9) in recognition of its conduciveness to meditative and reflective consciousness. At Full Moon the mind seems more naturally attuned to insight and vision than at other times, enabling those subtle whispers and inner messages to be heard through the temporary fusion of the unconscious and conscious levels of our beings. There is a greater clarity of perception available, an attunement and accessing of less tangible realms of existence, and an enhanced sense of relationship both within the self and with the external reality.

Yet whilst the seed of holistic vision is there to be contacted, its presence also stimulates the awareness of separation and the gap that exists between our present expression and experience and the potential reality of the vision. Part of this is due to the fact that the Full Moon is an opposition aspect, with Sun and Moon placed in opposite signs and houses, and so we are confronted with the problems of a dualistic situation – that of resolving stresses caused by disparate energies and spheres of life. The result is a state of heightened tension, one which many people find difficulties dealing with, as evidenced by crime and mental illness statistics. At Full Moon they experience their inner divisions and lack of integration even more acutely, activating their neuroses, psychoses or separative attitudes. Those who are more responsive to the holistic energy of resolution may conversely feel a greater need for relationship and social company at this time.

For the individual, there is the potential to apply the Full Moon phase to their own personal psychological dynamics, to enhance self-understanding by taking advantage of its reflective nature. For instance, a Full Moon with transiting Sun in Virgo, Moon in Pisces, is superimposed on an individual's natal 7th and 1st houses respectively. This could be explored as reflecting on the connection between relationships with others, the external world and individual expression and identity. Both Virgo and Pisces may stimulate thoughts of universal compassion and service, so the way to unfold individual potential and assert the nature of that unique identity could be through service to the greater community. The following month, the Sun in Libra, Moon in Aries in the 8th and 2nd houses respectively, could suggest another set of personally relevant themes to contemplate.

By developing this kind of personal approach to the lunation cycle, the individual will gain an insight into what is needed to resolve the opposing soli-lunar energies. Through such techniques, we effectively reprogramme ourselves to discover the balancing point between Sun and Moon. In addition, we gain a greater understanding of our relationship to the spheres of life indicated by the houses involved.

This is one way of gaining a more detached view of our established patterns of thought and action, and to receive new insights into how to adjust any that are not in harmony. Through a year's exploration of this lunation cycle, we pass through each sign and house, and this offers us a simple but effective approach to considering the range of energies at work within us.

Like the New Moon, the Full Moon can activate any planets that it contacts by aspect, suggesting those key issues that can be usefully considered as reflected by the particular planet, house and sign involved. The conjunctions are especially powerful, offering an opportunity to make a deeper contact to that planetary influence upon us, but from a contemplative perspective, seeing how it influences and directs our behaviour, recognising if we are repressing part of its nature or failing to exploit its true potential, seeing ourselves through that planetary filter, noting how effectively we integrate it into our lives and how well we express it in the world. Perhaps it suggests needs of that planet that we have not yet acknowledged, or how it could co-operate creatively with other areas of our nature. We can register underlying meaning and purpose slowly unfolding through our inner planetary pictures, moving closer towards the essence of our unique inner structure and wholeness of being. It focuses on that planet's reflections in the outer world, be they of people, activities or relationships, and suggests that they could be made more harmonious, creative, positive and meaningful if we choose. It may show how we unconsciously project this energy externally, and we may need to learn how to own our projections through inner clarity and reintegration.

The Full Moon is a time for pause; to look again in the greater light; to receive the illuminating inspiration that is released; and to take steps towards greater contact with others, instead of maintaining separation. We may receive the consequences of previous actions taken at the New Moon, or decide to initiate changes and actions at the following New Moon. Essentially, we must turn within at this time in order to receive the greatest benefits.

CHAPTER 8

Dragon's Head, Dragon's Tail:
The Moon's Nodes

THE MOON'S NODES ARE CONSIDERED to be significant in an astrological analysis, although, in the West at least, less is known about their action than about that of the planets. One point that may need mentioning is that, unlike the physical planets, the Nodes have no objective or tangible reality, and no physical mass at all. The Nodes are points or positions in space which indicate the intersection of two orbits, those of the Sun and Earth, and the Earth and Moon.

The Nodes have often been viewed with caution or even fear as representing the inexorable influence of fate and destiny. Older traditional beliefs – especially in Hindu astrology – tend to view the Nodes as signifying baleful and negative effects, as periodic releasers of karmic experiences linked to the Lunar Lords and the living presence of the consequences of previous lives in the cycles of reincarnation. The North Node was seen as an active principle, associated with Mars, and the South Node as one of Saturnian limitations and restrictions. The Theosophists also saw the Nodes as indicating karmic patterns, and contemporary humanistic and transpersonal astrology has developed these concepts further, so that the Nodes represent a symbolic pathway of individual unfoldment and spiritual evolution.

The Nodes essentially symbolise a fusion of solar and lunar influences, being 'created' by the intersection of the Sun, Moon and Earth orbits, and indicate the interface in the present life of the individual between the past (Moon, South Node) and the future (Sun, North Node). The nodal axis is seen as indicating the magnetic attractions of the past and the future, and the individual struggle to make evolutionary progress, instead of allowing a retrogressive motion repeating well-worked patterns of life to dominate. Fate and destiny are involved, both in the 'inheritance' of foundational personality patterns from genetic hereditary, race, nationality or reincarnational concepts of previous lives, and in the potential expression of such latent personality traits which can be exploited for personal and collective benefit and which reflect the progression indicated by the North Node.

Through the forming of an axis, the nodes are clearly operating within a relationship of solar and lunar forces. This implies the potential for integration and understanding of two distinctly different inner influences in the psyche. The Nodes are as important as the planets, through house, sign and aspect positions. They are two poles of one process occurring within the psyche, and like opposition aspects, can be interpreted as implying that the meanings of the axis house/sign positions are complementary, and that there is the potential for a radical restructuring and integration of their influences. This relationship of two spheres of experience and personal meaning needs to be worked with, so that the hidden potential becomes released into actualisation, and the past successfully gives birth to a developing future pattern and does not just stagnate.

The Nodes symbolise the effort and struggle between the involutionary and evolutionary forces present in our dualistic universe. For the individual, this results in the conflict between the attractions of matter and the magnetism of spirit; at this point in evolution, matter is more powerful, although many are beginning to resonate and respond to the higher magnetism of spirit. For the spiritual seeker, there is the alternating attraction to both poles. This is reflected in the ongoing process of alignment and separation between the solar spiritual energies and the lunar personality forces within the individual, a process of periodic integration and disintegration within the personality and within whole life-cycles, in an attempt to attain a higher unity.

Through the relationship to the past, and the questions arising as to how to progress towards a future destiny, the individual is confronted by their own personality patterns, beliefs, attitudes, values and talents. These become the parameters of movement in life, representing karmic limitations and lessons, whilst also offering a means through which understanding of life can be gained. The social dimension and collective responsibility is also emphasised, as the use of natural and developed abilities is considered. Barriers of isolation are dissolved, and each person becomes part of a world-wide group born under the same nodal signs who are participants in a collective effort to resolve the conflicting issues of the opposing signs, for their own evolutionary benefit as well as for world evolution.

The South Node's position indicates where we are unconsciously reflecting familiar life-paths, where there is an ease and lack of evolutionary friction. The North Node indicates the ways in which we need to stretch our inner potential, reaching out for unknown possibilities and attainments by consciously attempting to unfold our nature in terms symbolised by the North Node.

When the transisting Moon is moving away from the North Node towards the South Node, there is the potential for a positive and creative relationship with spiritual energies. Such times are suitable for activities associated with projects of individual–collective evolutionary development responding to inner guidance. This can include forming appropriate structures to contain and reflect the spiritual impulse, new organisational, organic or psychological structures. The intake of spiritual power can be highlighted and made more effective. The emphasis may be purely personal or have a collective intent, and is often concerned with the inner turning of the receptive lunar nature to fertilisation by solar energies, and can deal with issues of personal and collective survival or development needs, of the relationship of the individual to the environment and the potential application of human influence to planetary life and environment.

When the Moon is moving away from the South Node and towards the North Node, the emphasis changes to become that of assimilating the spiritual impulse received in the northern hemisphere, focusing away from the spirit towards personal and material concerns and the releasing of force. During this southern latitude of the cycle, the lunar function may be related to involvement in social groups devoted to political, social or spiritual activities, in an attempt to discover greater meaning in life through external association. But primarily, this phase is the working through within the psyche of what was absorbed during the time of moving through the northern latitude cycle, of inner and outer adaptation or experimentation, learning what can be applied and constructively integrated, and what fails to be positively assimilated and so can be temporarily rejected in some way.

THE NORTH NODE

The North Node has been called *Rahu* and *Caput Draconis* – the Dragon's Head in older traditions, and is the pole of the nodal axis which is attuned to the progressive, evolutionary, spiritual energies within the universe, those which can provide us with guidance and indicate beneficial directions by resonating with our destined future expressions of self. In Jungian terminology, it is the pole of individuation, representing the prospect of *becoming* and the potential of ongoing inner unfoldment. This node may symbolise a personal dream of what we would like to become, an ideal that attracts our aspiration and efforts to achieve.

The house and sign position of the North Node indicates a path of self-development, calling to us throughout our lives to move ever onwards in expansive growth, to alert us to our latent potential and to demand that we make efforts to release our innate gifts. The North Node points to new faculties, qualities and talents that can be revealed through us, and in so doing adds to our enjoyment of life and our contribution to the whole, giving us purpose and the promise of fulfilment. The key to our future development lies in our own hands; we choose whether or not to align ourselves with spiritual energies, or not to make the sustained effort that is required for genuine transformation.

In astrological traditions, the North Node implies positivity, the spirit, and a place or point of divine protection and providence, where personal success is gained through the deliberate use of the focused will towards spiritual integration. The role of the Moon in forming the nodal axis is perceived as a turning towards the spiritual light of the Sun, and becoming a reflective distributor of the true light of divine purposeful will. This is the challenge confronting the individual and symbolised by the role of the North Node in the horoscope.

It is as if the North Node is a voice from our future self, encouraging us to rebuild ourselves into a new pattern that is designed to be more responsive to evolutionary needs. It serves as a doorway to our future self, guiding us in the right direction for our personal evolution. This offers a new type of nourishment suitable for building the next stage of our development, to discover renewed life-purpose, new attitudes, guiding values, principles and ideals which reform the existing personality and enable us to become receptive to a higher awareness and vision, that of the underlying unity and integrated holistic nature of life.

Through accessing this North Node doorway, we can absorb those energies that give birth to our transformed self. Through this gateway come appropriate and fulfilling experiences which offer the possibility of growth. By being true to an emerging part of our being, we become more whole and integrated, evoking that connection to spiritual beneficence within ourselves which can create corresponding well-being physically, emotionally and mentally. It is the route to make possible faculties and abilities that previously lay dormant, awaiting the time when the personality is suitably rearranged and capable of expressing new talents. This can be through insights received from the holistic vision, through psychic faculties awakening, or greater effectiveness in life generally. In this context, the North Node has been associated with the cerebral cortex of the human brain, which is considered to govern the higher and as yet unfolded capacities of the human psyche and physiology, including the powers of thought, imagination, the interpretation and understanding of experience, and the ability of self-awareness and reflection, qualities needed in order for individuation to occur.

Entering through the North Node is 'fresh air', vital for healthy breathing and cleansing us of reliance upon stale, stagnant air which is steadily losing its vitality and ability to sustain life – those repetitive, unconscious habit patterns that we invariably develop over time. In order to move beyond existing patterns of behaviour which have become restrictive and inhibiting, the North Node needs to be activated through effort and determination. Its messages are regularly transmitted to us, from its natal position, through natal aspects, and in transits, giving us the opportunity to attune to our future self, listen to the guidance available and receive the intake of the lunar material of experience and adjustment that makes a renewal or rebirth of personality possible.

Greater fulfilment is obtainable through the North Node, even though we may pass through periods when we are struggling to express our higher vision, and we are too aware of a current inability to live up to an ideal. It is never easy to express nascent abilities and qualities; lack of confidence, insecurity and the restraints of the past are difficult barriers to transcend, especially if our old life-style seems to be in a state of collapse, as we become dislodged from the familiar environment of our South Node. In most aspects of daily living, we are faced with the choice of taking steps towards our North Node, by seeking to expand beyond existing limitations, by attempting to actualise our gifts and talents, by achieving a broader, more universal perspective of relationship with ourself and others; or to turn back, retreat towards our South Node and remain with the restricting and limiting familiar world of the static status quo.

Following the North Node calling, we may realise that many of our personal dreams may be directly related to expressing North Node energies and attitudes, that our dreams of a better life can be achieved through changing our life-style and inner attitudes to reflect that greater positivity and constructive vision revealed by the mystery of the Dragon's Head. Our ability for social adaptation and unity with others may be greatly enhanced by this new spirit, and a greater sense of satisfaction with life should be experienced; energies which have the effect of deepening unity and wholeness are deeply fulfilling for the psyche, healing and purifying the whole personality. Responding to the North Node offers scope for experimentation; here there is space for freer activities, from which considerable benefits may begin to accrue. The effort required may be equally increased, yet it is in the North Node house that the new personality will emerge as a fusion of the past and future personalities. There is also the possibility that aid may occur through others whose planets conjunct the individual natal North Node, so intimate or business relationships could take this indication into account. Within our own natures, transiting nodes or lunar progressions which aspect natal nodal positions may also be significant in indicating changes, help or hindrances in resonating to the North Node.

THE SOUTH NODE

The South Node has been called *Ketu, Cuada Draconis,* – the Dragon's Tail and is usually associated with the doorway to the past. It represents the turning away from and resistance to the power of the spiritual solar light, so that the powers of the energy vibration of matter dominate within the lower separative human nature. It is the polar axis of automatic behaviour, as distinct from individuated freedom of choice, in which prior conditioning factors determine decisions according to habitual patterns of reaction.

The South Node holds all the seeds of the past, all those

instinctive behaviour patterns that dominate unconscious personalities, forming rigid or compulsive actions and which may often derive from attempts to ward off threats to individual survival. The South Node symbolises the accumulation of experiences, attitudes, beliefs, thoughts and personal values which form the current life-style; these may have been derived from parental sources during childhood, from racial, social and religious education, earlier childish experiences and world perceptions, or reputedly from past lives. It is at this point that the individual establishes habit patterns through regular repetition of actions, and indeed it is through such experiences that our childhood understanding unfolds.

Evaluating the South Node's position by sign and house, or through planetary aspects, may indicate what was present in the personality foundations at birth. It is a sphere of release for these personality contents, a sphere of natural expression which may be dedicated to personal exploitation, or directed towards benefiting the collective. The South Node is the easiest area of life for the individual to expand in, releasing those natural creative seeds with relatively little effort required.

The South Node displays two faces, one positive and constructive, aiding the future progress of unfolding the North Node potential, and the other more negative and destructive.

The positive dimension involves those innate abilities that are easily expressed, almost without any conscious effort; gifts that are present without the need for great training, which may be that individual's greatest assets. A child musical prodigy like Mozart is an extreme example of this, exhibiting later sublime musical abilities with a problematic personality. These hereditary gifts can be effectively used for personal benefits, or be creatively applied to regenerate the personality through the potential of the North Node.

The more negative dimension is often the most powerful, and also one that everyone has to contend with during life, the pull back towards habit, inertia, unsociability and those familiar pathways of least resistance. In some, this can manifest as an evasion of life, perpetually poking the embers of the ashes of the past, looking backwards, reliving past experiences and denying present and future prospects. The search for a 'golden age' is a regression towards the South Node principle if it means refusing to make any new developments, and is just a desire to repeat an illusory ideal past.

There may be characteristics within the psyche that the individual resists because they do not fit a particular self-image, repressing them and projecting them onto others and the world. Failing to adjust to changing circumstances is a negative South Node trait, and both the house and sign positions indicate likely points of 'undoing'. The house indicates the sphere of activity where through repetitive unconscious actions and decisions the individual may repeat mistakes, experience the consequences and become trapped. The sign reveals those types of activities that may be reacted to in a passive, negative or unconscious manner, thus creating additional personal difficulties and restricting opportunities for development. In such cases, those largely innate resources remain unexpressed, possibly becoming dissipated or distorted through lack of application, and so turning into negative energies circulating within a self-frustrating individual. An incorrect response to the South Node involves persistence in following that repetitive path, resisting the prospects of growth and development, and becoming trapped by the energies of inertia. New opportunities fail to be developed or die stillborn, and the North Node contact diminishes through lack of alignment.

A common response to the pull of the South Node is to return repeatedly to familiar sources of pleasure, expecting them to satisfy again and again. This is an avoidance of growth; our inheritance needs to be built on. The Dragon's Tail can become a point of retreat, a sanctuary to shelter in when life becomes too demanding and there are fears of being unable to cope; if not abused, this can be beneficial as a resting-place in which to regroup and re-integrate personal resources and balance. The South Node can be a point of security and stability, where consolidation can take place within a beleagured personality that may be passing through testing times. 'Going through the motions' is a common tendency at such phases. It may help to build a solid foundation for individual expansion and utilising intrinsic capabilities, especially if attempting to use the South Node energies in co-operation with purposes designed to activate the North Node potential.

It must be recognised that the roots of the Dragon's Tail go very deep within the psyche, and the South Node has been associated with the instinctive imprinting within the brain, those survival instincts which often manifest as a fear of progress, entering the unknown, and those preferences for favouring the present or past to the future. There are defensive mechanisms that can be activated at the South Node, and if these demarcation lines are inadvertently crossed, then the sense of identity becomes threatened. It may be that past lives can be accessed through attunement with this position; and, conversely, that future lives awaiting manifestation in time and space may be contacted through North Node attunement. We may display tendencies to repeat mistakes, failing to learn through experience. Unconscious activity often creates compulsive behaviour which blocks learning and adaptation to new experiences, and will eventually result in a diminution of vitality, loss of meaning, and disintegration. New ways need to be found to make a more effective contact with the fertilising inner sources, instead of becoming imprisoned in the circle of our own unconscious repetitive behaviour.

Yet the South Node also sows the seeds of its own undoing. It does not allow the individual to become truly comfortable resting. in its embrace. Its search for the perfect repetitive action often stimulates the awareness of individual failings and imperfection of expression as the ideal is rarely reached, and satisfaction is held back until that apogee is attained. This is a spur to eventual progress for many, even though there may be genuine doubts about their capacity to succeed. Those who still resist attain only stagnation and atrophy of innate talents. It is this confrontation with the need to rework habitual South Node behaviour patterns that holds the key to future progress and attunement to the North Node, as the two poles slowly move into relationship and balance with each other. This is the goal that is to be achieved.

WORKING WITH THE NODAL AXIS

It needs to be remembered that we are dealing with an inner axis of polarity that symbolises one process within our nature, that of our current interface in the present, reflecting what has past and anticipating what is to come. The challenge facing us is to integrate the two nodes, so that they do not operate in relative isolation from each other. Instead of attempting to align ourselves exclusively with either polarity, we need to discover a new point of balance at the fulcrum of the axis. Attaining such a position implies that we are able to respond equally to each nodal impulse, and capable of assimilating the newer North Node energies into our South Node patterns. Such an ideal is probably impossible to reach, but the concept of it may be beneficial as a pointer to the direction in which we need to go.

The preference for many is to remain close to the South Node, making only tentative steps towards experiencing North Node energies; yet it must be realised that our current South Node pattern was once our North Node potential. The necessity for conscious co-operation and relationship between the Nodes is indicated if we wish to grow towards embodying North Node purposes. Our perspective has to be committed to applying South Node abilities as a springboard for aligning with North Node development; we need to look at our South Node to see how we can release new potential through that foundation, seeing the process as one of ongoing unfoldment. Raising the level of our awareness to the next spiral is one way. If we have a strong pattern of material possessiveness emanating from the 2nd house, then we could rework that into attitudes and values associated with 'stewardship' of resources and possessions, learning to share more in a variety of ways and breaking down and transcending a pattern of individual possession and acquisitiveness, or a purely personal exploitation of resources. In many ways, the concepts of the New Age movement involve this process, of moving beyond existing patterns and creating more inclusive ones; this is a step away from the South Node operating in society towards a North Node concept of a 'new world' emerging for the Aquarian Age.

It may not be easy to take this path along the nodal axis. We are being asked to transform the raw material of ourselves into a new human pattern. Radical life-style changes are quite likely if progress begins to be made, although there will be many temptations to look back again at the familiar, secure world that we may be temporarily leaving.

THE NODES AND THE NATAL CHART

By analysing the nodal positions, we may find a powerful key to rearranging the inner psychological dynamics of our lives. The two houses linked by the nodal axis indicate those spheres of life where there is the potential for integrating the soli-lunar energies within the individual psychology. The nodal houses are more individually specific than the sign positions, and it is through them that we particularly express the distinct nodal energies. The two houses stimulate us to recognise the inner conflict between the Moon's unconscious habit patterns, our conditioning and security mechanisms, our fears of the unknown and consequent self-restriction and inhibition, and solar issues of self-determination and conscious decision-making, mediating the inner prompting of spiritual inspiration.

The signs in which the Nodes are placed indicate how we naturally express our nodal energies. This will be more obvious in terms of the South Node, as the North Node is likely to be still relatively unexpressed as the alignment needs further opening. In addition, looking at the planetary rulers of the nodal signs and their house position may offer other spheres of life through which the Nodes can be channelled or activated. These may be secondary sources, but may provide indications of which planets could be used either to transform the South Node or awaken the North Node. See if they make aspect to the Nodes. The house containing the North Node is particularly important as regards personal effort being made.

NODES AND PLANETARY ASPECTS

Any planetary aspect made to the South Node tends to indicate that those planetary qualities are overemphasised through habitual repetition, that there may be powerful conditioning influences derived from the past or personal patterns and tendencies (these are often ascribed to past lives and karma). Conjunctions to the South Node may imply highly emphasised planetary qualities or talents, which may, however, also act compulsively and unconsciously, being difficult to assimilate and integrate successfully into the life structure. A planet conjunct to the South Node can seem as if it is an independent aspect of the psyche, acting like a subpersonality when activated by external situations. Any such planet requires a closer look, as it will operate at a deep level of the personality, often having a much greater effect than may be consciously recognised. They will condition our world-view, and influence our habitual personality patterns, but without our being fully aware of it. A reworking of our relationship to such planets is indicated, and noting their role to the rest of the chart can be useful keys to show how we are being self-restrained in various ways.

Any planetary aspect made to the North Node tends to indicate that those planetary qualities need to be experienced and developed more fully, as they may be new qualities and faculties that are to be unfolded. Conjunctions to the North Node may imply that it is through the influence of the planet that we can align ourselves with the energies streaming through the North Node, those which can reveal our life-task and evolutionary direction. Studying the sign and house of this conjunction will indicate the type of positive expression required by the individual for progress. The conjunction planet can provide a channel of attunement to the North Node messages, although it will also influence our interpretation of such messages. There is still the difficulty of integrating these energies, establishing co-operation between the two poles of the nodal axis, and learning how to express it. If a transpersonal planet is aligned with the North Node, then working with it can prove to be especially beneficial, once any initial difficulties have been overcome.

Aspects which include sextiles and trines support personal attempts at resolving the polarities of opposing signs and houses, and can be worked with in that way. They may not be especially strong, but the trine can provide the image of the triangular model which could be successfully used in integration and resolution of the energies involved. Squares indicate considerable friction related to the relationship of that planet with the Node, with inner frustration and restriction being likely responses. This is the midpoint, and can reflect the previous proposed fulcrum image, which through inner stress and tension encourages us to resolve the conflict rather than evade it. Releasing the energies of this planet may prove to be very empowering for us, and offer a means to transcend the polarity of the nodal axis. Squares often prove to be a stimulus to inner growth, and any planet squaring the Nodes may be highly significant for the individual. Oppositions often project the inner contentious issues out into the world and onto people as an externalisation of the psychological Shadow. If involving the North Node, then it is possible that projections onto people may indicate ideals, messages, qualities that you are expected to embody yourself; if the South Node, then these may be projections onto people that you need to see yourself as embodying now, that you need to re-own, and then transform into new patterns, thus enabling yourself to move forwards.

If there are aspects made by the natal Moon to the North Node, this implies that further assimilation and integration of lunar qualities is needed for development. There may be a need to express lunar qualities and faculties, or to contact the inner feminine, the feeling tone of life will be emphasised, and a lunar psychism based on receptivity highlighted. If the aspects are challenging, then this may indicate that the unconscious mind is resisting the North Node messages, and that adjustment is needed. If Moon aspects are made to the South Node, then we may have an exaggerated behaviour formed by unconscious habit patterns, where innate tendencies dominate us and we act repetitively without clarity of awareness. Our lunar qualities are too developed and attuned to South Node resistances, and a transformation of psychological patterns is necessary for future growth. We may be attracted towards collective groupings for a sense of security and stability, and prefer not to break away from social traditional behaviour and attitudes. Our self-identification may be with established mass social groups, such as a church or a political organisation.

THE NODES THROUGH THE SIGNS

North Node Aries, South Node Libra

The major issue facing you is the development of a distinct identity of your own, one which is not reliant on dependent relationships, derived from others' perceptions of you, or founded on their dominating attitudes, beliefs and values. Lacking a firm identity can lead to indecision and confusion, especially when challenged by important life-decisions, and you often prefer to allow others to decide for you. As relationships appear so vital to your sense of security and stability, you try to please those on whom you are so dependent; yet if this is misapplied through a lack of self-knowledge, then you can begin losing sight of your own needs, desires and aims. By nourishing and nurturing others, you may forget to take due care of your own needs.

You need to be wary of a tendency to be gullible and im-pressionable. You will need to outgrow this and take more responsibility for evaluating your own situation and options, or else that earlier tendency will continue to interfere with major decisions. At points of crisis, self-division will only bring additional confusion and pain, and instead of wanting to travel along either all or none of the available directions open to you, you will have to become more single-minded and decisive. You need to move in the direction indicated by your intuition, following that inner guidance. Through your faith in this you can unfold your potential in a unique manner, be true to your own nature, and in so doing, teach yourself to honour your whole individuality.

By being overly sensitive to others' needs, and tending to confuse them with your own unfulfilled desires, you may become prone to a loss of vital energies, leading to occasional depression. It becomes essential for you to acknowledge and assert your own requirements, and take responsibility for satisfying them, as these are important for self-nurturing, personal growth and integration. This is the crucial first step towards their expression and release. Whilst a concept of service to others may remain a motivating, inspiring force, your first priority must be to yourself, so that you achieve integration of your whole being, instead of fragmenting yourself through relationship dependency. Once this is achieved, you will be able to serve from a more effective perspective. When you attain a state of inner harmony, then the energies which flow from you will also express that quality, even though many people may find those energies uncomfortable due to their own disharmonious state.

Your new approach needs to be assertive in a way that also respects the nature of relationship, connecting self and others for mutual harmony and benefit. Actions need to be evaluated in terms of nourishment, so that you are being true to yourself and also co-operating with others. If you acknowledge your own inner nature, your relationships will be able to move towards deeper contacts, so that all partnerships are enriched through enhanced mutual understanding. Often that Libran energy is revealed when you try to balance out people, ideas and situations, mediating between opposite conditions, taking a centre position struggling to create harmony. The new balance that is indicated is one of self and others, involving an inner balance in your attitudes, becoming independent and asserting your individuality, whilst expressing an interdependence within relationship. This can be achieved through transforming your dependency traits.

North Node Taurus, South Node Scorpio

You will attempt to build a new set of personal values, to provide a firm foundation in your life. One of the difficulties facing you will be the influence of the Scorpio energy, which as part of the transformation will serve to undermine any foundations which are not capable of resisting its pressure. This can be viewed positively as an inadequate structure would not be safe enough for you anyway. Because you will experience this subversive action, you are likely to develop a defensive reaction towards those attempts to determine your life-style and personal values; eventually though, you should succeed in building a solid structure and benefit from the struggle to do so.

There will be a tendency for you to look for personal pleasure in the sorts of relationships which have seeds of joy and pain within them from the beginning; your choices determine which seeds will eventually bear fruit. It may be that in your younger days your choices were less suitable, and if they still are, then perhaps you should look closely at why this is so. It could simply be because you enter with your eyes closed, both to your own nature and needs, and to the nature of your prospective partner. Seeds of destruction may be present, and if they emerge amidst confusion, your Scorpionic energy expresses itself again. If you remain ignorant of this aspect of your nature, even more opportunities are created for the Scorpio energy to undermine your actions and directions, as it seeks to drive you towards greater self-growth and understanding. Learn how to see it as a wise friend helping you (although a little roughly at times) and then you will be able to use its power to achieve your new objectives.

It is likely that you will experience periodic crises (turning/decision points) in your life, stimulated by this brooding inner revolution, and conflict is inevitable, especially in closer and more intimate family relationships. You are not always moderate, sometimes having a mistrust of others, which can also lead to friction. This can arise from tendencies to scheme and manipulate, which can be automatically unconsciously projected onto others, and you see or imagine them doing the same to you. Many of your problems stem from yourself, and you will have exchanges with others where through your own actions, you 'force' them to react to you in ways which serve to confirm your previous perception of them, reflecting your own preconceptions. Once you observe this phenomenon, you can begin to change as you learn to see that more hidden inner side of your nature in action.

Due to your inner intensity, you may experience strong feelings of anger and frustration when things are not going your way, and the tendency may be to vent these frustrations on those closest to you. You need to find and develop suitable channels of expression for this potent energy to be released in a positive and creative way. As has been noted, it can be a difficult energy to handle correctly, and one of its main uses is to resolve inner conflicts and dilemmas. Perhaps by learning to trust life and others more, distinguishing between needs and wants, you may discover that you are surrounded by all that you really need, but have not fully recognised that fact. You are looking for stability, and can by your own choices and reactions begin to bring calm to your turmoil or stimulate it into renewed activity.

North Node Gemini, South Node Sagittarius

The main themes here include the search for freedom, and the needs for knowledge, understanding, meaning and purpose in life. Often, you will feel uncomfortable within society, as your impulse for freedom is so powerful that you will react strongly against any attempts to restrict and limit you, and much of your energy is devoted to retaining that free independence, especially if you feel threatened. This can lead to problems related to issues of commitment or relationship, and this inner impulse needs to be acknowledged by yourself and by anyone intimately involved with you. You may tend to justify your evasive actions by an attitude of self-righteousness, but this can become destructive to your social relationships unless you choose to co-operate with others.

This pattern of selfish naivety needs to be modified, and you may become aware that most of the tendencies in others that you dislike are actually reflections of patterns within you that you have failed to accept and understand. A more searching process of self-enquiry is necessary, as it may be that your expression of freedom can only be gained at the expense of another's freedom, resulting in a future restriction for them. Is this what you want? And is it a denial of the freedom impulse present in everyone? Perhaps a re-evaluation of the effect of your actions on others is required.

A greater focus may be needed in your life, as by diversifying your interests and efforts too widely you may fail to complete things unfinished or skimping on quality. A clearer vision of your purpose may be needed, and that tendency to rush completion in order to feel free again may be preventing a satisfactory end product. One lesson that you may have to learn is that through a frantic search for freedom you actually create an opposite reaction, culminating in a position where less freedom and fewer choices are available. Look at your life, see if this has been occurring, and note whether your results have been different to your initial intention.

It is in the development of your mind that a deeper freedom can emerge, through study, knowledge, understanding and the emergence of a life philosophy and purpose. That Sagittarian impulse towards freedom needs to be transformed into a mental search, and this may develop later in life as you become aware that your earlier education was inadequate to your needs. As the energy becomes more internalised, you are likely to develop a greater affinity for cultural expressions of the intellect, particularly for language. The issue may be how that accumulation of knowledge and information is being used, and whether you are capable of applying it in daily living.

Forging this into a personal belief system is the next step, and as you begin to unfold a sense of meaning and purpose in life, these beliefs will be tested in the fires of experience. Vision generates direction, and serves as a unifying centre to the individual, both fulfilling the Sagittarian needs and offering a focus for the Gemini juggling of facts and information. Mental stimulation will become more important for you, as will learning and communicating your discoveries. Through these, new routes for social relationship may form, in which your interaction is more purposeful and less egotistically evasive. Gaining a higher perspective on your personality and life will transform your attitudes, and you may find that you can settle more into deeper relationships. Freedom is the goal for everyone, freedom to be themselves; you are not to deny your impulse towards this state, but it should be consciously moderated by insights so that ideally positive results are created for all, as the challenge is to be both socially constructive and individually free.

North Node Cancer, South Node Capricorn

The challenge here involves the confrontation with the rigidity of the Capricornian influence on your personality, especially within your expectations of respect from others and your secret feelings of self-importance and superiority. Much of your sense of identity is associated with your social relationships and prestige, and it may be that most of your attitudes and actions are coloured by your hopes that they will enhance your social position; this becomes a major determining factor in your choices. The nature of your social acquaintances and relationships is also likely to be similarly influenced by that need for social status.

It is social image and 'face' that must be upheld, and you find any public loss of dignity or respect extremely traumatic. In several ways, there is an insecurity of identity hidden away, a need for the acknowledgement of others to help you to define your own identity and to feel good about yourself. Take away the attention and respect of others and you may rapidly deflate. You like to feel wanted and important, and may assume responsibilities that are too great for you, and then stagger under the weight of the burden, becoming a martyr and expecting both admiration and sympathy from others. Failure is seen as anathema to you, and you hate to admit any personal shortcomings as that diminishes your self-respect; intolerance of failure spills over into the rest of your attitudes, and your assumed standards may lack an understanding of human fallibility, even though you may not always attain them yourself.

In maintaining that self-imposed personal image to others, there can be a tendency to evade situations where failure may occur or inadequacy be exposed, even to the extent of psychosomatic illness resulting from inner conflicts and pressures. You prefer to impose control and management on life and those around you, and this can create family tension at times if it becomes oppressive.

Your world-view tends to be fixed and preconceived, with evaluations of others made by looking through these imposed filters of opinion, attitudes, beliefs, values and standards. Many fail to match your purist and self-righteous ideal, which perhaps secretly pleases you and satisfies that tendency towards assumed superiority that may be present.

Yet the question is, does this life-perspective fulfil you, or are you involved in an ongoing struggle to retain it intact as a support and protection for a less self-assured personality? You know that you dislike anyone probing your personal life beyond the boundaries that you choose to establish, and that you become highly sensitive to any criticism, often preferring to withdraw into your armoured shell rather than engage in open and honest confrontation. Do those barriers really help you, or do they actually imprison you, restricting your appreciation and enjoyment of life within a rigid personality structure.

The Cancer North Node is offering a way out from the impasse. Attitudes of assumed superiority always have the result of diminishing contact with life and restricting relationships, and often end in the delusions of an inflated ego, especially if power over others has been achieved. You need to break free of those self-imposed barriers between yourself and others, learn how to give more, acknowledging and helping to fulfil the needs of others instead of only being prepared to take their approval and admiration. The feminine aspects of your nature need to be expressed more fully; you need to give sustenance, to be receptive, to value relationship and communication, to be sensitive to the struggles of humanity instead of feeling content sitting on your pedestal. Once you can accept, understand and express your emotional nature more fluidly and honestly, a greater personal integration can occur, and the rigidity of those misapplied Capricornian tendencies can dissolve. Admitting that even you can be wrong sometimes is a step forward. You need those waters of emotion to transform and heal you, so that your life can become more enriched and relaxed, free from the obsessive need to control, manage and manipulate, and so you can begin to value people and feelings more. If you can make this shift, great benefits are yours to take, and you will have the opportunity to perceive and relate to life in a new satisfying light.

North Node Leo, South Node Aquarius

For your personal unfoldment and growth, you will need to become more self-expressive and focused in applying your will, so that your energies are aimed towards a purposeful direction. This can be a major challenge for you, as there may be a tendency to dissipate energies in several directions at once, partly due to this lack of future focus and planning. You may need to realise that present thoughts, actions, values and attitudes have their consequences in future experiences. The key is understanding that what we do today creates tomorrow, and that a favourable future depends on our choices and decisions now. We build the future edifice on the foundations of today. If our choices now are misguided, then we will have to face the inevitable consequences and likely suffering later.

In order to achieve this new and clarified life-direction, you will probably have to step out from the consensus mass consciousness of society indicated by the South Node Aquarius. This does not mean becoming eccentric or socially alienated: rather, it is a step towards becoming more self-reliant and independent, taking greater responsibility for your own choices and life-path. The positive gains of this can include a more stable sense of identity, self-knowledge and understanding, and the emergence of a genuine and deep self-confidence. Moving beyond unnecessary self-doubts, you may realise that once you determine that life-direction, then there are relatively few obstacles to block your progress or distract you from eventual achievement. Asking others for guidance may be unwise, and could weaken your own determination or send you in the wrong direction; instead, you need to seek guidance within. Once this life-direction is clear, then you will discover that meaning and purpose are present, and pursuing that task will engage your will-power.

Yet this is not a self-centred path that you are searching for; it is one which combines greater independent self-expression with the awareness of social relationship and interdependence. Your growth will benefit others as well as yourself. From your new perspective, you may feel free from many of society's usual preoccupations. Building a personal value structure is important, and you will try to stay true with those guiding life principles which offer a firm inner foundation from which to live.

It will be through the North Node house that the new creative direction will be focused and expressed, and as your new world-view unfolds, you will feel inspired to share your beliefs more widely. Your sense of a heart embrace of society will deepen as your feelings of responsibility and contribution expand. That humanistic idealism and altruistic spirit will shine more clearly, and you will try to transform yourself more towards that ideal, so that your direction becomes a contribution to the larger world. The issue is individual and group growth, and may be concentrated on themes of social fairness and equality. Once that focus is attained, you may move towards a role as an inspirational leader in some capacity, attempting to stimulate beneficial change within established traditional practices and thought. This may generate mixed reactions, especially as certain attitudes may be a little before their time, and therefore difficult for most people to absorb. But it is essential for you to retain your independent spirit, so that your transformation into enhanced positive creativity indicates one which society can also make. For yourself, directing your energies in ways which are in accord with your true nature will bring deep satisfaction. There is a joyous energy present when one moves closer to being oneself, and this wild joyous spirit can be yours; but you should never forget the existence and needs of others, because your path is formed by living your humanitarian ideals.

North Node Virgo, South Node Pisces

One of the major challenges facing you is that of relating your inner nature, with its emotionally sensitive perceptions, to the outer world, in a way that becomes creatively positive and which forms a bridge between the spiritual and the physical. The Piscean trait of dependency may emerge as reliance on others to define your life-direction, perhaps through earlier social and parental conditioning, which will also influence your own perception of your nature and identity.

Your weak spot is your emotional nature, and you will be highly compassionate, strongly feeling the suffering and pain in the world through an empathic attunement to the anguish of others. This leads to an attempt to minimise pain for others, and will be displayed in efforts to be diplomatic and tactful, often by not saying – or even inwardly acknowledging – what you really do feel and think. You try to mould yourself in ways which avoid giving offence to others, but in doing so, you can damage your inner integrity and confuse yourself by ignoring the strengths of your own feelings and reactions. A combination of sympathetic sensitivity and inner/outer evasion can begin to drain and distort your energies and solidity of identity, leaving you more open to be abused by unscrupulous characters.

Those emotions will dominate your judgements and decision-making, and you may need to gain more clarity as to your real needs, desires and thoughts. Saying 'no' to others often poses problems, and your resolution is easily undermined by others appealing to your vulnerable emotions and persuading you to change your mind.

There can be a tendency towards escapism, day-dreaming and fantasies, retreating into an ideal and perfect inner world. This is the conflict between illusions and the external reality, the interplay of the Virgoan dream of perfection and the Piscean dream of idealism. A misapplication of these can lead you into a trap where your ability to deal with the world is impaired. You need to assert your own reality more when confronted by others, acknowledge that your own individuality is of equal importance, and become less passive and self-sacrificing in attitude. You can contribute much to society when you begin to work with your strengths, which can be derived from an idealistic vision which is applied in daily life to benefit others and to enhance the quality of the world. A concept of service can be developed which embraces an understanding of how to serve, when to serve, how to receive from others, and how to recognise those whom you can benefit.

You may display a high degree of idealism, but until you achieve self-confidence, you may limit your manifestation of these ideals, or even give up making the effort. Yet it will be the lessons that you can learn from these struggles that can strengthen you; disillusionment is often the most effective teacher. The challenge is that despite the pain and the struggle, you continue to maintain that dream of peace and love ruling the world. You have to live out your own beliefs, principles and idealistic vision in the outer world; they have no validity if they remain as dreams, and need testing in the fires of daily experience. It is a grounding of your sensitivity, spirituality and vision of the ideal world that is required; even in a small way, it is a step forward. Facing the conflict between illusion and reality, you will always search for a better state for yourself and others; much enlightenment can come to you when you realise why people tend to suffer so much, but in this is also the key to your own suffering. The more conscious you can become of your own nature, the less you need to lean on others; the more you test the applicability of your beliefs in real life, the more your understanding of your ideals can develop in a pragmatic and practical way. You may find that applying your imagination – perhaps through the techniques of creative visualisation – is especially beneficial in self-healing and transformation, and within that Virgoan impulse to serve through working for the community in a manner which corresponds to that Piscean vision of fulfilment for all.

North Node Libra, South Node Aries

This indicates that you may have to learn more about the lessons of co-operation in relationships, and how you can give to satisfy the needs of others. You should become less preoccupied with your own needs and sense of identity and focus on how you can work to make all your relationships more meaningful and harmonious through conscious co-operation, rather than expressing an egocentric and selfish attitude.

You are likely to experience a competitive drive, preferring always to be first, but this powerful individualism and pioneering spirit is not really meant to benefit you: it is meant to enable you to give more to others. There is much in life waiting for you to stop and recognise its presence, and you would benefit by actually taking time to listen to other people who can reveal to you other aspects of life that in your eagerness and haste you had never registered or considered of any value. It is ultimately of little use to drive yourself on when you do not really know why or to what objective you are aiming towards. You may need to stop and re-evaluate your direction and aims in order to direct your energy into a clearly defined purpose.

Your energy may often be experienced as restless and impatient, and you will note that you often change your mind and find it difficult to remain single-minded about any course of action, investigating each new possibility that arises but rarely knowing exactly what you are looking for. Each direction that you choose to take may seem unfulfilling, a cul-de-sac, a destination which allows little rest or permanence. What you may need to realise is that you cannot be an island: you need other people. Until you learn how to share and to give, then you may find that everything you achieve falls flat, because it is not meant for you alone. Indeed, you may pass through phases when it appears that life is against you, with many painful confrontations to chip away at your ego. It may appear that you are failing to receive your desires, and it becomes frustrating to see others around you apparently making progress towards achieving their desires and needs. Even though you begin applying more effort, your aims seem to move further away. What may be necessary is a transformation in your outlook, so that your efforts are no longer devoted exclusively to your own benefit, but benefit others too. Instead of feeling envious, you should be pleased for them; until you truly base your life on co-operative sharing, and in a sense, turn it around, then you may stay frustrated in receiving satisfaction for your own desires. You will probably react against this lesson, but that would be your own free choice, and an expression of a contrary nature.

In your social relationships, you will often find that you stand in a central position as 'referee', and you will have to learn how to help others to resolve their problems without taking sides; here you will learn about and encourage the application of co-operation as an energy of goodwill and harmony. You may learn a great deal from marriage, with its potential conflict between partners and opportunities for creative co-operation, and it may represent the dilemma which faces you during this life. It is likely that you already register the fact that your relationships could be more satisfying and meaningful, and that they do not revolve around your needs alone; your intense self-regard must expand to include all others, and once you see and accept that life could be much better by sharing with others, your life will become a more harmonious and fulfilling one.

North Node Scorpio, South Node Taurus

This indicates that in order for you to move beyond those restrictive and resistant patterns symbolised by the house position of Taurus, certain radical changes in your attitude may be required. These are likely to be related to Taurean possessive tendencies or material possessions which are seen as helping provide stability and security in life. The desire for pleasure, comfort and home enjoyments can deepen materialistic patterns, so that your needs involve possession, and a corresponding diminution of real enjoyment of things that you do not possess. Contentious issues may arise from this possessive impulse, over material items, or over people and family matters; relationships may be detrimentally affected if this tendency becomes excessive or fails to be consciously modified. People rarely like feeling owned by anyone, and a family grouping is one sphere where this authoritarian and commanding role is both easily applied and abused, particularly by emotional or forceful manipulation of circumstances in your favour.

It may be difficult to avoid slipping into a repetitive habitual life-style, especially when you have created one protected from the vagaries of change and disruption. This is the Taurean placidity, a ruminative enjoyment of stability and security. Yet even that accumulation of possessions will begin to weigh heavy, restricting freedom, and eventually the undermining Scorpio energy of transformation will begin to shake those foundations. If much of your sense of identity has been displaced into external possessions, then this may become a vulnerable area, demanding change.

You may take time and be a slower learner than most, relying on the absorption of established and traditional social attitudes for your perspective on life. Through moving at your own pace and learning in your own manner, you develop fixed foundations which you rely on for security and as a barrier resisting external influences and change. Yet you may need to form a new centre of personal identity, one which is based on the higher values of a less self-centred position. A reorientation is necessary, from the outer world towards inner self-possession and self-understanding. This becomes a new assertion of self-esteem, value and power, but not in an exploitative style, and is based on inner security rather than on external supports, habit patterns and possessions. Personal talents and material resources are applied for constructive practical action, consciously directed towards building a new life-style.

An understanding of the tension between the Taurus resistance to change and the Scorpio impulse to transform is necessary. You may find that at some point the Scorpio energies undermine your efforts to create stability, by somehow frustrating them or making you discontented with your achievement; this will encourage you to transform those behaviour patterns into less restrictive and more open forms. Such experiences may prove to be uncomfortable, and may lead you to 'burn your bridges behind you', releasing the ties of the past and being receptive to the new future experiences. That dependency on inner repetitive patterns of thought and action or external possessions may be dissolved by the Scorpionic transformation. It is not a negative experience, despite your reactions to its impact, but one which is designed to liberate you into new freedom. The degree to which you have to release current life-patterns will depend on your resistance; the more you resist, the more you will have to 'pay' for transformation. It is a form of rebirth that awaits you, and may be unavoidable. The old has to be replaced by the new, and you may be advised to welcome this transformative crisis whenever it arrives, because it is for your own benefit, even though intitially you may not choose to perceive it in that light.

North Node Sagittarius, South Node Gemini

Your Gemini energy tends to make you restless, striving for stimulation and diversity of interests and experience, and encourages an active life-style. Whenever you feel restricted in any way, whether at work, in relationships, or in those attitudes, thoughts and emotions you are permitted to express, you begin to feel extremely uncomfortable, and will look for a way to change the situation. Your mind is alert and very receptive to that multitude of impressions and information that you absorb from daily life and other people, yet due to these quicksilver changes of attention you may find concentration difficult to maintain.

Changeability is strong in your personality, resulting in indecision and regular changes of mind and emotions. That mutability of nature is displayed in the way your personality seems to change according to the company you find yourself in. You find evaluation of choices challenging, as you perceive the virtues of opposing decisions and actions, recognising that from each perspective, each option presents a valid position. This inhibits your decision-making ability, as you fear that moving to either position will lose the value in the other. Personal decisions are difficult to determine, and when you are in the situation of evaluating the viewpoints of others, you often take the easiest way out, which is to agree with whichever one is the most persuasively and powerfully expressed. The danger with this is that you may lose sight of your own beliefs, values and feelings.

You find discrimination difficult, and try to resist giving commitments because you are likely to change your mind too often. Refusing to make responsible choices, you try to be agreeable to all, or else echo the attitudes of whoever you are with, only to change again chameleon-like when with others. This may add to social acceptability, but can be damaging to your own potential and deeper nature. The Sagittarius North Node indicates that you need to develop a more personal unifying life-philosophy that can act as a foundation in your life, a belief or purpose which offers meaning and individual clarity, rather than moving with the winds of superficiality, diversity and mutability.

This becomes the issue of direction, and it is probable that you will at least be in your late twenties before you begin to accept the need for a more purposeful life-direction, and then start to look for it; guiding indications may come from an influential older person. One important step is to modify your reflective nature, to become more capable of determining your own attitudes and feelings, irrespective of whether or not they are pleasing to others. Neither with all sides nor agreeing with none leads anywhere; and you have to find your own light. Changing this habitual pattern may not be easy, but you will benefit from progress towards being yourself. Joy will be released as you feel free to express your own nature, and it is liberating to be natural and real without any compulsion to agree with others. Take those tentative steps to release the past, and to enter the present and future as yourself, because you have much promise and much to offer. At least then you will realise that whilst a coin has two sides, it is just one coin, and that whilst life has a multitude of faces, it is just one life.

North Node Capricorn, South Node Cancer

The Cancer South Node suggests that you will be attracted to the past, looking back to your roots, reliving old experiences and memories, and retaining childlike, escapist habits and emotional responses. There is probably a degree of immaturity present, which can manifest as a resistance to viewing the whole of life, a preference for seeing life through a selective filter which cuts out that which is undesirable or painful. Maturity involves seeing the whole, and not turning away from facing those parts which you pretend are not there; and this is the challenge facing you, the growth towards greater maturity and responsibility.

You may feel dependent on others, and maintain sentimental attachments to people and nostalgic possessions, trying to preserve all relationships from ever ending or even changing. Often this dependency becomes a reliance on others for solving your problems, rather than an assumption of personal responsibility, and one extreme form may be the generation of psychosomatic illness in order to receive attention and support. Your feelings are highly sensitised, and these are vulnerable if relationships fail; your natural reaction is to cling on, hoping that things will improve. What is necessary to you are those feelings of being loved and taken care of, and you rarely spend time analysing the nature of any relationship or why it failed. Your interest is in personal satisfaction and the fulfilment of emotional nourishment; the path of self-discovery may appear too dry to appeal to you. The concept of changing yourself in order to improve the chances of successful relationships does not initially attract.

The past has a strong hold over you, and you may indulge in dream memories of a 'golden age'. Due to that attraction to the past, you may become involved in activities which maintain the past in the present; this could involve you in traditional attitudes and ways of life, by supporting the old ways and resisting more modern viewpoints. You may try to avoid the obligations of the present as they imply the responsibility of creating the future. Only you can face your own future, and it is by conscious choice in the present that you can build your chosen future; by avoiding this action now, you leave your tomorrow dependent on circumstances beyond your control, and lose any sense of meaning and life-direction.

The way forward is to become self-nurturing, taking responsibility for your own choices and actions by accepting the need for maturity. Learn how to look forward more, let go of that accumulation of memories, feelings and childlike needs which you have used as a place of retreat and a means of inner support. Through maturation, a new destiny awaits you, and it is the fear of the unknown that you are trying to evade; yet through such an evasion, you may unconsciously create conditions that are difficult for you, which in themselves will still drive you towards maturity, but which will do so with more attendant pain. This is not to be a negative destiny, and in fact it holds seeds of great personal potential and benefit for you once you openly confront and acknowledge the new path. You'll discover a new inner strength, stablised emotions and self-sufficiency as you move into this new phase of growth, and life will seem less threatening and much more enriching as you open your eyes wider to the diversity and complexity of the modern world.

North Node Aquarius, South Node Leo

The challenge facing you is the movement away from a self-centred preoccupation towards one of greater connectedness and contribution to society. As you have a tendency to feel yourself to be the centre of the universe, this potential shift in attitude may pose difficulties. You may need to transform that egocentric perspective, breaking down any attitudes of assumed superiority and any belief in the inviolability of your own ideas and opinions. That Leo South Node is likely to enjoy recognition or social attention, and you may be attracted to basking in the reflection of the company of people who have some public or local fame, as it can amplify your belief in being special. You may attempt to apply your will-power to fulfil your desires and ambitions for self-gratification and personal advantage alone, with the house position of the South Node denoting the particular sphere of personal desire and endeavour. Yet, feeding your pride and having to maintain your dignity may become restrictive for you, standing in the way of experiencing a deeper feeling of interdependence with life.

Self-assertion will come naturally to you, but you may find that by being too dominating you create problems within closer relationships, and unless your assertiveness can be matched by an equally strong partner, one whom you learn to respect, there may be an inherent source of conflict present. This could come from any attempts to impose your will, to such a degree that a progressive fragmentation of your partner's individuality occurs under the impact of your energy, which may force them either to submit passively or leave in order to reconnect to themselves. This dominating energy may not be expressed in a deliberately conscious manner by you, but may be 'received' by a partner through the psychological environment in a purely subjective manner. Pay due regard to your influence, and note also those times when your will is thwarted by others or by circumstances, and observe how your reaction is rarely graceful in defeat – you will probably have a tendency to brood in resentment and wonder why your will-power failed to work.

You may need to discover the essential values in life, so that you stop wasting energy in unfruitful directions, and begin applying it towards what offers greater personal meaning and benefits others too. Sometimes you may rush off, chasing romantic dreams, but determining what is important has to come first. Once you clarify what is personally important, then this insight can serve as a life guide; to reach this stage, though, may require a confrontation with experiences that reveal the consequences of unsatisfactory choices, aims, values and directions.

The fundamental conflict will occur between personal desires and the potential contribution that you could make towards the creation of a more caring and humanitarian society. This is the pull of Aquarius, asking you to join the world-wide work by using your talents, gifts and energies to benefit others, rather than just for personal aims. Once you succeed in releasing all that is personally inessential and limiting, and manage to refocus your attitudes, then you will be free to explore new horizons. This is the real direction through which you can satisfy that need to feel 'special', as your nature is suited to exploring the uncharted lands of the future. The image of a 'pathfinder' is apt and indicates your way in life. You need to find the cause which is inwardly summoning you to follow the Aquarius energy, because that will give meaning and purpose to life, much more than chasing your desires. This cause will reflect the vision of a new society, based upon universal brotherhood, and you can choose to contribute to this in either a small or a larger way; the main task is to share in the group work. Aquarius promises you a special adventure; this will be a challenge to your will and your belief in being special, and will be quite capable of satisfying your ambitious drives, making full use of your potential and resources – yet it will also be a uniquely personal experience.

North Node Pisces, South Node Virgo

The house position of the Virgo South Node will be an area that is especially liable to reflect your tendency towards individual rigidity and repetition of habit patterns and fixed attitudes. This fixity in the face of a changing life and world is starting to feel limiting and restrictive to you now, even though it is an automatic set of reactions that is activated during daily life; you recognise that your responses are not often spontaneous or free, but are habitual and predictable. The problem is that you do not know how to become free of these binding inner personality patterns, may be afraid to break free, and would not know how to respond to life without their protective barriers, as you rely on them for a sense of security. With the Piscean North Node pointing the way forward, you may find that a series of confrontations and experiences in life undermine your preference for structure and order, or reveal its inadequacies. Through shifting circumstances, your rigidity of response may prove unable to cope with challenges, causing you to awaken slowly to the need for a radical change within your self-perception, attitudes, values and beliefs.

Sometimes you feel that the world can be a threatening place, and you often hold mixed feelings about people too. Part of this arises from an insecurity of identity, and a fear of relaxing your guard, so you attempt to protect yourself by establishing barriers of caution and distance between yourself and others, and by distancing yourself from experiences. By generating this barrier of separation and maintaining those restrictive habit patterns, you may also be creating states of dis-ease and health problems associated with the centre of your body. If you cannot trust life, you may amplify forms of tension and stress related to those needs for caution and rigid order, and may trigger off actual physical disease in your body, or psychosomatic illnesses. This can create a vicious circle by making you more certain that the world is an unhealthy place to live in, so long as you fail to become conscious of the probability that through your own attitudes you are contributing to your own ill health.

You may need to accept the totality of your whole nature more, so that any tendencies towards repression do not create additional inner conflicts and tensions. One vulnerable area could involve the relationship between your emotions and your sexual expression. This may be influenced by your dominant moral views and attitudes of relationships and sexuality. You may feel uneasy with your feeling responses, perhaps having a tendency to withdraw emotionally from intimacy, and an inner refusal to become too emotionally involved in relationships due to that fear of emotional pain. If this occurs, then greater self-enquiry and modification of habit patterns may prove beneficial.

Your Virgoan tendencies towards mental analysis and separation may begin to be limiting, imparting an excessive seriousness to your world-view, and diminishing both your sense of proportion and your sense of humour. That analytical, dissecting approach can work against you, in that you observe the pieces of the puzzle but are unable to comprehend the whole picture; if you become too involved with the separate pieces, you may also lose the prospect of peace of mind, as the rearranging never ceases.

It is by attuning to the Pisces Node that the lessons of trust and faith in life may be learned. That endless pattern of separating and categorising life into a multitude of fragments and attempting to order it into sectional life should be transcended. Life is a whole, and you are interdependent with the world; there is no real separation, and this understanding will give you peace of mind. The stimulus for this movement may be the dissolving of your plans for an ordered life. You need to search for a unifying approach to life, one which unites the pieces instead of emphasising them. For this proposed radical change, you will have to be prepared to release the past and habitual Virgoan tendencies so that you can embrace the Piscean experience of the unified mind at one with the world.

THE NODES THROUGH THE HOUSES

North Node 1st House, South Node 7th House

This indicates that your main area of personal development involves focusing on issues of identity and relationship. The 7th house South Node suggests that you have a tendency to become dependent on others, and in so doing, submerge your own identity in the process, perhaps by acquiescence to their will, desires and needs. You may lack self-esteem, as often your self-image is reflected by others' perceptions and evaluations of you. This can obviously be misleading and tends to create a distorted picture of self, particularly as you allow their views to influence your behaviour. Yet relationship needs will play an important role in your life, and you are liable to devote much of your time and attention to satisfying them.

It is likely that you need to become less dependent on others, and to build your own sense of identity instead of relying on others to define it for you. Through self-understanding, you can live by your own light, but until you can achieve this, the probability is that you will remain too highly influenced by the wills and desires of others. Through your desire to please, you have denied and repressed aspects of your own identity, needs and desires, and through your tendency towards self-sacrifice you have lost contact with your deeper identity.

Whilst you are correct in believing in the virtues of co-operation and harmony within relationships, being too submissive to other more assertive personalities becomes damaging, and there are other ways of relating that can be beneficial to all concerned. Discovering this alternative path is the challenge facing you. You may have to begin to assert your own nature, needs and desires, and hopefully you will be able to do so in a harmonious way. You may find that due to previous reliance on others in deciding courses of action, when you start being self-assertive you enter into conflict with those who have up till now taken you for granted. They may find it difficult to deal with the new you that is emerging as you respond to the 1st house North Node energy. Such difficulties must be faced and relationships rebalanced and adjusted; reverting to a submissive or passive attitude will be detrimental.

Ideally, you will balance the growth towards expressing your full identity with an openness to the richness and complexity offered by relationships. Initially, this may cause relationship challenges, and your style of assertion may be damaging at times. Moderation may be required, especially if you suddenly attempt to embody a 'new you' overnight, or try to become dominant over others. You will need to be aware of how you are treating others, as you move from being passive to being more active in relationship, and balance will be necessary as you unfold your personality and attempt to harmonise your needs with those of partners. For some, the transition could involve the dissolution of older patterns of relationship, and the formation of new ones suitable for the new phase of life. Growth will not happen overnight, and will come slowly and with considerable effort. But have faith: your struggles will prove to have been worthwhile in the end.

North Node 2nd House, South Node 8th House

The 8th house South Node is liable to create an inner pattern which is related to protecting personal secrets, which may be associated with feelings of undefined guilt and individual insecurity. One approach to your need for self-protection is likely to be the weaving of misleading webs around yourself, almost from a fear of letting anyone get too close to you. This insecurity will influence your relationships, and there may be fears of social condemnation of your attitudes and personality if they become revealed. Usually these fears are unfounded, yet they do create inner stress and pressure, affecting your social communication and often causing you to withdraw from more open and intimate contacts.

You may have a tendency to undermine things, as you probably lack firm personal values, and this has a negative effect on your sense of identity. You tend to challenge the value structures of others in a manner which undermines them, dislodging them from their own secure foundations. Lacking definite values yourself, you fail to appreciate their role in creating stability in the lives of others. Often, through no deliberate action of your own, you can have a disruptive effect on others.

You may feel that you are not socially acceptable, although your own peculiar isolationist stance is a prime contributor to this, as are your deeper insecurities; but simultaneously, you also desire to be a part of that society which another part of you is rejecting. Pain may arise from those feelings related to fears of social rejection, and through avoidance of these, you withdraw from deeper social involvement. The danger is that these feelings can create a vicious circle, making you want to undermine people and society deliberately, to punish them for your own lack of social adaptation and integration. Feelings that you deserve more than you receive, coupled with a knowledge that you are failing to make a suitable effort, create contradictions which generate suffering, inner discord and dissatisfaction.

Sexuality will have a high profile in your life, and much attention will be devoted to its expression. Yet a change of attitude may be required, especially if you are using sex as a means of obtaining power over others, or as a means of working out aggressive energies. Through deeper and more honest sexual experience, a path towards enhanced harmony with others could be discovered, by which much of your relationship negativity and confusion could be transformed.

It is essential to align yourself with the 2nd house North Node energy, learning to develop and build the foundations of your own personal values and world-view, based on what is personally important to you. You need to look honestly at yourself, define your values and seek to apply them in daily life. Once you learn to respect and honour your own values, you will cease to undermine those of others, and instead respect them too. As you begin to achieve success in recreating yourself, relationships will also improve and become more satisfying. You will discover a new affinity with society, and through acceptance, much of that self-rejection and disruptive pain will be dissolved. You can benefit greatly from self-directed changes along these lines. Human nature is much more flexible and amenable to change than is often realised; choosing to change will offer considerable insight into your own nature, and you could become of great use to others in helping them to effect a positive transformation in their lives.

North Node 3rd House, South Node 9th House

One of your major tendencies is the urge towards freedom, whether it is physical freedom and the need to travel, or a freedom of the mind to explore, enquire and satisfy its curiosity. You will probably feel this as a restless energy, perpetually striving for release from all restrictions. Yet there is a lack of a fixed direction or purpose; you will find it difficult to rationalise those needs for escape and change that agitate you so much, and others, too, may find your attempted explanations less than satisfactory. You need to understand this pattern operating within you, and choose to control and direct its impulse, or else this could prove damaging to any life-style, relationship or employment stability.

A main focus for learning will be in the sphere of relationships, and you may lack a real understanding of people and ability to interact with them. Even though you may be involved in relationships, you retain a tendency to desire freedom; how this is expressed is very important, for you and for others. Often, you will feel that relationships become limiting after a while, but as your need for freedom is often expressed selfishly, you may find that a discipline of staying within a relationship and living with that feeling could begin to help you understand yourself more. You may be afraid of losing this freedom, but modifying it may enable you to enjoy other benefits. A good relationship is priceless, enabling both partners to enjoy life and develop in their own unique ways, and it could be this joy that you lose in deciding on freedom at any cost, because it is inevitable that your experience of a selfish freedom will not be all pleasurable.

Your social friendliness and flexibility will help to create a variety of relationships, and this can be a source of experience which aids you in attaining a greater understanding of others. Yet, allied to your search for freedom, it could also encourage you to enter affairs without too much forethought. Surrendering to this impulse could complicate your life, leaving many issues unresolved and causing pain and confusion. Your future well-being could be affected, due to giving in to the temptation of change without fulfilling any obligations or responsibilities.

Mentally, you will absorb knowledge easily, accepting a range of information from all sources, whether from formal study, which is likely to be of great value to you, or from people and places. Such information can be of value to others, and you can gain enjoyment from sharing it with those in need, and you fulfil a useful function at the same time. You may be attracted to becoming a teacher of some sort, yet one who disseminates rather than evaluates and interprets, due to your difficulty with piecing together disparate pieces of information into a coherent whole. Decision-making or judgements may not be a strong point, as you always wait for more information to come along, which may influence your choices; often circumstances will decide for you.

The essential lesson is to understand your urge for freedom; learn how to express it in a right manner within social relationships and your life will be enriched and lead to greater harmony. Fail to apply it correctly through selfish expression, and your freedom will lead to greater suffering for yourself and others.

North Node 4th House, South Node 10th House

Your conscious personality tends to be dominated by a regard for your own importance, authority and executive ability. You will feel that you have a higher social standing than most around you, and that they should give you the appropriate deference and respect. Translated into action, this implies that you may feel that certain tasks are beneath you. You will have an aura of dignified aloofness which can distance you from others. How accurate are these feelings of self-importance? Are they just reflections of self-deception coming from those 10th house patterns of the South Node? To some extent, these feelings arise from a need to be in control, and the ideal position from which to achieve that is as a leader or authority; you dislike having to follow someone else's lead, or defer to the authority of others, especially as this can imply that your inner feelings of command are mainly illusory.

This issue of authority is one which you need to confront. You will often assume a role of protector, through attracting others who, due to passivity and personal weakness, need someone to rely on, and this role will suit your attraction to domination and leadership. Through your authority role, you often succeed in evading aspects of your real nature, although it does also offer you additional challenges which can help you to grow and mature. Authority implies greater responsibility, and you may need to feel convinced that you have the ability to succeed in such a role.

Part of your need derives from a deeper personal insecurity, which may have been formed during your childhood, perhaps by your parents seeking to instil in you a belief that you would one day become a leader or attain a position of authority. If these expectations fail to materialise in adult life, then a growing dissatisfaction may develop, as life fails to match the absorbed hopes and dreams of parents.

There may be problems within your own adult family, related to some choice between family obligations and your work, especially if you rise to a senior and responsible position. You will tend to be adept at organising for others, but in doing so leave less time and energy for integrating your own nature through self-understanding. This may be most noticeable in the expression of your emotional nature, an area of yourself that you tend to feel uncomfortable with and try to avoid. You may have difficulty in coping with emotional problems, tending to hope that they will just go away. You regret that you cannot organise them!

Your main area of growth can occur when you fully accept that you have emotions, and seek to understand and express them naturally rather than suppressing them. You will be better valued by others and your family if, over time, you can allow your emotions to flow more easily, instead of maintaining your role-playing. Your achievements can be considerable, especially through a career and work, but you should strive to achieve for its own sake, rather than just for the 'applause of the audience', as that will serve only to reinforce you in your role. You need to establish new and deeper roots within your own nature, and become less dependent on others to provide you with external meaning in your life.

North Node 5th House, South Node 11th House

The issue that confronts you with this placing is the exploration of creativity and imagination, the discovery of the potential of the dreaming mind and how this can be applied in life. Releasing and expressing that latent creativity will enrich both your own and others' lives. Your mind and subjective life will fascinate you, and you will often be inwardly preoccupied. Day-dreaming and you are very close friends, and considerable energy will be directed towards imaginative stimulation, designed to work out and elaborate your more inventive dreams. Your inner life can develop into a tapestry of imagination, dreams, desires and fantasies.

Yet this ability is a two-edged sword; it can enrich a life, adding an extra dimension interwoven with the physical reality, or it can become a conditioning force, distorting your reality through attempting to rule and direct your life, trying to force you to act out those fantasy roles. Care does need to be taken, ensuring that you remain a master and not a slave to this creative process, which can become powerfully obsessive. You may tend to avoid living fully in the present, becoming lost in dreams of an ideal future or in an alternative, compensatory reality where you get what you are denied in the here-and-now material world. You may allow this to happen because your present reality fails to match your projections, and it becomes too painful to confront the reality that your dreams fail to materialise. You prefer to associate yourself with friends, partners or groups which enhance your dreaming tendency, whose attitudes are basically supportive to you, or whose interests offer material for your imagination. Often you may be tempted to rebuff and reject those who try to confront you with your present reality. Eventually, the abyss between your dreams and actual reality will stand out in stark relief, and this will pose a direct challenge to your progress.

Once you stand before this abyss, you cannot avoid this confrontation. You wish that there could be no abyss, because that limits your imagination. Looking around for a way forward, you may become attracted to exploring psychology or the occult in order to gain a deeper understanding of the nature of mind. You are searching for ways to discover the power and ability to create your own future in accordance with your favourite dreams. By studying, observing and experimenting with your own mind and imagination, you can become aware that it is by dreams, thoughts and imagination that life is unfolded – these are the roots of all choice and decision-making – if the will and application are potent enough to manifest your wish. This is the concept behind the technique of creative visualisation, a powerful method of transforming oneself and one's life-style.

You may note that it is difficult to manifest purely enough, and that many dreams are too selfish and thus become distorted in the process of becoming real. You need to understand this process of 'creative wishing', and the most effective way is by experiencing the results of the wish in real life. Thus you begin to learn how to control and direct this ability in order to create those situations for which you are willing to take responsibility. Ideally, you will discover that your dreams and imagination should be directed for the benefit of others as well as yourself; selfish dreams will eventually stand revealed as offering no lasting enrichment or satisfaction. Basically, the creative process consists of the ability to manifest one's thoughts – an important psychological and magical skill. Considerable self-knowledge is required, since it is a power that can be dangerous if abused; the only effective safeguard is to apply it only for the good of others.

North Node 6th House, South Node 12th House

This indicates that there can be a slipping back into the depths of mind and beyond across the perimeter of the unconscious mind, moving past logical and rational thought and tapping into the irrational and imaginative sources. You tend to be inwardly orientated, often having a distracted air about you as you create situations through which you can avoid total involvement in the mundane world. This could be a form of escapism, an evasion of responsibility and duty; more positively and creatively it could give rise to meditation, contemplation and an expression of the artistic spirit. Its effects depend upon individual application. You may often feel that life is like a dream, but this depends on how effectively you can separate your inner journeys from external reality.

This absorption into your own mind does affect your daily life. You may not be too efficient and organised at work or performing your home tasks, and through a diversion of interest towards those inner realms, tend to leave work unfinished, claiming the excuse of insufficient time. You could benefit from being in an organisational structure which necessitated greater self-discipline, so that you could learn the benefits of careful planning and the application of a focused will.

There may be a variety of inner fears and indistinct worries that afflict you, preoccupying your mind and making you feel sorry for yourself. But through assuming greater responsibility for yourself, becoming more positive and developing a trust in life, you can banish these fears, and in so doing feel confident and free enough to face the real world. You are quite capable of doing this, but that established habit of avoidance may prevent you, and you prefer to retreat into that private inner world, especially at times during your relationships when you believe that your love is unnoticed and unappreciated.

You will feel a need to be helpful to others, but you may be reticent in moving beyond your protective shell. Your usefulness depends on the degree to which you can pass beyond your own restrictive patterns. Your way forward involves reaching out to embrace life, accepting your own nature, and building bridges of communication with others.

There may be a phase of illness – affecting you or someone close to you – which will serve to teach you that much illness is psychosomatic, being caused by inner states of disharmony within thought, attitudes and values. This can be through emotional blockages which generate physical side-effects, tensions and stresses. If you can succeed in perceiving the cause behind the symptoms, and make a deliberate effort to transform and resolve the problem, then amazing healings can occur. You may then be drawn towards healing work generally, and indeed you could have latent healing abilities. Linking your abilities of observation and empathic contact to your own personal emergence and unfoldment, and adding a more positive outlook, could help transform you into a healer, especially in the field of complementary medicine. Once you have dealt with your own problems, you should experience a greater sense of purpose and fulfilment as you share yourself with others.

North Node 7th House, South Node 1st House

You will have a tendency to assert your independence and unique individuality, and this can become detrimental to the success of your intimate relationships and general co-operation with others. Self-preoccupation is highlighted by the 1st house South Node, and this concern with your own needs often makes you unconscious of the reactions of others. You insist on travelling through life in your own way, and can fail to pay attention to the wiser advice of others. A need for freedom is felt strongly, and whenever anyone seems to pass beyond that inner demarcation line and demands your commitment, then you feel that your independence is threatened. The tendency is to react against such inhibitions by asserting your own individuality, often by extracting yourself from the relationship. This could indicate divorce, separation, or relationships characterised by considerable freedom and space between partners.

You may have to become conscious of the selfishness that you often express, look at yourself honestly, and begin to discover how to give freely to others, instead of taking just for yourself. There may be a lack of harmony between you and the world, a lack of a free-flowing energy of relationship; this can lead to the appearance of some form of ill health, physical or emotional, which could be used to gain sympathy and get your own way, manifesting perhaps as a psychosomatic illness.

Through your individual assertiveness, you will be mainly a loner, believing in your own self-sufficiency, and you will rarely accept any indication that you have failed in anything. Probably you will prefer to feel at the centre of things, holding an important supervisory role, and if you do achieve this, you will feel secure. The point, though, is that it is from such a position that you are asked to learn how to be more considerate to others, and how their needs are to be met as well as your own.

The challenge facing you is to learn to give to others without thought of personal gain. Fundamentally, you are a strong, confident person, but one who tends to take more than share; learn to give to those in need and your life will be enriched and your relationships renewed. In fact, you will discover that you have much of value to share with others – and, of course, they with you. It is likely that you will find that when you are acting from a basically selfish standpoint the results of your actions will fail to satisfy, or cause suffering for you or others. The creative and positive way to transcend this tendency is to risk sharing and to give freely; your perspective needs to widen beyond yourself, and your future growth and happiness depend on you opening to others, and on experiencing the joy that can occur in true relationships.

North Node 8th House, South Node 2nd House

You may find it difficult to change your established ways, even while recognising that they are leading in the wrong direction; you tend to continue regardless, mainly because it is the only path you see, and you will attempt to convince others that your way is right. In many ways it is, because it offers the potential for you to realise what is driving you and it encourages you to change, especially when negative results begin to occur.

You find a substitute for real purpose and fulfilment in the acquisition of material goods; you tend to value yourself according to your possessions. This desire nature of yours often prefers quantity to quality, but is rarely satisfied for long. It needs to be transformed if you are to gain real, lasting satisfaction from life.

You tend towards extremism in most things, and you often invalidate any progress made in your life by burning your bridges behind you, preventing any chance of returning to the past and old habits by ensuring a commitment to your chosen direction. Potentially, such action can lead to positive results, but these do not just come about by themselves; they require conscious effort.

You require some type of inner transformation but may have difficulty in generating consistent energy to stimulate change; additionally, there is always the element of possible chaos in all of your behaviour emanating from a misapplied 8th house energy (Scorpio link) which can undermine many of your intentions.

Relationships are important for you, although you may have a tendency to look for social status through them. There is the possibility of some confusion in respect of sexual matters/identity/activities, and you may not always feel at ease with the insistent demands and requirements of the physical nature, and this can lead to inner resistance, stimulating friction and conflict. You may feel wary of your sexual nature, which gives you an image of self which you may not fully accept or integrate easily into your consciousness and everyday life. You can tend to keep this aspect of yourself apart and at a distance, and yet it is both an essential part of being human and a powerful need which must somehow be satisfied.

If you seek more transformative values for yourself, this will lead to a moderation of any unconsciously rooted excessive behaviour patterns; you need to become more open to the values of others so that your own become less narrow, and so that you become more understanding and tolerant. You need to review your attitude towards possessions learning that they are mainly for use and do not enhance the true value of a person, and that in themselves they do not satisfy or fulfil. The emphasis should be placed more on quality, both of the person and of possessions. You may find that you have to let go of much that you have considered meaningful, even though it has failed to give you inner peace or happiness, and circumstances may require that you be stripped of the past in order for you to learn more appropriate attitudes and values. If this occurs, see it as a potential for positive renewal, as it is an opportunity to change yourself so that life can be enriched by a more moderate and balanced approach, rather than being directed by any compulsive and unconscious tendencies.

North Node 9th House, South Node 3rd House

The emphasis here is on communication, relationships and the development of mind, particularly in terms of acquiring information. Relationships may become a source of conflict and confusion; you may not always feel at ease in them, preferring to break free from complications. As you are basically mentally focused, you feel less comfortable on emotional and physical levels, and sexual unease may be present. This may be because you are less physically preoccupied than many, and so the physical expression of relationship is less pronounced in your awareness, and sexual needs do not generate your main motivations or desires. You will learn to accept sex as a natural part of life, but within a context which values other aspects of life more highly.

You can enjoy being alone, pursuing your interests undistracted by others, yet there is also an impulse operating which is continually reaching out for communication and relationship with others. Balancing these tendencies can cause difficulties at times. Often people with emotional problems turn to you for support, finding that your detached mental perspective is calming and helps them gain a more rational viewpoint from which to deal with their agitated emotions. You enjoy this role and try to be helpful, hoping that your support and advice can be used by them for positive results; you are very careful with your advice, and try to ensure that it is not misunderstood.

Sometimes your tendency to be diplomatic and neutral has negative effects on you. Your attempts at being non-confrontational can make you lose sight of your own thoughts and feelings; if this does occur, then it may be better to become more partisan and true to yourself, ensuring greater clarity. This could become more of a problem as your social life builds an ever-expanding web of relationships and contacts, and it becomes inevitable that you will inadvertently upset someone now and again. This stimulates relationship conflict, and makes you confront your own inner doubts; if your diplomacy has involved you in some degree of dishonesty, then you will realise the futility of attempting to interfere with genuine communication.

Keep conscious control of your life, or else you may experience phases when its speed appears to increase and you are running on a treadmill just to stay in the same place. This could be through a social whirl, or a mental whirl, and feel increasingly uncomfortable, and could lead to symptoms of ill health and problems in decision-making. You are not always adept at decisions, as you prefer to gather all possible facts and details prior to deciding, and the difficulty is that you tend to believe that there are more facts to accumulate, and so postpone the decision. Using your intuition could help here.

To you the world is a treasure trove of knowledge and information, and you want to accumulate as much of its wealth as possible. Your need to understand will be a lifelong preoccupation, with your interest spanning many fields of human knowledge. Your mind never rests in its search for more pieces of the human jigsaw. At least through mental journeys you will explore the world, although physical travel may also be highly appealing to you, and will broaden your perspective. It may be that success will come to you through leaving your area of birth, or through foreign contacts.

You may need to focus your information-gathering, so that you begin to create a synthesis that indicates something of importance about the human condition and the nature of life. If you can do this, it will give extra meaning to both your own and others' lives, as you begin to concentrate more on inclusive ideas and less on fragmentary facts, and as your vision deepens, your ability to communicate will become more effective.

North Node 10th House, South Node 4th House

The South Node in the 4th house indicates that personal roots, foundations and family life will play a very influential role in your life, possibly demanding a great deal of your time, attention and energy in order to meet family demands and obligations. You may feel that the family duties are restrictive, inhibiting your freedom and options of expression, or that satisfying the economic needs of family life becomes a heavy burden. Feelings of resentment may accumulate if you begin to believe that your efforts are unappreciated. Your role of service to the family is likely to be crucial, perhaps due to your being the sole money-earner and home-keeper.

Much of your identity is tied to your family roots and foundations. This may arise from the dominant influence of parental attitudes which have strongly conditioned your adult values, and so still persist in guiding your life and decisions. Such attitudes may include powerful established social or religious belief structures, which have become firmly embedded in your conscious outlook. You will find it difficult to move away from these foundational attitudes, even if you want to.

Either in your childhood, or in later adult life, there is the possibility that the family unit may not be complete in the traditional sense of two adults. Perhaps you experienced the early loss of a parent, and so had to shoulder more responsibilities at an earlier age, or in your adult family, a partner may be unable to fulfil their parental role fully, and so leave you with additional responsibility. Facing the demands of parenthood will also be a challenging task for you, as you may have to struggle to perform both adult roles for the family. Yet emotionally, you are deeply tied to your family links, even though you also react against their sometimes oppressive nature. The family tends to stabilise your life, defining your life-style and daily experience. It also absorbs most of your energy, but you cannot imagine life without it – except as a lonely void.

The area of conflict for you is that between selfish and selfless desires, between your own needs and those of family members. Generally, you shrug your shoulders, take a deep breath and carry on by applying self-discipline. The lesson that you are learning by moving through those trying and testing times is that of service to others, which will require a degree of self-sacrifice. You try to nourish those with whom you are in close contact, and help them to grow, but your experience is leading you towards a fuller expression of this beneficial influence in the greater community or society in which you live. Through performing those challenging family duties, you have been learning to become more competent, decisive and self-assured.

You will emerge from your trials as a pillar of strength for others to draw support from. Accepting this self-sacrificial role consciously will deepen your capabilities, and your emotional maturity and acceptance of responsibility will expand correspondingly. The likelihood is that through various routes, your influence will expand beyond the family parameters into the greater community, perhaps through inspiration or even by the achievements of your children. It may not seem a glamorous path, and may be very hard work, yet in learning to transcend the personal desire nature in favour of benefiting others there lies a key to positive transformation, which will gradually become apparent, especially in later years.

North Node 11th House, South Node 5th House

From the 5th house South Node comes an enjoyment of the pleasures of life, creativity, love affairs, and a self-centred style of expression. Your creative imagination often weaves many colourful webs around your actual reality. The world you create is a stage on which players perform their chosen roles, chasing private dreams and adventures, and following their desire natures. Arguably, there is some accuracy in this perception of life, and certainly it lifts human existence above a more mundane perspective, infusing it with a glamour and fantasy that can enliven and enrich. Yet the danger can lie in using this as an ʰ.ʰ.ties, in your preferring to live a romantic and heroic drama. ʰsed and noticed by others, to ɪs helps create your attraction n audience; anonymity is not to be ignored. Love affairs are ɪ on your need to be loved by le stage for your performance, ɪch you can depend, at least ɪtic interludes divert you from ɪon in life, as the by-ways of ɪtive. In love, you tend to make ɪacrifice for love – to be seen by to turn any relationship, at least ɪt passionate drama. You can fall ɪpact is only superficial, and you rmative depths of love. Ultimately,

ɪrit at play within you, but one that is naively and almost ɪɪɪɪɪɪ.ly self-centred, and which desires constant company or a supporting cast to entertain. Much of your waking life is spent in creative, imaginative and romanticised dreams which are projected onto the world and people; in several ways they serve as a protective barrier. Yet it is your aptitude for dreaming that can offer you greater self-development and opportunities to attain insight and understanding into the real meaning and influence of 'dreams' in life. Personal dreams can enhance creativity and actualise your desires, yet if you attempt to use your will to force events against the tides of life, then failure is most likely. Dreams can also bring you messages from within, trying to guide you towards understanding the reasons for your actions and experiences. If you can register such impressions, then you can adjust your direction and use of your will, bringing it into harmony with the direction indicated. Noting such impressions from dreams or intuitions can be an important step to take, as guidance arises from within, although many fail to listen sufficiently to that quiet inner voice.

Until you begin to reorientate your self-centred focus, you will tend to experience a sense of discontent and feelings that you are missing something vital in life, even though you attempt to colour much of your life with brighter hues. Seeking to be free of personal ties, you succeed only in making more. Your sense of ego and pride may create problems, through excessive self-preoccupation, especially within relationships, and your need for more stops you appreciating what you already have. You need to become more aware of others, and to see them not just as supporting players, but recognising their needs, desires and dreams as being just as important as your own. That romantic vision of life may need to be modified so that reality is not lost, although that childlike view of life can still be refreshing to more jaded viewpoints. The new direction involves applying your creative imagination to dream of a better world, not just for yourself, but for everyone.

Friendships and group involvements are likely to be important in expanding life for you, and a possible commitment and dedication to some idealistic vision could be the key enabling you to move beyond that self-centred focus into performing a more important role, one that improves the quality of life for others too. In learning how to conjoin your creativity with social needs you could discover the powerful mystery of creative dream. It has generated the whole universe, and by our small use of it we have the power to transform our own lives and the world.

North Node 12th House, South Node 6th House

From the 6th house South Node, the realm of work will be influential to your sense of well-being, and the implication is that you will feel restricted and limited, creating dissatisfaction and resistance. This can arise from earning a living in ways that fail to interest you, or which do not take advantage of your talents and gifts, and which constrict those opportunities for personal development. Your employment may experienced as boring and stultifying, offering little job-satisfaction, and these frustrations can cast a dark shadow over the other areas of your life. You may need to invest more effort and attention in changing your working environment if this is the case, perhaps pursue a different career, or change the priorities in your life; seek a positive and creative alternative to follow.

You will prefer to see order in the world, and adjust your own life-style accordingly, failing to comprehend why much of life appears to be chaotic, illogical or unnecessary, and why people tend to make most of their own suffering as a consequence of their own attitudes and choices. Sometimes you feel yourself to be superior in this respect, although if your work sphere is not satisfying, then you too are creating your own suffering instead of changing it.

There can be inner pressures building up, due to repressed feelings of anger and resentment, and you may feel sometimes that life is failing to reward you for your efforts. Try to avoid this build-up or else you may create health problems caused by festering unreleased emotional energies, which can result in physical or psychological illness.

You will feel uncomfortable if you have to impress people, and being in any situation where this is necessary will tend to generate feelings of 'selling yourself out'. What will be of most value to you is to come to terms with your inner self, because it is by looking inside that you will discover your answers. You may need to learn discrimination regarding what is truly important to you, that which is meaningful and lasting, and that which is impermanent. Defining your priorities can be very revealing, and an important step in the direction of making your life-style harmonise with your essential nature; such a step can lead to radical changes. Instead of reacting against certain aspects of life with which you disagree, a rechannelling of your energies to enable you to understand your own nature can then lead you towards building a life which suits you, and which draws out those qualities and abilities that you knew were there but had not been able to express before. If this can be achieved, then the sense of personal satisfaction and fulfilment will be great. The key to this lies in your own nature, as it is likely that the world will not easily afford you opportunities, and you may have to move in an independent direction.

You should avoid the fragmentation of life if possible, trying to see and experience it as a unity, moving freely with the winds of change. Provided that this can be done with a corresponding degree of growth in compassion and understanding for others, there is considerable potential for you to realise more meaning and purpose. It may require some substitution of assumed values with more appropriate ones, but you do have the character to succeed if you dare to apply your will to build what has been revealed by that inner examination of your priorities. Just looking out and feeling dissatisfied is not the answer, and will only lead to more resentment; turning within and changing can reveal a new direction for you to follow.

CHAPTER 9

By the Light of the Magical Moon

As the ancient wisdom of the East, and the Western magical, hermetic and pagan teachings began to be resurrected through the efforts of the Golden Dawn organisation, Blavatsky and other pioneers, the archaic power of the Goddess began to emerge from the darkness of the collective unconscious. The feminine Moon principle commenced her slow and steady procession back towards the light, ready to seat herself once more on the dual throne of the Queen of Heaven and the Dark Queen of the Underworld.

Sigmund Freud responded to the subterranean rumblings and shone his psychological light into the inner darkness. What he found lurking there became the basis of modern psychology; in opening the trapdoor on the boundary of the conscious mind, he discovered new inner realms, the unconscious levels of mind. By his probings he unleashed a human Pandora's box, unearthing the complexity of human nature through tapping into the rich vein of associations and foundations symbolised by the inner Moon goddess.

His analysis indicated that early childhood experiences and relationships with parents were influential in the unfoldment of personality, and that instincts, sexuality and past events were major factors influencing our behaviour. He used the term Id to describe the collective, unconscious aspects of mind which accumulated around inherited, instinctive impulses of the individual, especially childish memories and fantasies. He defined the Oedipal complex as related to infantile sexual attraction to the parent of the opposite sex, and a negative reaction against the other parent.

His vision of an unconscious mind was that of a primal level of the psyche, motivated by instinctual urges, chaotic compulsions and sexual impulses. The image of the possessive, devouring Mother is present in Freudian theory, and is an archetypal image in mythology, most religions and magical traditions. Freud was exploring the unconscious roots of the individual and delving into the inner lunar realm, areas of which are associated with heredity, ancestry and collective instinctual life. The path that he was taking was that of a descent into an underworld, searching for those inner complexes that constellated various unconscious patterns of behaviour that were both inherited and unfolded in response to childhood experiences.

From the pioneering psychological work of Freud, the investigation into human nature has taken many routes in deepening our understanding. In several ways, modern psychology has only been rediscovering secrets of the psyche that have been known within the esoteric mystery schools and in the inner sanctums of world religions. The work of Carl Gustav Jung, in particular, has been of immense significance to contemporary psychology, and equally illuminating to our insights into the archetypal roots of mythology, legend and several esoteric paths. His studies of symbolism and its relevance to inner transformation and the potential healing of disparate parts of the psyche, and his realisation of the necessity for meaning in life, have made a major contribution to the development of New Age thought. The spheres of astrology and alchemy have benefited from his approach to exploring the unconscious mind, and most psychological and humanistic astrology is indebted to his insights.

Jung realised that hidden in the symbolism of alchemy, Gnostic thought, and the religious myths of Egypt, Greece, Christianity and the East were profound spiritual teachings and insights into the nature of the human being, and that underlying these myths were the luminous presences of archetypal beings which had been recognised by the ancients as gods and goddesses. The Magna Dea, the Earth and Moon Goddess, cast her silvery light over many ancient cultures, and Jung saw that modern man needed to reintegrate the feminine back into his nature and civilisation in order to prevent social imbalance occurring. He proposed that one approach to resolve this lack was the contacting and integration of the inner anima, one of the guises of the feminine principle.

Over the last thirty years, psychological techniques and schools of though have greatly diversified and begun to spread out into society. Many basically balanced and well-socialised individuals now use, and benefit from, psychological techniques, whereas at one time such techniques were only employed by professionals treating the clinically disturbed. The former group of individuals are searching for greater self-understanding, meaning and purpose in life, and have expanded the concept of self-therapy in new directions. There has been a proliferation of ways emerging, including gestalt, encounter, psychosynthesis, transactional analysis, psychodrama, primal therapy and rebirthing. This shift to people choosing to explore their own psyche was often stimulated by a need to deal with the power of their own emotional and feeling responses to life. Perhaps by experiencing failed relationships, conflicts directed at parents, over-sensitivity to the world environment, or a lack of fulfilling meaning in their lives, they all began to recognise that they could benefit by self-understanding.

For many, the biggest challenge was coming to terms with their emotional depths, confronting feelings that had been repressed, learning how to release blocked energies and hold their inner darkness to the light to be acknowledged, healed and dispersed, peering down into their unconscious self and opening the way for conscious integration to occur. People were recognising that from early childhood there can develop a tendency to bury and hide hurt emotions, to restrain anger and frustrations and constrict behaviour to that which is socially acceptable. By adulthood, our scope for expression has been limited and aspects of our nature have been unconsciously repressed for fear of punishment and rejection. Effectively, our opportunities for loving, freedom of choice and creativity have been diminished or distorted. Openly sharing our deeper feelings and emotions becomes difficult; we even have problems admitting them to ourselves. This results in a lack of real communication in relationships and problems in finding a fulfilling life-style. People realised that somewhere along the way they had lost touch with the essential vitality of their lives.

Such issues are related to the concepts of the astrological Moon, and represent a natural and collective response to the stirrings of that psychological archetype. They embody a personal need to deal with the emotions and instincts, by understanding the way in which we experience our feeling responses to life. By participating in self-therapy or human potential workshops, people found that gaining a new perspective on their emotional nature – perhaps by cathartic release of repressed energies, or by restructuring their habitual response patterns, values or hidden childhood conditioning – could create a renewed sense of vitality and self, almost amounting to an experience of rebirth. Primal therapy theorists believed that through reliving the actual traumas of birth, radical individual change could be stimulated.

Parallelling this psychological movement, the old traditions were also re-emerging, with a renewed interest in paganism, witchcraft, shamanism, alchemy, the Western Mysteries, the Grail paths, and the Celtic revival. The esoteric and magical dimension of the Moon Goddess was becoming activated in the world, resulting also in the new assertiveness of the feminist movement and the increasing focus on the nature of ancient matriarchal cultures and Goddess worship. By the light of the magical Moon the promise was that of cycles of renewal and transformation through attunement to the power of the divine feminine; this appeared to be an attractive antidote to the imbalance of patriarchal attitudes and masculine dominance. As the silver rays of the Goddess began to light the inner realms of the collective unconscious, awareness also turned towards the social exploitation and misuse of the planet. An ecological vision started to form, and the idea of green spirituality emerged into public view. The realisation is slowly dawning that if we create an inner wasteland by our lack of understanding and integration, then collectively we will create an ecological disaster and a planetary wasteland. The Goddess has returned with her images of the Moon, the Grail, and the Cauldron of Transformative Inspiration for our use in the great work, the *magnum opus*. It is apt that it was from the Moon that our first vision of planet Earth was attained; it is a reminder of our roots and home, an image of the one planetary ecosystem.

WICCA

Contemporary Wicca or witchcraft is a revival of an older tradition derived from paganism, and from nature and fertility worship, where the Moon Goddess is the primary deity and an assertion of the feminine principle is to the forefront of the religious symbolism. In most Christian countries, witchcraft is still commonly perceived as almost satanist in essence, a dangerous and sinister left-hand path; the word 'witchcraft' evokes an automatic negative reaction from many, but that arises only from ignorance, misunderstanding and an effective Christian propaganda machine. Patriarchal Christianity has tended to deny the power of the feminine for centuries now, and is not about to change its tactics of continually associating the lunar cults with evil and sinister rituals; even the word 'sinister' is derived from the name of the Babylonian Moon God Sinn. This is a travesty of interpretation, and a deliberate distortion of the older spiritual foundations of Wicca, and is only designed to maintain the supremacy of the patriarchal Father-God symbolism and attitudes within this culture.

The resurgence of Wicca has partly been through the interest of the international women's movement, which has begun to look again at the images and roles of women throughout history. For many women, the realisation of the ancient spiritual power of the Great Mother and Universal Goddess was a revelation. There was the opportunity to reconnect to a feminine power source, one that both gave birth to worlds and sustained them. Uncovering the repressed Moon symbolism gave them keys to the acceptance and understanding of their own femininity, and the opportunity to assert their own womanhood with confidence. The belief in the previous existence of matriarchal cultures which were more peaceful and more in harmony with nature suggested a socio-political model that could be brought about by feminine power and qualities.

Through the restoration of the Goddess image and the assumed model of the matriarchal state, women are inspired to see themselves as being equally divine in essence as men, differing not in spiritual status but in that their aspirational pattern is that of the Feminine rather than of the Masculine principle of Deity. A new inner relationship with their female bodies has developed; they have begun to see themselves not as a vehicle for the satisfaction of male needs, but as a sacred and holy gateway for the mysteries of life and death. Their fluctuating inner emotional and physical menstrual cycle is also seen as natural and holy, and the power of their emotional and feeling natures is increasingly seen as something to be honoured, accepted and expressed as a purifying release of energies.

Like the Goddess, women have the power of creation and nurturing in their possession, as well as the destructive and devouring nature which is unleashed in order to liberate. By perceiving her nature as one with the Universal Goddess, woman can become a mediating priestess, acknowledging her own strength, the potencies of her body, emotions, mind and imagination, and move beyond constricting social parameters of behaviour; she can assert her need to become whole within her femininity.

The Goddess of Wicca is immanent in all creation; everything is perceived as sacred and honoured as the embodiment of the Goddess or Mother Nature. It is an assertion of universal life present in each form, embracing without preference, non-discriminating in its shared abundance for all. Wicca is primarily a religion of ecology and natural harmony between all outer kingdoms of Earth nature, and also within the inner levels of each individual. In this, it provides a healthier role-model for spiritual aspiration than does a religion which views God as transcendent and beyond nature, and which views the planet as having been created purely for man's benefit, to exploit as he pleases.

Whilst the rising Goddess has been most attractive to women, her path is also important for men as it indicates the way towards experiencing and integrating their own inner feminine, by consciously accepting the validity of their sensitivity and feelings, and allowing a psychic and intuitive quality to be expressed through them. There are an increasing number of men attracted to the pagan and Wicca paths. For them, the Moon Goddess serves as a beckoning image of the anima, summoning them to take the inner journey into her transformative underworld.

To enhance sensitivity to the rhythmic cycles of universal life, Wicca celebrates an eightfold ritualised festival cycle, known as the Sabbats, connecting inner and outer cycles and based on the solstices, equinoxes and cross-quarter days which invoke both the Goddess and her consort the Horned God. These are termed: Yule (winter solstice), Brigid/Candlemas (February), Easter (spring equinox), Beltain (May Eve), Litha (summer solstice), Lughnasad (1 August), Mabon (autumn equinox) and Samhain (Hallowe'en, 31 October), the Wiccan's New Year. In addition, the lunar phases are also recognised as offering times when receptivity to the subtler energies is at its strongest.

These become apt times for witchcraft and magic, and all craft rituals are essentially magical rites, designed to reawaken those inner Moon goddesses and gods, open doors to the secret, hidden, spiritual realities and to amplify those psychic and intuitive powers which are often latent within the human mind. The word *wicce/wicca* is derived from an Anglo-Saxon word meaning to shape and bend, and this is an aim of magic – sensing, receiving and shaping those forces which generate creation, and becoming aware of the alternative realities which coexist within our own consciousness beyond the scope of the rational and logical mind. The Wiccan belief is that the visibility of the Moon presence and light transmits forces, which, whilst invisible to human eyes, can be perceived and experienced through inner ritual and imaginative meditation. Moon magic is often experienced in terms of intuition, inner visions, scrying and divination, enchantments and disguise. As a 'keeper of dreams' the Moon plays a role in dream creation; some people experience more evocative, colourful and interesting dreams near to the time of Full Moon, or dreams which appear to be attempts at conveying symbolic meanings or guidance.

A Wiccan conception of the relationship between the unconscious and conscious mind sees the unconscious as having direct experience of the outer world, through the holistic awareness of the right brain hemisphere. Conscious awareness of this, however, is filtered out by the left brain activities of classification, analysis, abstraction, and verbal differentiation. The unconscious mind communicates through sensations, emotions, feelings, instinctive drives, intuitions, dreams and visions, symbolism and psychosomatic responses. These equate closely with aspects of the astrological Moon interpretations especially when struggling with individual repression. Wicca conceives that the way of progress is through the union of left and right brain activity – that is, through integrating the two distinct types of consciousness. In an archetypal setting, the fusion of masculine and feminine principles evokes the images of the black and white pillars of the Tree of Life and the path of equilibrium which descends through Yesod, or the images of the mating Shiva-Shakti of Hinduism, and the joining of the Goddess and the Horned God. The result of the interpenetration of the conscious and unconscious minds is the androgynous magician, whose mingling of both positive and negative energies opens the gates of eternity.

The waxing moon becomes a time of beginnings in Wicca, a seed time, a return from sleep or death and a new awakening or rebirth. The subtle power of the tides increases, so it is considered the time for spells involving growth, increase and work in the outer world, for starting magical training, for recharging continued workings, and for unfolding practical psychic and divinatory skills. As the symbolic light will grow brighter from this phase, it is appropriate to work with spells of healing, whether of physical, emotional, mental or spiritual suffering, so that the magic strengthens the recipient's vitality and ability to cast off disease. Meditations on the waxing moon may include contemplating the power of generation, growth and the importance of sowing right seeds. The latent potential of new ideas and opportunities is noted, and the outpouring of as yet unshaped ideas and plans may be registered prior to the challenge of manifesting and anchoring them in form and reality.

At Full Moon, covens traditionally meet at the *esbats*, a time for practical magic and study of Wiccan teachings. It is the point of flood tide and the peak of the Moon's power, the culmination of the seeds of change and the release into the world of her abundant fruits. The Mother dominates as the nourisher and nurturer, the manifestation of what was started at the New Moon. The Goddess is at the height of her glory, and the lunar light illuminates the mysteries of the dark. She is seen as the equal of the Sun, her complementary polar nature.

The waning moon becomes the phase of the dark, the ending of the cycle, the death before the renewal of life, the ebb tide and the hidden moon. This is the subsiding phase of the tidal energies, when they turn inward again. Any illness or personal discomfort can be imagined to be waning and decreasing now, and those anxieties safely released prior to leaving the sufferer capable of accepting the renewal at the next waxing phase. Deeper inner awareness, focus and sensitivity may be attained, with the potential of more rewarding and helpful realisations being grasped. Connections to the anima/animus figures may be easier to achieve at this phase, as personal attention naturally looks within. The natural process of life can be acknowledged, with an acceptance of the need for endings in order to generate new beginnings, and a recognition that life and death are two poles of one axis embodied in human nature. The power to transform stagnating, unintegrated or imbalanced areas of one's life may begin to rise, and instinctive wisdom stored in the body or unconscious mind may suddenly appear accessible.

The Goddess is perceived as mutable, a shape-shifter rhythmi-cally transforming her form and face, allowing no single image to define her or limit her transformative and embracing nature. She becomes a source of inspiration, a creative fertilisation of humanity. As a Wiccan chant states, 'One thing becomes another in the Mother'; things flow and interpenetrate in mutual receptivity. So she becomes the Triple Goddess, known in her disguises as the Maiden (New Moon), the Mother (Full Moon) and the Crone or Wise Woman (Dark Moon). In the Celtic tradition she was recognised respectively as Rhiannon, Arianrhod, Ceridwen, becoming 'She is all things to all men'. An alternative version of this replaces the Mother by the image of the Nymph, who is a seductive siren and sexual temptress, reflecting the need of sexual attractiveness prior to becoming impregnated by the passionate man. A valuable interpretation of the Triple Goddess is the perception of the virginal Maiden as the natural, instinctive mind; the Mother as the mature, rational and practical mind; and the Crone as the intuitive and inspirational mind.

It is the Crone's realm that is most feared, even by the Goddess's own devotees, let alone the followers of solar religions. This is the Underworld of old age, deep mysteries, wisdoms, prophecies, divination, death and resurrection; this is the realm of Hecate, the Dark Queen of Midnight, who possesses the power to give blinding insights which inspire or madden, whose uncompromising and unforgiving nature challenges even the strongest, and who shares the magical secrets of banishing all ills and anxieties. In her black realm, the Crone stirs her Cauldron of Inspiration, ready to offer the sacred brew to any who genuinely desire to receive the inner knowledge of gnosis and the experience of the Goddess. Hecate only helps and advises those strong enough to descend into her underworld, because it is only those who are capable of encountering her dark and sinister mysteries. The Crone aspect is the real source of the Goddess's promise of liberation, for 'her service is perfect freedom'.

THE DESCENT INTO THE UNDERWORLD

The tradition of the UnderWorld has recently been reformulated and presented as a magical path towards transformation and initiation, and is derived from archaic and archetypal mythic patterns present in several objectively extinct cultures. It is currently being perceived as an inner realm of consciousness which is inhabited by archetypally symbolic figures, which we are able to experience and explore if we take an inner journey through guided meditations or pathworkings. These approaches are becoming increasingly popular as a means of contacting that 'treasure house of images' and to awaken inner energies and powerfully evocative symbols within the psyche.

There are three aspects of the realm of the Moon Queen of the UnderWorld; it is the place of new generation, the giver of fertility, as life grows in the dark of the soil; it is the place of the dead, where we travel to when we leave our earthly forms; and it is the place of regeneration, where the secrets of human rebirth, initiation and immortality can be attained. The inner journey can be made on the ancient Moon Boat of the Goddess, and the ways into the hidden world are discovered by the illumination of moonbeams revealing those concealed entrances into hills and caves descending into the earth. These paths are commonly found in pagan legend, and all indicate that the way is inwards and downwards, often towards subterranean caverns where the Goddess is discovered, or where sacred wells or pools have the reflections of stars shining within them.

The UnderWorld is considered to be an inner realm associated with the land of the individual's physical birth, and which embodies that particular native tradition and set of symbolic imagery. This is the source of ancestral and racial myth and legend, where the keys to understanding the coded tales are kept, and where nature magic and the power of Earth's chthonic foundations can be tapped. The role of ancestry is highlighted, with the wisdom of the past passing into the land and being stored there. Contact may be made with the ancestors, either literally, on some level, through inner sensitivity to the physical embodiment with the land and specific sites, such as barrows and burial chambers, or through a psychological exploration interpreted as embodying the inner knowledge and lore of the individual and collective unconscious mind.

The image of a magical tree is often present in the UnderWorld, representing a boundary between worlds, an ancestral soul, or a source of initiation and transformation. The tree symbol is an archetypal one, and was present even within Chaldean Moon worship and in the biblical story of Genesis. The art of 'summoning the ancestors' is a means of receiving wisdom, advice and magical powers from the inner worlds (or from the collective and genetic heritage). Traditionally this is performed by priestesses, seers and shamans. It is often associated with particular physical sites, where invocative rituals or inner journeys can make contact with the ancestral sacrificial guardian of that place.

The sequential stages of descent into the Underworld equate to stages of ascent in other traditions, and all represent a passage beyond boundaries of life and death towards a rebirth and transformation into an entirely new state of consciousness. Wiccan and Celtic traditions are especially concerned with the wheel of life–death–rebirth as indicated by their Moon and Goddess symbolism.

The UnderWorld journey tends to move from the dark moon to the full, suggesting that the path to light is first through inner darkness, or that the way to heaven has to pass through hell, reminiscent of Christ entering the underworld to liberate the prisoners before he became resurrected. The initiation in the depths is cathartic in essence, releasing those repressed dark shadows and powers within human nature, destroying the artificially inflated and separative personality, dissolving the false masks and misplaced identifications, and liberating the real self into light. On that journey there may be contact with inner female beings, who are reflections or aspects of the Goddess, and through relation with them, transformation may occur as a result of the negative power of the left-hand feminine potency which stimulates personal breakdown and reassembly through initiation. Symbolically, this is reflected in the Grail myths, in which the loathsome lady (the unloved, unintegrated anima-Goddess-Crone nature) can only be redeemed and transformed into a great beauty by the knight succeeding in his spiritual trials. It is interesting to note that on these journeys, two of the UnderWorld's totem beasts are the hound and cow, both attributed to the Moon.

Through this type of initiatory process, the implication of the dark Moon and the path into the UnderWorld is that humanity can re-establish contact with the natural life only by descending deep into the roots of being. At that point the Cauldron of Ceridwen and the Crone distils the holy elixir by which life is renewed. Here we rediscover the legends of *soma*, the drink of inspiration and ecstasy which leads to the higher Moon initiations of consciousness, and is derived from realisations associated with the dark Moon and the Moon tree and from the opening of the unconscious world to the light of conscious understanding. Hidden within the dark robe of Isis (the garment of form, matter and the UnderWorld) lies concealed the deepest revelations. To ingest *soma* is to share the food of the gods, and be granted the power to transcend death, become immortal and to create. The liberated Moon becomes 'the self of nourishment' and as the unconscious and conscious minds become one and the inner barriers dissolve, a new self emerges from the caverns, a Moon initiate, and one who is connected to the feminine powers and has succeeded in integrating the opposing polarities within their psyche. A new child of light is born, listening to the guidance of their 'inner daemon' and to the wisdom of the Goddess.

QABALAH AND THE MOON

In the esoteric system of the Qabalah, the ninth sphere or Sephiroth on the symbolic Tree of Life is known as Yesod, which is attributed to the Moon. For the astrologer, what is significant about Yesod is that it can be worked with qabalistically in order to attain a deeper personal understanding of the magical Moon. Yesod is associated with the unconscious mind, which is seen as the symbolic Yesodic repository of 'The Treasure House of Images'. Part of the Yesod sphere is connected to the psychological areas explored by Freud in his examination of the influence of past experiences contained within the unconscious mind, where repressed emotions and blocked energies may lodge. The message is that the residue of the past conditions choices, decisions and experiences in the present; if the past is retained in a distorted and unintegrated pattern, then it can slowly become a stagnant and fetid pool tainting the whole psyche, with obvious negative effects on the future.

The experience of Yesod has been called 'The Vision of the Machinery of the Universe', and this concerns the relationship between the subtle etheric web and material form. In myths the Moon was connected to the mystery of form and the seed of life, and the Yesodic Moon is seen as performing a task by which a containing etheric framework is generated to emmesh particles of denser matter together into distinct forms. It is an energy of integration which serves to co-ordinate molecules, cells, particles in ways which create an organism, which is a structure built and held in place by the etheric web during life, and is the foundation for all physical manifestation. Yesod has been given the title 'Foundation' and is an underlying root of matter and human consciousness, transmitting higher energies and precipitating them into human levels so that we can use them to create ourselves and the world. Similar to the astrological Moon, the Yesodic Moon acts as a binding force, defining personality and forming repetitive and rigid habit patterns and tendencies, which are protective in nature and when consciously opened to receive the higher spiritual energies can be transformed.

Yesod is considered to be the sphere of magic on the Tree, and this connects to the lunar goddesses of antiquity. Moon magic is intimately associated with the rhythmic and cyclic pattern of the universe, and magical activity is aligned with the etheric machinery of the universe. It involves the nature of magnetic response, and the science of invocation and evocation. Primarily, this magical approach to the Yesodic Moon is concerned with the purification and unification of forms, enabling humanity to contact and apply those higher spiritual forces that have to pass through the Yesodic sphere before they can manifest on Earth. These forces include the energies of the astrological Sun and the transpersonal planets of Uranus, Neptune and Pluto.

When meditating on the sphere of Yesod, the potential of the magical use of the treasure house of images arises. The inner Moon contains the source-realms of esoteric traditions, where the experienced Qabalist can make contact with the images of alchemical, Celtic, Wiccan and UnderWorld paths amongst others. By deepening our understanding of Yesod, we can learn how to access and apply symbolic imagery within the unconscious mind which can help inner transformation and psychological healing. As all ancient traditions recognise, this approach to working with the inner Moon unlocks doors to personal realisation and spiritual inspiration, and is one of the most powerful sources of magic.

FULL MOON MEDITATIONS

More and more individuals and groups are participating in the cyclic ritual meditations at the times of each Full Moon. Whilst this may have its roots in earlier pagan and Wicca traditions, a powerful re-emphasis and renewed impulse for such meetings has been derived from the teachings of Alice Bailey and the Tibetan. The modern conception of meditating at the time of the Full Moon is that people can subjectively link together across the world, transcending any religious, cultural, social and political differences, and join in focused group thought, aspiration, prayer and meditation for the purposes of world service.

Such gatherings or even individual solitary meditations are signs of the developing Aquarian group consciousness, through which, by working together as planetary group it is possible to open channels to a successful invocation of energies of light, love and spiritual direction which are vitally needed by humanity in the efforts to build a world characterised by unity and goodwill and the recognition of the unified human family. Often the mantric words of the Great Invocation are used as a focus for this receptive meditation, although this is not essential for contacting the spiritual potencies available for absorption.

Full Moon meditations are a response to the realisation of cyclic phases and rhythms in the universal life-force, and create a yearly pattern of twelve Moon festivals, linked to the zodiac, designed to constitute an ongoing revelation of divinity and to establish the divine attributes within the consciousness of humanity. It is as if a doorway opens at the times of the Full Moon; the image is that of a band of golden light extending between the Sun and Moon, which completely irradiates the lunar surface and makes possible certain spiritual inner realisations. This phase of deeper meditation and the opportunity of enhanced spiritual contacts constitute an approach that can be utilised by the occult White Brotherhoods and by humanity, and involves the magical science of invocation and evocation.

By Full Moon, the Moon has reached maximum visibility to Earth, and we receive more light and energy than at any other period in the lunar month. There is an opposition alignment between Sun and Moon, and in the greater illumination available to Earth then, the potential is for humanity to contact and align itself with the higher spiritual energies. This is part of the universal rhythm of periodicity, and at Full Moon we naturally open our psyches more to the amplified energies being transmitted to Earth. In that enhanced light, we have an opportunity to become more conscious of ourselves, our universe and the interrelationship between the parts and the whole. As the outer light intensifies by the Moon's reflection of the solar light, then correspondingly our own inner Moon and Sun align themselves to illumine the inner soul. During that Full Moon phase, prior to the actual time, either one or two days of conscious attunement, purification and preparation may be made. On the day of the Full Moon, meditational contact is made, allowing the energies to flow into and through the personality, receiving, grounding and embodying any insights and understanding. On the day after Full Moon, the outbreath or outflow into daily life is released until the commencing of the next lunar peak four weeks later.

Essentially, adopting the meditational Full Moon cycle is a religious act, and, as Alice Bailey has stated, 'Religion is the name given to the invocative appeal of humanity and the evocative response of the greater Life to that cry.' Each Full Moon is a point in time throughout the yearly cycle when people of the world can voice their demand for relationship with God and the spiritual dimension of life, as well as for a closer relationship with each other. The image is that of a vertical line ascending to spirit, and a horizontal line of service and unification with humanity, the cross of the initiate. The invocative outgoing stream of concentrated human energy telepathically reaches the awareness of spiritual beings, who then respond by releasing constructive, positive and beneficial energies to be used in the transformation of life on Earth.

Even within many established religious traditions today, major festivals are often determined or related to Moon phases and zodiacal signs. The technique of Full Moon meditations is a development of this spiritual tendency. Amongst the twelve lunar festivals, three are considered to have a greater significance. These are the Full Moon of Spring, associated with the Christian Easter festival, the time of the Risen Christ and the energy of Love; the Full Moon of May, the Wesak festival, the time of the Buddha and the energy of Wisdom; and the Full Moon of June, the Festival of Goodwill and World Invocation Day, when the spirit of humanity aspires to right human relationships and to conformity to the will of Deity and the evolutionary plan. On that day, there is the opportunity to give recognition to the spiritual essence of humanity.

Apart from those practising pagans and Wiccans, who offer due regard to the Moon Goddess at such phases, there is little obvious emphasis given to the Divine Mother in Full Moon meditations. Yet the energy of the Divine Mother is present and active, especially in the need for the meditator to develop inner receptivity in order to be fecundated by the descending spiritual potencies. The meditating and mediating group collectively generates a chalice, grail or invocatory funnel, magnetically evoking a response from the divine focus of their aspirations. Consciously adopting this rhythmic cycle can help to bring each individual into alignment with a natural universal energy flow, stimulating greater sensitivity to the influence of the Moon, as well as contributing to world-wide spiritual consciousness by participating in a timeless ritual.

THE HEALING MOON

The healing power of the Moon is released by our conscious integration of aspects of ourselves that have become repressed, denied and thrust away into the darkness of the unconscious self. For many, the Moon has become absorbed within the Shadow of the psyche, partly forming aspects of the total personality that have been rejected, and which fail to fit an idealised self-image, those traits and tendencies that we may like to pretend are nothing to do with our natures.

Contemporary psychological techniques are aimed at making the unconscious mind conscious, by shining a light into the darkness and so illuminating the unknown, and whether realised or not, are following in the footsteps of the esoteric explorers. This is the passage into the dark side of our divided wholeness, and as physical birth begins in the inner darkness of the womb prior to emerging into the light of earthly birth, so does the spiritual rebirth process commence in the darkness of the unconscious mind, passing through the traditional dark night phases of the soul.

The task confronting us is the rediscovery of part of our nature that has been lost, and a stemming of those unconscious tendencies that are perpetually splitting off aspects of ourselves under the pressures of daily living. What actions do we need to take, and what changes in attitudes and self-expression may be necessary?

The fundamental transformation requires the embracing of our Shadow self, the acknowledgement and recognition of our darkness without condemnation, rejection or additional denial. This may include facing our emotional wounds, our stunted instincts, our darker passions, our anger and frustration, our failures, our deepest needs, our feelings of rejection and loneliness, our negativity, our fears, and our lack of meaning, purpose and direction. We ask ourselves, 'What is wrong and unsatisfactory about myself and my life? And what can I do to change this?' Attempts to impose control and rationality on life may often fail, even when superficially the life-style may be one to be envied; it is that inner malaise that becomes increasingly debilitating, as energy disperses through an unintegrated and unfulfilled self.

The lunar energies offer deep healing and vitalisation if we can tap into their roots, which lie within the deeper levels of our being. This is the downward descent into the primal psyche, which may pass through levels of inner chaos and emptiness, and areas where the source energies of our emotions, feelings and instincts have their roots, powerful, wild and unrestrained. Their vitality and force may shock us, as we are so used to controlling and harnessing these vital forces through social and personal conditioning, and we may shrink away from facing their real natures and acknowledging them as existing within ourselves. It is a real test and initiation to pass, deliberately and consciously, through that gateway into darkness, to enter the realms of the black gods and goddesses, especially after prolonged repression of the 'black' by the 'white' solar light consciousness. But as our reality is dualistic, we must accept the validity of both the light and darkness within our self, and create a new type of conscious identity.

There is no path towards experiencing greater unity and integration that does not pass through the realm of the Goddess Luna, and this requires the fusion and dissolving of artificial barriers between the conscious and unconscious minds. Wholeness is the equal embracing of light and darkness, and taking this journey is a consciously sacred act, even though one of the major challenges may involve the passing through realms of madness as the separatist rational confronts 'inner demons and devils'. They are of our own making, and we perpetuate their existence. They can be liberated by transforming the demons into friends and re-owning those aspects of our nature that have become poisoned by our rejections and denials; in doing this, we may discover that new strengths are released within us for creative expression, as well as our feeling more unified.

As our shadow projections are reabsorbed, we can begin to see with greater objectivity, and the power of our emotions, feelings and instincts becomes re-balanced and capable of a positive, creative and dynamic personal expression. We realise the dangers in repressing feelings and emotions, and begin to look for safer and more constructive ways to release the wounds of our inner child. We can learn how to nurture and mother ourselves, and heal by acceptance and forgiveness those wounding shafts of our past. The gateway of darkness can become the way to enhanced opportunity and the prospect of understanding the secrets of inner healing; reliance and trust in inner guidance replaces any external dependency on authorities and social conditioning. We can see by the illumination cast by our own inner light as the full moon rises in the darkness.

By choosing an openness to our inner darkness, we succeed in reawakening the Queen of the Night in the Underworld. By erecting defensive walls against the darkness, the only possible result is imbalance, separation and self-wounding; by working with the lunar forces, a potential redemption is possible for both the personal and the collective.

In rediscovering individual foundations, we can reunite the energies of both Water and Earth within our being, as both these are associated with the lunar power, and are connected to archetypal patterns of the cycle of life–death–rebirth. Our watery feelings and emotions are dependent on our earthy bodies, and it is through this relationship that such techniques as body-work and massage can be so effective in releasing physical–emotional stresses and tensions locked within our physical forms.

The Moon may demand a surrender to 'the ground of being', which can equate to the patterns of Mother, Self and the Earth, and it can be this releasing of the dominating solar control of self that liberates the renewed creativity and fertility of the lunar energies. As is recognised by artists, occultists, lovers and mothers, the new impulses emerge only when conscious control is transcended or relaxed. Thought is affected by opening to the Moon, as stranger types of inspiration may flow with profound concepts being more easily grasped, and intuition may flourish as an exaltation of released instincts and inner guidance. Creative ideas possess additional power and depth, displaying a luminous, compelling, imaginative quality, and expand apparently of their own volition to embrace more and more.

As the personal roots stretch consciously downwards into the individual unconscious, the prospects for healing increase, but this is only through valuing the darker side of our being – a point that can never be stressed enough, as it is the key to spiritual integration.

CHAPTER 10

The Evocation of the Equinox

DURING THIS CENTURY, HUMANITY HAS taken great strides in exploring the mysteries of the seeds of life – from the medical and biological knowledge of the genetic components of human life, to the developments in artificial insemination and 'test tube babies'. On a different level, we see the discoveries of the quantum physicists who are slowly exposing the almost intangible building blocks and foundations of universal form cohesiveness, striving to locate the infinitesimally minute source of life. We are attempting to unlock the secrets of the Moon Ark of the Covenant, and much still remains to be disclosed.

Yet as we have discovered, the realms of the Moon Goddess spans several distinct levels, those of the Heavens, the Earth and the Underworld, and the symbolism and patterns inherent in the astrological Moon point to many different but complementary directions. In exploring the astrological Moon, we open the gate to many ancient and sacred mysteries, which, like the 'midnight sun', are only accessible when we descend into the Moon temple and cross over into the dark side. The archetypal powers that reside beyond and within Moon symbolism are very real and potent; and working with our astrological Moon beyond mere superficiality will begin to touch their existence

As Dion Fortune once commented, 'a goddessless religion is halfway to atheism', and as the balance within Christianity has swung towards acknowledging only the masculine and Father God and a denial of the divine feminine, many in the West have correspondingly matured with an imbalanced world-view of reality, one that has been negatively reflected in patriarchal social conditioning. The result has been individual and social fragmentation, losing the feminine principle of connection and relatedness, in both personal and collective lives and within the inner consciousness.

The Temple of the Moon Goddess awaits our arrival, if we are willing to claim our heritage of the powers of love, fertility, receptivity, sexuality and regeneration. The Moon is not only the Goddess of women who are searching for transpersonal symbols capable of strengthening aspirations to accept their full femininity; but as old traditions indicate, she is also present to initiate men into the dark mysteries of the sanctuary of transformation. There we can stand face to face with the eternal mystery, experiencing the ordeal of rebirth, and moving beyond the limitations of mental control and restrictive denials by confronting those powers of instinct, feelings and emotions unleashed from their imprisonment by ourselves, as the self stands revealed in a stark glory. We learn the Moon lesson and principle, that by loving form and all that seems lowest within us, we can be transformed by a spirit of acceptance and attain a vital healing insight into the transmutation of matter; that divinity exists equally in the lowest as in the highest. As the Gnostics say, 'to go up or down, it is all the same', that a descent corresponds to ascent, and that real movement beyond the separate personality leads to a release from ego, opening to the transpersonal and spiritual perspective. As Ishtar declared through her joy-maidens 'A prostitute compassionate am I', a unification of the lowest and the highest.

To attain the ever-renewed life of the Moon, those secrets of the rhythmic life-process of creation–destruction, and the patterns of cyclic becoming–expansion–diminishing–dying, sacrifice must be offered to the Goddess. For all, the depths and peaks of emotional intensity need to be experienced and explored, and there are few harder challenges than being torn apart by the wild hounds of the emotions, and then remaining capable of withstanding the revelation of the Dark Goddess at the apex of vulnerability. The old esoteric phrase, 'fear death by drowning' can refer to the descent into the emotional waters and the depths of the unconscious mind. Life always demands sacrificial phases, even in the sacrifice of parents when they have to release their children to live their independent adult lives, or that of the daughter who has to turn away from her father in order to assert her next step in uniting with a man in marriage, or of the son who has to 'reject' the mother to discover his own identity and be ready to discover his female partner.

In walking the road of the crescent, we can unite and integrate the past, present and the future, by building conscious bridges between levels of our being represented by the Underworld, Earth and the Heavens, the triple realms of the Moon Goddess.

Within a dualistic world, the only way onwards is by the resolution of opposites, and this is the stage represented by the path beyond the Temple of Moon Initiation. In the apocryphal 'Gospel to the Egyptians' Christ states to the disciple Salome, 'When the two become one, and male with female neither male nor female . . . then the two shall become one flesh,' and this becomes the road of all spiritual alchemists, that of the sacred marriage, the *mysterium coniunctio*.

In alchemy, this is symbolised in the images of the inner marriage of Sun and Moon, the Red King and White Queen, and the prospect of transmutation arising from their mystical conjunction. As the Moon Goddess is the primal image of birth into the mysteries of life, it is only though her gateway that progress can be achieved. For the alchemist, each male is a reflection of the archetypal Logos principle or God, and each woman reflects Eros or the Goddess, and it is through the inspiration of the inner opposite that a guiding companion is discovered; hence the outer parallel of the partnership of the *frater mysticus* and *soror mystica* on the alchemical quest, and which reflects the inner unification that is the ultimate aim of that path. The male alchemist enters the UnderWorld containing his hidden feminine principle, seeking the Goddess; and the female alchemist enters the UnderWorld of her hidden masculine principle, seeking the God (or the Horned God of Wicca). In Christianity, the parallel imagery is that of the nun's symbolic marriage to become the bride of Christ, who is described as the bridegroom of her soul. The contentious issue of the opposites is a root source for many myths and legends, and reoccurs in many esoteric traditions.

Alchemy proposes that the Great Work involves a 'mating' of opposites on every level, a fusion of negative and positive forces so that a reconciliatory union of the microcosm and macrocosm can be attained. Through this *coniunctio*, the universal (individual and collective) 'body of light' can be recreated from the previous phase of evolutionary disintegration and fragmentation across multiple levels of existence.

The stages of this reunification process within the individual or the collective involve three phases. The *Nigredo* is the entering of the darkness, the time of the wounded Grail King and the psychological and physically infertile Wasteland. Christ enters the tomb, descending into the UnderWorld for the healing release of its inhabitants. The Body of the Moon God Osiris is scattered and dismembered by the evil Set. Disintegration occurs, and the realisation of fragmentation and lack of wholeness becomes paramount. In reaching 'rock bottom', the realisation should be made that each lost piece of self needs to be rediscovered, transformed and reintegrated into the personal jigsaw of self, and that acceptance is the means of re-owning cast-away aspects.

The phase of *Albedo* emerges, which is that of the healing power of the White Queen, where a re-forming and restructuring can begin, founded on the crucial realisations and changes stimulated by the Nigredo descent, and symbolised by the efforts of Isis in regaining the scattered parts of the body of Osiris, and the attempts to fertilise herself. The final phase is the *Rubedo*, which is the resurrection of the glorified body of greater unity and integration, the body of light, and the rebirth of Osiris, now transformed into a Sun God. It must be understood though that this triple cycle is an ongoing path of spiritual development, and that the seeker or alchemist has to pass on this path many times on various levels in their efforts to bring light to the darkness. The path of the triple cycle *Nigredo-Albedo-Rubedo* is periodically repeated and experienced as the inner psychological 'burning ground' or phase of individual transformation and modification between each level of attainment or initiation.

Yet what is reborn now is a new fusion of Sun and Moon, Logos and Eros, Osiris and Isis, as a result of the transmutation of the alchemical elements through separation, purification, transformation and recombination into a new pattern of primal unity. Horus, the inner spiritual hero-child (the alchemical hermaphrodite), is born as a consequence of the path of alpha-omega. By the balancing of Sun and Moon principles, a state of creative equinox is achieved, where the energies can flow smoothly between spirit and matter with diminishing distortion, and the vision can be whole and unified, not partial and biased.

There is a recognition that, in common terms, neither light nor darkness can ever win any victory, as both are interdependent in nature. Solar light fails to penetrate the inner worlds and the subterranean caverns of the unconscious or Underworld, and the solar faculties of analysis, categorisation, definition and differentiation are unable to comprehend a level in which 'one thing becomes another, in the realm of the Mother'.

The importance of the stage of *equinox* is still to be fully understood, and requires that we move beyond dualisms of Sun–Moon and patriarchy–matriarchy into a new type of thinking and perception. The Aquarian Age is not meant to see a new version of either male- or female-dominated culture; neither polarity should be dominant and repressing the other, as this only perpetuates the previous conflicts and generates the collective unconscious through repression. Aquarius is the stage of group consciousness, uniting masculine and feminine qualities into an integrated and unified planetary humanity where only the soul vision of fused spirit-matter predominates.

Images for this future evolutionary step exist in archetypal symbols of the old traditions, such as the Tao or the Qabalistic Tree of Life. The Tao embraces within its containing circle the polar opposites of the feminine attributes of yin and the masculine yang, yet the real secret is the consciousness of the Tao, the Way. Similarly, the Tree has twin pillars of polarity, the masculine pillar of Mercy and the feminine pillar of Severity, yet the path of the arrow's ascent/descent is that betwen Kether and Malkuth (Spirit and Matter) placed on the Pillar and Path of Equilibrium. The theme of equilibrium between positive and negative energies constitutes one of the major magical mysteries and spiritual revelations, as in the Buddha's Middle Way.

The embracing of duality through the descent into the Underworld, the encounter within the Moon Temple, and the alchemical fusion of King and Queen are the stages necessary to generate our transfigured Hero-Self. As more individuals tread this path of Moon and Sun, and succeed in releasing their own spiritual light, then a new phase in collective society can begin to emerge. If a word is needed to distinguish this embryonic culture that is gestating in the planetary womb, then the vision embodied in *uniarchy* is a next step in holistic evolutionary progression. *Uniarchy* is derived from 'uni', meaning one, composed, consisting or characterised by one, and 'arch', meaning rule of the first. Loosely translated, uniarchy implies the rule of the one, the spiritual source beyond dualism, the root of both gods and goddesses, and the first universal principle of unity; the Tao or Equilibrium.

A society characterised by a uniarchal perspective, would be one akin to Aquarian group consciousness, a joint collaboration of equal respect mutually given to both men and women, where all human qualities are acknowledged, respected and applied to enrich all planetary life, recognising the immanence of deity and the unity of Earth and humanity. This is the soul vision of oneness that is our immediate goal, and it is to guide us towards this goal that the Goddess has awakened. Individually and collectively we are summoned to invoke the universal equinox, and to receive the vision of a successful descent of the equinoctial evocation when light and darkness are balanced and consciousness becomes one, as matter and spirit awake to the realisation that they are the two poles of the axis of life. The overshadowing new culture awaits our participative endeavours in making it real on Earth.

Through the Queen of Night, we can discover the light of the midnight sun, and then all our lives will be inwardly lit, radiating and illuminating the way. Or else we can live in darkness. Choice confronts our every step. It is the human dilemma, and can only be faced by each one of us in the depths of our being. There the Crone stirs the bubbling Cauldron, always waiting for a traveller to arrive, ready to share her magic brew. Can you hear the Goddess calling you? Are you ready to share her Mysteries?

Index